# On the Margins

# Studies in Indian Sociology

*Series Editor:* Jacob John Kattakayam

## Other Volumes in the Series

**Volume 1**
Indian Sociology: Issues and Challenges
*Editor:* L. Thara Bhai

**Volume 2**
Changing Caste: Ideology, Identity and Mobility
*Editor:* Surinder S. Jodhka

**Volume 3**
Agrarian Change and Mobilisation
*Editor:* B. B. Mohanty

**Volume 5**
Themes in Sociology of Education
*Editor:* R. Indira

**Volume 6**
Sociology of Social Movement
*Editor:* D. R. Sahu

STUDIES IN INDIAN SOCIOLOGY

VOLUME 4

# On the Margins

## Tribes, Castes and Other Social Categories

EDITED BY

**Abhijit Dasgupta**

SAGE

Los Angeles | London | New Delhi
Singapore | Washington DC | Melbourne

*First published in 2012 by*

**SAGE Publications India Pvt Ltd**
B1/I-1 Mohan Cooperative Industrial Area
Mathura Road, New Delhi 110 044, India
*www.sagepub.in*

**Indian Sociological Society**
Institute of Social Sciences
8 Nelson Mandela Road
Vasant Kunj, New Delhi 110 070

**SAGE Publications Inc**
2455 Teller Road
Thousand Oaks, California 91320, USA

**SAGE Publications Ltd**
1 Oliver's Yard, 55 City Road
London EC1Y 1SP, United Kingdom

**SAGE Publications Asia-Pacific Pte Ltd**
18 Cross Street #10-10/11/12
China Square Central
Singapore 048423

Published by Vivek Mehra for SAGE Publications India Pvt Ltd, typeset in 10/12 pt Adobe Garamond by Star Compugraphics Private Limited, Delhi.

**Library of Congress Cataloging-in-Publication Data**

Studies in Indian sociology.
v. cm.
The first six volumes in this series are a collection of articles that have been published in the Indian Sociological Society's biannual journal Sociological bulletin; the seventh volume is a collection of select ISS presidents' addresses.
Includes bibliographical references and index.
Contents: v. 1. Indian sociology: issues and challenges/edited by L. Thara Bhai—v. 2. Changing caste: ideology, identity, and mobility/edited by Surinder S. Jodhka—v. 3. Agrarian change and mobilisation/edited by B. B. Mohanty—v. 4. On the margins: tribes, castes, and other social categories/edited by Abhijit Dasgupta—v. 5. Themes in sociology of education/edited by R. Indira—v. 6. Sociology of social movement/edited by D. R. Sahu—v. 7. Indian sociology over the years: selected presidential addresses of All India Sociological Conferences (1967–2010)/edited by Jacob John Kattakayam.

1. Sociology—India. I. Thara Bhai, L. II. Indian Sociological Society. III. All India Sociological Conference.

HM477.I4S78 301.0954—dc23 2011 2011038663

**ISBN:** 978-81-321-1624-0 (HB)

---

**SAGE Team:** Shambhu Sahu, Puja Narula Nagpal, Vijay Sah and Rajender Kaur

Dedicated to the memory of the late Professor G. S. Ghurye,
Founder President of the Indian Sociological Society

# Contents

# List of Tables

# Series Note

The Indian Sociological Society (ISS) has successfully completed six decades as a professional body of individuals united for the cause of Sociology. It began as a small organisation in 1951 under the initiative of Professor G. S. Ghurye at the University of Bombay. Around the same time, a formally registered body, All India Sociological Conference (AISC) was started in 1955 under the leadership of Professors D. P. Mukerji, Radha Kamal Mukerjee, D. N. Majumdar and R. N. Saksena. In 1967, these two groups were united under the common banner of the ISS at the Seventh All India Sociological Conference held at the Tata Institute of Social Sciences (TISS). The conference was inaugurated by Professor G. S. Ghurye and presided by Professor M. N. Srinivas. After this unification, ISS became the lone professional national body of sociologists in India. Since then, regular conferences have been organised, attracting scholars from all over India and importantly providing several young sociologists a platform for their professional and academic growth. Just one year after its inception, the ISS started a biannual journal—*Sociological Bulletin*. It has become an internationally reputed journal in Sociology known for its academic relevance and authenticity with wide acceptance among academicians and professionals.

With the ISS celebrating its Diamond Jubilee in 2011, the Managing Committee has decided to reprint the articles that were published in the *Sociological Bulletin* as a series of books under different themes. We have already published a series of books in 2001–05, with Professor B. S. Baviskar as the series editor, as a part of the Golden Jubilee Celebrations of the Indian Sociological Society. The series was wholeheartedly accepted by academicians and students. The impact of the new series is assured by the fact that the articles that are getting reproduced were highly sought after by academicians and students of Sociology following their publication in the *Sociological Bulletin*. The fact that some of the articles that will appear in this series are several decades old and hence have fallen out of our immediate reach increases their value immeasurably. The publication of this series is also an attempt to commemorate the contributions and contributors of ISS to both the discipline of Sociology and society.

The series titled as *Studies in Indian Sociology* will have six volumes. Each volume comprises an introduction by the editor and a foreword by an advisor. The editors of all the volumes took great pains to select the papers to be included, aided by the expertise of the advisors. As soon as the idea for the series was conceived, we consulted the stalwart sociologists in our midst as well as promising young social scientists. They offered their valuable thoughts and observations on the broad topics each volume should cover and the articles that could be included. Despite several constraints, the editors have included 12–15 articles each per volume. We are certain that the volumes will prove to be an intellectual treat for the readers of Sociology books. The themes coming under this series cover varied sociological dimensions. They include: *Indian Sociology: Issues and Challenges* (Editor: L. Thara Bhai, Foreword: T. K. Oommen); *Changing Caste: Ideology, Identity and Mobility* (Editor: Surinder S. Jodhka, Foreword: Dipankar Gupta); *Agrarian Change and Mobilisation* (Editor: B. B. Mohanty, Foreword: D. N. Dhanagare); *On the Margins: Tribes, Castes and Other Social Groups* (Editor: Abhijit Dasgupta, Foreword: Virginius Xaxa); *Themes in Sociology of Education* ( Editor: R. Indira, Foreword: A. R. Vasavi); *Sociology of Social Movement* (Editor: D. R. Sahu, Foreword: Partha Nath Mukherji).

*On the Margins: Tribes, Castes and Other Social Groups* (edited by Abhijit Dasgupta and foreword by Virginius Xaxa) is the fourth volume in the series. For the past several decades, there have been different studies examining the very relevant theme of marginalised communities and their social life. These have examined the nature of marginalisation in both the pre- and post-independence periods, and have covered different regions of the country. The authors of this volume have taken into account the scheduled castes, the scheduled tribes, the backward classes, women, workers, refugees, minorities, physically challenged persons and other groups on the margins. The 12 essays in this volume explore different aspects of marginalisation among some of these groups. They show how from the margins of Indian society they mobilised themselves to take an active part in social protests, and raised their voices against discrimination in different spheres of social life. Ghettoisation of Dalits and their voices from the margins is the focus of some of the essays in the book. Very little is known about the social and political isolation of Adivasis. Some essays deal with the nature of isolation and exploitation of Adivasis. Although most authors in this volume deal with Dalits and Adivasis, some scholars have brought to our notice class-like exploitation, especially of migrant workers in cities, those who are working either in the formal or informal sectors. Two other categories that have been included in the volume are refugees and physically challenged persons. This means that the editors of the volume have tried to bring out a comprehensive view of different marginalised communities.

I hope that this contribution from the ISS on the occasion of its Diamond Jubilee Celebrations will be an invaluable asset to Sociology students. These works by our renowned sociologists cannot be reproduced or replaced as these are also, to a certain extent, products of circumstance and a time that has gone by; they are to be preserved and made use of in the further growth of Sociology.

I would like to thank Rekha Natarajan, Shambhu Sahu and Ashok R. Chandran of SAGE Publications for their initiative to complete this endeavour on time. I express my words of thanks to the Managing Committee members of the ISS and also the members of the sub-committee who identified the themes and editors of this series. Let me also thank all the editors and their academic advisors for their immense amount of time, effort and expertise invested to materialise this volume. I also appreciate the work put in by two of my research scholars, Charles Varghese and Sheethal S. Kumar, in the completion of this volume.

**Jacob John Kattakayam**
Series Editor
*Studies in Indian Sociology*

# Foreword

As a part of Diamond Jubilee Celebrations, Indian Sociological Society (ISS) is bringing out a series of publications of papers published in *Sociological Bulletin*, its official journal. The publications are organised around certain themes, and one of the themes is the aspects of marginalisation, which Abhijit Dasgupta is editing. I am happy to write a foreword to this volume.

It is not clear if marginality or marginalisation can be conceived as a concept, as it tends to be too wide and general and therefore may not be very fruitful for theorisation. However, it has captured the mind of the scholars as an idea and has emerged as a powerful frame of discussion/discourse in recent years. Indeed various social science and humanities disciplines have organised their teaching and research around this idea. Marginality or marginalisation is a multidimensional idea and hence can be located at different planes of social reality. As an idea, it is invariably relational but the meaning underlying it is far from identical. Broadly it emerges in two distinct contexts. One is comparitive and the other is structural. Marginality in relation to things valued in society, for example, level of development refers to one kind of marginality or marginalisation. The other marginality is rooted in the structure of inequality that has generally assumed the forms of class, power, status and gender. It is in this sense that the idea of marginality has been more widely explored and discussed in various disciplines. More often than not, however, the two meanings of marginality are intertwined with each other. Marginality can thus be studied along various dimensions and along different axes.

The editor in selecting the chapters for the volume has taken the broad view of the idea of marginality and hence has been able to bring together the multiple and complex dimensions of marginality prevailing in Indian society. Aspects of marginality included in the volume cover caste, tribe, labour, slum, displacement and disability. Tribe and disability have even been compounded by an added dimension of marginality, that is, gender.

**Virginius Xaxa**

# Introduction

*Abhijit Dasgupta*

Sociological studies on citizenship and welfare states, by and large, highlight the point that material deprivation is the most common cause of marginalisation, since material resources are unevenly distributed in a society. Sociologists in India brought to our notice that other factors such as discrimination based on castes, ethnic divisions and population displacement are as important as material deprivation. During the last six decades, *Sociological Bulletin* has published a large number of articles that dealt with different marginalised sections of the society. These contributions explain at length why some communities are on the margins of the Indian society. In this volume, marginalised sections have been identified among castes, tribes, industrial workers, women, refugees, ethnic minority and physically challenged persons. The authors examine the complex nature of marginality, socio-economic life of the marginalised, and their role in the Indian politics. Some of these chapters explain the factors that led to the marginalisation during the colonial period and explore why they continue to play an important role in independent India. No studies on marginalisation would be complete without an understanding of voices of resistance of those who are on the margins. Some authors in this volume have examined this point.

Marginalisation can be understood at three levels: individual, community and global. The contributors in the volume have concentrated more on the marginalisation at the community level. At the same time, they observe that these three levels cannot be kept in watertight compartments, as they often overlap and interact in a complex way with each other. Marginalisation of dalits, tribes or ethnic minority can hardly be understood without taking note of how it is linked with wider national and international politics.

## Dalits and Tribes

Dalits remain on the margins of the Indian society in spite of measures taken for them by the state. Marginalised sections of dalits mostly belong to castes with lowest ritual standing, outside the varnas, and victims of social and civil disabilities. In the sociological literature, these sections are also known as 'harijans', 'scheduled castes', 'outcastes', 'untouchables' and the like. Without going into semantics of these different terminologies, let us use the concept 'dalits' since it has gained popularity not only among the scholars but also among large sections of the oppressed in the caste system. As per the 2001 census, dalits constitute nearly 36 per cent of the total population. In some regions they are numerically significant, e.g. the Mahars in Maharashtra, the Pariahs in Tamil Nadu, the Chamars in North India, and the Namasudras and the Rajbangshis in West Bengal. It has been noted by sociologists that numerical dominance helps dalits to gain certain economic and political powers that are hardly available to those who are small in numbers. A vast number of such dalit communities experience occupational segregation, restrictions on their movements in public places and other disabilities. In contemporary Indian society they are the 'excluded' ones. They are excluded because they are denied access to spaces, e.g. temples, and schools. They live in segregated residential areas, e.g. in *cheris* in the state of Tamil Nadu. This may sound a bit paradoxical in contemporary India since the Indian Constitution upholds the principles of equality, educational opportunities, affirmative action programmes and universal adult franchise in order to protect the underprivileged and deprived sections of the society. The constitutional measures have contributed only marginally to the development of social, political and economic lives of dalits. Empirical studies on dalits show very little change in their everyday life as far as constitutional rights are concerned. Some have shown how dalits encounter atrocities for breaking caste rules at the hands of those occupying higher position in the caste hierarchy. The problem of the marginalised dalits needs to be studied against this backdrop. The formation of caste organisations has added a new dimension to dalits' struggle against social oppression and has far-reaching effects on dalits and their struggle for social justice. The movement of the Pariahs in Tamil Nadu, the efforts of the Ezhavas organisations to establish their own temples and schools marked a new beginning in the movements of dalits in the country. Caste organisations helped them in achieving their goals. In the early part of the twentieth century, the Namasudras in Bengal distanced themselves in an organised manner from the *bhadralok* (elites) dominated *swadeshi* movement in Bengal. In Maharashtra and many parts of South India, dalit organisations rejected sanskritising claims to higher status, and developed their version of the history in which upper-caste 'Aryans' are seen as alien conquerors. It is imperative to study the history of the struggle from the perspectives of dalits. Scholars hardly take note of this dimension.

One more point merits our attention. Many scholars are of the view that proselytising religions like Christianity and Islam offer an opportunity to dalits as well as to tribals to escape caste oppression and raise their social status. The history of the proselytising role of Islam goes back to the Mughal period and conversion to Christianity began during the British rule. Conversion to Islam and Christianity continued in independent India. In Chhattisgarh, the Satnami Christians point out that their interest in Christianity grew out of a sense of social inferiority and their desire for social status and respect. Many Satnamis found in Christianity resources for social assertion, physical resistance and legal protection against litigation. It offered an opportunity to alter existing power relations. The community's foray into education, practice of modern medicine, recognition of the status of women all became symbols of pride and belonging. Many such examples can be cited from the north-eastern states and Kerala. However, this is just one side of the story. Many sociologists are of the view that proselytising religions do not offer emancipation; on the contrary they complicate the position of dalits. Proselytisation in some cases led to the marginalisation of dalits. Conversion to Buddhism has hardly improved social status of chamars in many parts of North India, the label of neo-Buddhist exemplify their marginal social position.

In an overview of the condition of dalits, C. Parvathamma is of the view that ritual purity and pollution separate the untouchables from others, which means that they could not be incorporated into the mainstream in Hinduism. This has not changed even after Ambedkar's neo-Buddhist movement. There is hardly a movement which attempts to influence the minds of the people with secular agenda. She argues that religious ideologies act as opiate to masses. The constitutional benefits have covered only a fraction of the scheduled caste population since most of the deserving ones are hardly aware of their rights. Sometimes the forward groups among the backward dalits enjoy most of the benefits. Moreover, she points out that the electoral politics and affirmative action programmes have ended up in dividing the dalit community, and there is a need to re-examine the position of different section of dalits in India. The history of the movements of dalits in India suffers from an elitist bias. John C. B. Webster noted in his chapter on dalits that there is a need to re-look and re-examine the historiography of dalit movements. In his view, the writings on socio-political movements of dalits hardly present dalit voices, and this genre of writings hardly takes note of the fact that dalits are the main actors of their struggle, they oppose discrimination, atrocities and segregation on their own. Webster tried to explain different facets of dalit struggles that began during the British period, and continued in independent India. Dalits in other religions were part of these struggles. He finds it difficult to accept that if dalits convert to another religion they cease to be dalits as he argues that this is highly compartmentalised view of Indian society. The problems of the Christian dalits need to be studied within the context of the dalit history. The recent attempts to study dalits within the Marxist theoretical framework that lays emphasis on class miss out many important dimensions in a caste-based social system.

Socio-cultural marginality of dalit slum dwellers is the focus of Victor D'Souza's chapter. He critiques Oscar Lewis' theory of 'culture of poverty', which states that poverty in general and slum life in particular have a number of associated traits related to family structure, interpersonal relations, value systems and spending patterns which transcend national boundaries, and have been handed down from generation to generation along family lines. Once this culture is formed, it perpetuates itself. The theory, D'Souza argues, does not take note of how the dominant sections of the community are dependent on these slums, and how their interests are served by the perpetuation of slums. Socio-cultural marginality can be empirically defined by taking into account factors like the position in the caste system, and that they are representing a different culture. With case studies from Punjab, Surat and Hyderabad, he redefined slums in terms of economic poverty of the residents, their socio-cultural marginality and deteriorating housing and environmental conditions. Dalits are marginalised not only for their position in the caste system but also for acute poverty and segregation in slums.

For a large number of socio-political and geographical factors, tribal communities in different parts of the state are not fully integrated with the rest of the country. Barring a few exceptions, many tribal communities occupy more or less similar position like dalits. It is a well-known fact that the policies of protective discrimination and the universal adult franchise helped many tribal communities to move up in the social ladder. However, as these programmes are not inclusive enough, many tribes remain isolated. Development projects hardly take note of their plight. It was often argued that the programmes of development would facilitate integration of the tribal communities with the rest of India, but they hardly succeeded in doing so. Many development projects both in the hills and the plains ended up uprooting a large number of tribal communities. According to official estimate, nearly 7 to 8 million tribals have been displaced as a result of development projects. The state programme to rehabilitate and resettle displaced persons has hardly made any headway. State intervention in controlling water, land and forest have adversely affected almost all sections of the tribal communities. Tribals who depended on natural resources for their living now find their traditional natural environment in ruins. Land alienation in the tribal belts is a perennial problem, as non-tribals have entered into tribal land in a big way in order to exploit natural resources. This in turn has radically transformed the traditional lifestyle of the tribals. The marginalisation of tribal communities needs to be examined against this backdrop.

In a theoretical chapter on tribes and their integration with the non-tribal communities, B. K. Roy Burman highlights the significance of understanding problems of social and psychological integration. He notes that the structural relations between the tribals and non-tribals in an ideally integrated society cannot conform to any rigid pattern. Unless we see the tribal problems in a larger context, the integration of the tribals with the rest of the society will remain a myth. Economic and cultural development by themselves do not lead to solidarity. On the contrary, by rousing ambition the development process can create a situation of mutual distrust and competition. Therefore, economic and cultural development have to be supplemented by other programmes. We know far too little about the women tribal workers and their struggle. By being women they are doubly disadvantaged, first within the family and second within the community at large. Ritambhara Hebbar deals with women and the land problems among the tribals in Jharkhand area. She highlights the point that the denial of land rights to Ho women is premised on the under-evaluation of women's work on land and forests. The state policies towards forest, and specifically towards the tribal women, are alienating not only Ho women but also the tribal communities in the entire region.

## The Working Class

The labour market in the country has taken a gigantic form in recent years because of rapid economic growth. Massive expansion has taken place both in the formal and the informal sectors. Several projects have been undertaken in big cities and towns that now require huge labour force. Migrants are moving from villages to cities and towns as they are attracted by better living and earning opportunities in these areas. Land alienation and depeasantisation in the rural areas forced some of the laborers to move out of their villages. The workforce in the informal sector has a marginal existence in the cities; they live in slums and hardly interact socially or politically with others. Today the formal sector employs only 7 per cent of the labour force, whereas the informal sector has expanded fast and uses nearly 93 per cent of labourers.

An informal sector is considered as that part of the workforce that falls outside the organised labour market. Thus, it would include occupational categories like construction site workers, street vendors, stall keepers, porters, hawkers, rickshaw pullers and the like. Two points are particularly worth noting about the informal workforce. First, most of these labourers are outside the ambit of any legal protection. They do not come under labour laws, and the terms and conditions governing their relations with their employers are extremely harsh. Second, one-third of the workers in the informal sector are women. This makes gender-related issues in the informal workforce particularly significant.

The policy of structural readjustments and globalisation had many unintended consequences on the labour force. Large-scale layoffs, lockouts, sharp fall in the real wages of the labourers are quite common in recent times, both in the formal and the informal sectors. Sociologists who have studied textile workers in Gujarat have shown how displaced workers in the formal sectors are now joining the informal sectors, and thereby creating more crises. Massive import of industrial products and technological equipments from countries like China has made Indian workforce completely redundant in many sectors. Capital investment on the development of industrial infrastructure has not succeeded in absorbing displaced and unemployed labour force.

Sociologists in India have taken note of the marginalisation of the working class in the organised and unorganised sectors of the industry. Migrant workers in cities live in segregation and with indignity. Four chapters in this volume explore different dimensions of exploitation of the working class. With the rapid changes in the economy, massive development projects in cities and towns and industrial growth, the study of the condition of the working class assumes special significance. N. R. Sheth in his chapter tries to highlight this point. According to Sheth, there is a mismatch between the industrial growth in the country and the practice of the ideals of social justice. It is now well known that poverty implies denial of choice. In human society, commitment to alleviate poverty is considered as a primary goal, and those who are denied choice deserve special attention. This is why Sheth notes that our sociological imagination deserves a composite frame for a comprehensive view of human development, the development that includes an inclusive growth model. It should ensure that benefits of growth reach the poorest sections of the society. The problems of the working class merit special consideration today because of the sweeping changes that are taking place in the country as a result of liberalisation and globalisation. The emergence of a new labour force and labour contracts has caused irregularities and uncertainties of income and social security. Labour displacement, layoffs and closures are common.

A process of pauperisation and alienation is clearly visible among the working class in the country. Trade unions have done little to improve the bargaining power of the workers.

Sheth observes that the condition of the working class in the unorganised or informal sector is particularly deplorable. They constitute nearly 90 per cent of the total workforce. Employees in this sector are not protected by any labour law, and as such their position is particularly vulnerable as compared to the workers in the organised sector. The problem of women and child labour deserves special mention because they fall prey to the recruiters of labour force in the unorganised sector. With the rapid growth of infrastructure in cities, the condition of the unorganised labour force has become extremely complex. They live in shanty towns and in *jhuggis* near the construction site. They are mostly migrants because urban labour force would not take up ill-paid jobs under miserable conditions. Maren Bell Winkel in her work on Berwa construction workers in Delhi examines how dalits live in *jhuggis*. Berwas come to Delhi from the eastern part of Rajasthan, and they are recruited by the middlemen who act as conduits between the workers and the management. Middlemen prefer to bring their known relatives and fellow villagers to construction sites as caste and kin ties allow them to maintain control over a vast number of workers. Winkel brings to our notice that female workers outnumber male workers in the construction sites. Another finding that merits attention is that the residents in the *jhuggi* colonies although divided on caste and communal lines show a sense of solidarity. Muslims live side by side with lower castes and dalits. Untouchable Bhangis are allowed to draw water from the tap whenever they want, without any restrictions. In urban areas they do not follow many rites and rituals like in villages. When they follow them they do so in an diluted form. This is what anthropologists describe as 'compartmentalisation of behaviour'. The percentage of workers at the construction sites have increased at an alarming rate in recent years. Biswajit Ghosh critiques the view that workers in the unorganised sector are hardly organised and they rarely protest against the management. Although these workers remain on the periphery, they too raise their voice at times with the help of the trade unions against discriminatory policies of the management and the state. The workers in the book-binding industries in Calcutta are well known for their struggle and resilience against the management. These are the voices from the margins, and they do merit our attention. Although the bindery has not yet been covered under the minimum wage legislation, unionisation of workers and movement against the management has helped them to get fair wage. They are also paid for overtime work. With the coming of the left parties into power in 1977, the bindery workers' union gained a new lease of life. Trade unions of the left parties, especially the Centre of Indian Trade Unions (CITU) led new workers struggle in different sectors of the industry. They turned their attention towards unfulfilled demands of the bindery workers. Economic gains come about with political costs. The workers who showed an extraordinary determination to fight against the management now hardly care to keep it up.

## Marginal and Liminal Categories

Finally, the volume includes chapters on other marginal and liminal social categories. In this respect the case of the refugees merits special attention. A refugee is one who owing to well-founded fear of being persecuted for reasons of race, religion, nationality, membership of a particular social group or political opinion is outside the country of his nationality and is unable or unwilling to avail himself of the protection of that country. The number of refugees in the country has increased. In 1947, India received nearly 26 lakh refugees from West Pakistan, and between 1947 and 1970 nearly 70 lakh refugees arrived in the eastern region from East Pakistan. The problem of the refugees took a new turn in 1971 when 10 million Bengali refugees arrived in West Bengal and other north-east Indian states, e.g. Assam, Tripura and Meghalaya to escape war for an independent state of Bangladesh. In 1983, over 1 lakh refugees took shelter in Tamil Nadu. State policies towards refugees often isolate them from their hosts. They constitute a liminal category as they are neither rooted in their own country nor in the country of asylum. It may be noted that in recent years the concept of 'refugee' includes not only those who flee their countries but also displaced in the country of domicile or the internally displaced. Development projects like construction of dams, highways and industrial units often displace thousands of people. The creation of special economic zones (SEZs) by means of forcible land acquisition is also an important cause behind population displacement. Internally displaced persons suffer from the same predicament as those who take asylum in another country.

Like refugees two other categories deserve special mention here, they are 'foreigners' and 'outsiders'. The former refers to illegal immigrants or infiltrators mainly from Bangladesh to various parts of north-east India, whereas the latter includes all those who migrate to a state which is not their original place of residence, e.g. Tamils and Biharis in Mumbai. It is difficult to know how many foreigners are residing in the north-east, especially in Assam.

In 2000, an official report informed that some 300,000 illegal immigrants enter India each year, or 850 persons per day. In 2001, the Government of India estimated some 12 to 18 million illegal immigrants residing in the north-east. Criminalisation, humiliation and deportation are common as far these immigrants are concerned. They are the 'illegal aliens', 'the law breakers' and 'potential terrorists'. In the absence of appropriate measures to block entry of illegal migrants, it is becoming increasingly difficult to distinguish between an illegal immigrant and an ordinary resident of the state. In Mumbai, immigrants who come for different occupations from various parts of the country are treated as 'unwanted' and 'burden of the state' by some political outfits.

From the 1950s, sociologists have been working on the refugees, ethnic minorities and physically challenged persons. Kanti Pakrasi examines some aspects of family life of the refugees in West Bengal. According to Pakrasi, with the exodus the structure of the family among refugees changed in a big way. Displaced Bengalis struggled for preserving family life, keeping intact as far as possible patrilineal, patrilocal and extended families. But poverty and the scarcity of space stood in the way in maintaining an extended family. High-caste families generally found it easier to keep the old extended families; it was difficult for the lower-caste families to do the same. However, he notes the prevalence of any particular type of family among the refugees concerned were was not linked with their migration from rural or urban areas of East Bengal, it was also remotely connected with their residences in cities or town in West Bengal.

T. K. Oommen juxtaposes the case of the refugees with two other categories known as 'foreigners' and 'outsiders' in order to explain marginality of these different categories. Oommen notes that foreigners are alien citizens who migrate to another country for better economic opportunities. They are different from refugees who normally flee their country due to a fear of persecution/victimisation in their homeland. Outsiders are seen as intruders by the locals, crossing their own administrative units and cultural regions. Political events, e.g. partition of the country in 1947 and the emergence of Bangladesh in 1971 have greatly influenced the position of each of these categories. Two contrasting pictures emerge in the study of refugees from West and East Pakistan. In the case of the Bengali refugees, marginality remains a perpetual problem. They live in ghettos in the state of West Bengal. In contrast, the history of the refugees from West Pakistan is a history of quick economic success and cultural accommodation and assimilation. However, if one takes a look at the refugees who arrived in West Bengal in 1971, at the time of Bangladesh war of liberation, one is bound to notice a sense of isolation and marginalisation in their case. In about 10 months (between March and December 1971) nearly 10 million displaced Bengalis crossed the border and sought asylum, mostly in West Bengal. They were physically isolated in refugee camps and dependent on doles for survival. Segregation, physical hardships and insecurity made them a truly 'marginal' category. But this was a temporary phenomenon. The emergence of Bangladesh offered them new hope. This is why Oommen observes that although they were marginalised as they were proscribed from participating in economic and political life, this unique situation led to the emergence of collective shared identity, we-feeling, and cohesion. As pointed out, the term 'foreigner' is particularly popular in the north-eastern states in India where it refers to migrants from Bangladesh and erstwhile East Pakistan. They supposedly pose a threat to local culture and social life and hence encounter threat and violence. Therefore, some Assamese political groups argue that their fight is only against non-Indians staying illegally in India and not against people from rest of India who are residing in Assam. In some metropolitan cities, political outfits, e.g. Shiv Sena in Mumbai and Kannada Chaluvaligars in Bangalore have identified outsiders as the main source of social tensions. White-collar employees and professionals, the industrial working class and large workforce in the non-formal sector are often targeted by the 'sons of the soil'.

Finally, it may be emphasised that marginality and mainstreaming have been an important area for research in many countries as far as the physically challenged persons are concerned. Nilika Mehrotra points out that disability is gendered, culturally constituted and socially negotiated. Her main focus is on the nature and form of disability afflicting the individual and social life of women in rural Haryana. Studies have shown anti-women attitude in Haryana expressed through abuses, folktales and stereotypes. It was noticed that girl children and women remain discriminated as far as food consumption and health care are concerned. Mehrotra notes that a girl child with a disability would be totally unwanted in such a society. Various acts adopted by the state from time to time ignore the gendered realities of everyday lives of physically challenged, both within the family and outside. These are just a few selected essays on marginality that came out in the *Sociological Bulletin* during the last six decades. These are truly path-breaking essays and are unique not only for rich ethnographic data but also for theoretical precision and conceptual clarity.

# PART I

# The Socio-cultural Marginality: Dalits and Tribes

# 1

# The Weaker Sections of Society: The Scheduled Castes in India

*C. Parvathamma*

It is interesting that intellectuals specially sociologists in India have started thinking about the weaker sections in the country. In the present paper I confine myself to the Scheduled Castes, one of the weaker sections. The term Scheduled Castes given currency in 1930s is a blanket term including within itself hundreds of castes and sub-castes which constitute a hierarchy among themselves and in relation to the Hindu castes. The regional, linguistic and cultural differences add to make the picture more complex and complicated.

The world of caste and practice of untouchability have been subjects of serious thinking and research over the past few decades. They have also provided opportunity for reformists and revolutionary social movements historically. In post-independence India and also during the British regime, untouchability in particular has made the Government to assume the role of social workers.

The origin of untouchability remains obscure even in a society like ours with vast literary traditions. In the Vedic period Varna-Ashrama Dharma no doubt carried occupational attributes though much less rigorously and these got themselves crystallized in due course. The Post-Vedic period, the Epics, Puranas and Upanishadic times in particular, laid the firm foundation for the elaborate proliferation and development of the Indian social structure. The several law givers also contributed their mite, in particular the writings of Manu stand out as a beacon light on the horizons of Indian caste system.

Birth became the decisive criterion of membership in the caste—Occupational attributes of caste became more pronounced and carried values of rank and status. Some occupations were of high status and rank, others carried low rank and status. Groups following particular occupations came to enjoy social position commensurate with caste occupations. For instance, priesthood and scholarship in sacred literature carried higher values thus enjoining superior position to the Brahmins. Scavenging and leather work correspondingly carried low social status. Multiplication and classification of castes and sub-castes as well as occupations continued unchecked since then, resulting in a social hierarchy.

The caste system with its social hierarchy and implicit inequality of status and rank, in religious, educational, economic, political and juridical relationships among caste groups has been in existence from the earliest known historical times. At the top of the hierarchy are the Brahmins; untouchables come at the bottom end. Ritual purity and pollution as part of Hinduism have pervaded all the walks of life. A gradation or hierarchy of values obtains in most mundane things as well. Food, cloth, metals, in a word, everything that surrounds human life carry values, not necessarily always based on their utility. High rank is usually associated with economically costly items like silk cloth, precious metals like gold and silver which at least in past only higher castes could possess.

Practices, which were initiated with such elaborate value system associated with them, in the course of time, ceased to be voluntary. They became part of the tradition, customarily enforced and later supposed by public opinion and ruling powers. In all this, higher the status of caste, greater were the rank and privileges, in ritual, educational, economic, political and juridical powers. The lower castes were reduced to utter subordination devoid of many privileges and occupied the lower rungs of the hierarchical ladder.

Hinduism and the caste system are so much intertwined with one another that together they cover all the temporal and spiritual aspects of life. The educational, economic and political aspects of life belong to secular sphere and are associated with achieved status. In the Indian context, these areas of life have been subjected to and controlled by the religious and caste values to such an extent and are so loaded with notions of Dharma and Karma that people are generally afraid of transgressing the boundaries. A poor Brahmin and a rich untouchable are hardly comparable in terms of status and rank even under the present changed circumstances.

The supremacy of the religious values and Brahmins as the only authority being supposed to have mastery to interpret their religious implications gave them a definite edge over everybody else as custodians of all knowledge. Life on the earth and life after death, as developed in the theory of Karma and transmigration of soul coloured all secular and spiritual activities.

By and large, one sees the ascendancy of Brahmanical values throughout the centuries and these are held against all odds. In fact, the legendary attribute of the curse of the Brahmin, the worst that could be invited by anybody, seem to have held the sway. No one really tried to seriously challenge his spiritual authority and power. All the protest and reform attempts made from time to time historically amount to 'rituals of rebellious' which hardly meant a serious threat. The various political powers themselves were dependent on the advice, blessings and good offices of the Brahmins. Hence the Brahmins as a class and the Brahmanical values as a category have enveloped all aspects of life and continue to persist.

In all this the most deprived and depraved class of people are the untouchable group with a conglomeration of castes and sub-castes within it. In ancient India it was just an emerging category which got crystalized with the passage of time. In medieval period, even under the impact of Muslim rule, their position was by no means better off. Conversion to Islam in some ways ushered in changes but hardly brought about structural changes.

The British who succeeded the Muslim rulers took time to realize the intricacies of the Indian social structure. Since they were interested in the political consolidation of their position, their openly declared policy was one of 'non-interference' in the social and religious matters of the people of India. Christianity which came to India, like Islam, from outside, added another dimension to the existing social categories. Conversion to Christianity by lower castes and upper castes for several reasons did not help to bridge the gulf between them. The pre-conversion caste status, rank and values continued and loomed large influencing all kinds of social intercourse.

The indigenous reform movements starting from Buddhism, Jainism, Sikhism, Brahmo Samaj, Arya Samaj, including Veera-saivism in South, rebelled against caste rigidities and other social evils. The founders of most of these movements themselves came from upper castes and as one could glean, the results of these attempts to reform Hinduism could not really succeed. Preaching against caste differences and discriminations, aspiration to establish social equality and justice at best helped the middle range caste groups and not the really the downtrodden to raise their status.

Ritual purity and pollution, the barrier which separates the untouchable groups from others in India meant that these people could not be incorporated into the mainstream in Hinduism and largely remained so even under the impact of foreign and indigenous movements including that of Ambedkar's neo-Buddhism. It is noteworthy, how all these attempts were conceived and covered with religious ideology. There is hardly a movement which attempted to influence the minds of the people minus the religious idiom. In this sense religion—old and new—provide and act as opiate to masses. People are generally susceptible to religious ideologies. It is far more easier to win over people by giving a religious appeal and character to a movement than merely trying to introduce changes in the economic and political arenas.

The Scheduled Castes and Tribes, their problems, have assumed new dimensions in the post-independence India. Historically, they have been an ever-growing menace to national and social integration. Each of the conscious and unconscious attempts made to eradicate the evils of caste system has made the system much more vulnerable and monstrous to the downtrodden groups. The situation can be compared only marginally with their counterparts, the Negroes of America and South Africa and similar groups elsewhere.

For the present, I will briefly touch upon the coming to limelight of the woes of the group, largely by the efforts made by the late Dr. Babasaheb Ambedkar and the controversy between Gandhi and Ambedkar that resulted in the Poona Pact. During the post-independence period, in contemporary India, under parliamentary democracy, these issues are of vital importance precisely because the problems continue unabated and are becoming sources of social unrest in spite of protectionist policy adopted by the Government.

During the Independence Movement the National Congress remained largely oblivious of the fact that there were social groups in the country which were scorned at and relegated to a position worse than of animals. The leadership in the Congress again was largely confined to upper castes and richer sections. They hardly perceived the sufferings of the lower and lowest groups. Social inequality and injustice at its worst afflicted the untouchable caste groups.

From among the neglected sections there arose Ambedkar as a champion and spokesman of the millions of dumb human beings. When he made his demands on behalf of the untouchable groups the ruling British Government conceded political representation to them by the Communal Award. Gandhiji and the Congress were quick to grasp the implications of the same. Already staggered by the demands of Muslims, the Hindu leaders were not at all in favour of recognizing the demands of untouchable separatism.

Gandhi promptly undertook fast unto death for the withdrawal of the Communal Award. Ambedkar was finally coerced to sign the Poona Pact to save the precious life of Mahatma by sacrificing the cause of millions of untouchables. Though all this is a part of history of the struggle of Indian untouchables under a leader who had sprung up from among them by chance coincidence, the cause of untouchables was furthered in the hands of Ambedkar as the chairman of the Constitution Drafting Committee.

Ambedkar was forced to agree that untouchables were Hindus and that their conditions had to be ameliorated from within the social system. Personally he was bitter against Hinduism and the caste system and became a Buddhist in the last days of his life. But he made a fresh bid in the Constitution to provide measures for the betterment of these communities. The lot of the millions of illiterate poor untouchables needed a national awakening both among the untouchables and the caste Hindus. Therefore, the solution to the problems was visualized at national level and not just at State levels.

A series of measures were provided to combat against social evils consequent upon social discrimination and the practice of untouchability. Social discrimination is loaded with differential values, often supported and sanctioned by religious beliefs and practices. Provisions to eliminate discrimination, and to establish social equality have to be supported from other possible sources. Social inequality and discrimination are inherent and therefore ascriptive. It is hardly possible to alter ascriptive values by legislation.

In the Constitution economic, political, educational facilities are incorporated for the upliftment of the secular position of the untouchables. Ambedkar seems to have believed that as the process of modernization sets in, acquired status and the values associated with it would gradually displace values and status based on ascription. The tensions which we are witnessing in contemporary India between the Scheduled Castes and non-Scheduled Castes may be rightly described as a clash between the traditional and emergent values.

The achievement-oriented tradition still has to take its roots. But before it could become possible, the middle-range clean upper castes which have emerged as dominant groups in all the States as a result of the linguistic reorgnization have come to believe that if this transformation is allowed, they would be the losers for good. Hence, fierce attempts are made to thwart all well-intentioned Government policies meant to uplift the Scheduled Castes.

Access to public places like temples, tea shops, drinking water places and places of essential services like hair-cutting salons are frought with extreme difficulty in contemporary India. The Scheduled Caste population is spread out and is essentially a minority in almost all the villages in India. These people can hardly hope to assert themselves to avail the constitutional benefits. That each one should know one's place in the hierarchy, has such a stronghold in the minds of people that any attempts by the low caste people to break this barrier is resisted by all upper castes in addition to, sometimes, by other religious minorities in the village situation.

Political reservations are given in from village panchayat to the parliament. The party leadership has vested interest in maintaining the same. In fact a good number of Indian political parties, national and regional, conform closely to the patterns of caste groups in the country. The Scheduled Caste members in political parties remain essentially subordinate to the party bosses. No Scheduled Caste leaders worth the name are allowed to grow within the political parties and they are all contained and curbed effectively.

Political reservation and representation is a constitutional obligation. It is also a vote-catching mechanism for successful political parties. The! Scheduled Castes are lured to vote by promising them many returns. The Scheduled Caste political leaders are bound and regulated by party interests overlooking sometimes interests of their castes. This has created two different situations. The Scheduled Caste politicians firstly do not wish to be identified as Scheduled Caste leaders, presumably on the same lines such as there are no Brahmin or other caste leaders. Secondly there is a growing tendency among the Scheduled Caste politicians to overlook and brush aside the problems of Scheduled Castes precisely because 'general' votes in 'reserved' constituencies outnumber the Scheduled Caste votes. As such the politicians from these caste groups need not be under an obligation to the voters of their castes. The access to power enhances the secular status and rank of Scheduled Caste political leaders. So the class-mass differences are inevitable amongst themselves.

Political reservation and representation minus the emergence of effective leadership among the Scheduled Castes is a tragedy. Given the political mechinations, unscrupulous methods, bossism, exploitation, corruption and favouritism, it is an uphill task for a Scheduled Caste politician to emerge as an effective and generally accepted leader. Social values die hard. An ambitious and aspiring Scheduled Caste politician can be cut underneath his feet. Rivalry and pitting one against another, exploiting sub-caste differences etc. can be used as political weapons to contain them eternally by caste Hindu politicians. The political game is an important mechanism in democracy. The economics of politics is frightening and it is very difficult to visualize whether Scheduled Caste politicians can ever reach a bargaining position, get weaned of their dependence and have access to real power.

The various provisions made in the Constitution to bring about economic benefits have touched only the fringe. All kinds of economic assistance have roused the anti-Scheduled Caste feelings among the non-Scheduled Castes. The knowledge of availability of these benefits itself is limited to a small and negligible number in urban/town and rural areas. It is only the vocal and advanced sections among the Scheduled Castes who have availed themselves of most of the benefits. These are the people who have also acquired other forms of assets and influence and wield some power.

Since nearly 90 per cent of the Scheduled Caste population is scattered in rural areas, they are the ones who are the worst hit and continue to suffer. The knowledge of the Constitutional benefits is known to about 10–15 per cent of those in rural areas. Similarly economic benefits either in the form of land, house-site, building material, loan and so forth have proved much more deterrent. The land reform-ceiling and distribution of surplus land among the Scheduled Castes has led to much ill-feeling among the non-Scheduled castes. One wonders whether this measure could succeed at all at any time. In many cases it has let loose the anger and wrath of caste Hindus besides continued circumvention of the law itself.

Segregation based on caste lines in residential pattern is an age-old practice and very little could be done to curb this in rural India, though in towns and cities it could be tackled and set right. Distribution of house sites and construction of Janata Houses by the Government, though laudable, unfortunately have now thrown the Scheduled Caste people, further away from village location. This means again total segregation. Further, the new locations and their Scheduled Cases inhabitants can be easily held to ransom by irate villagers. Settlements can be set on fire, people beaten up and all kinds of atrocities directed without affecting the rest of the village community.

Dependent as they are economically, the Scheduled Caste population has to eke out their livelihood by selling their labour. That their economic vulnerability can be totally exploited by the villagers is born out by many instances of total boycott of the Scheduled Caste population in villages. In Karnataka this was reported recently from a remote village in the Bidar district. The police officials who went to the rescue of these people were humiliated and beaten up by the villagers. The State Government denied anything like that while the press and others who visited the village came out with stories of horrible woes and sufferings of the Scheduled Caste inhabitants living in constant fear of death.

Abolition of bonded labour and redeeming the borrowers from the clutches of local money lenders,, similarly have yet to produce the desired effects. Land distribution among the Scheduled Castes by Government has led to resentment and increase in physical violence and burning down of crops. In fact every effort made by the Government to create opportunities to make the Scheduled Castes economically viable and sound have led to increased jealously and hatred among the non-Scheduled Castes. All these are conceived as a direct threat to undermine the upper castes. Slightest attempts on the part of the Scheduled Castes to assert themselves and their claims for Constitutional privileges have led to clashes.

Actually the Constitutional benefits have covered only a fraction of the Scheduled Caste population, while most of the deserving among them have not even the slightest idea of these benefits. The publicity, bordering on propaganda, given by the Government agencies regarding the benefits in a way has been responsible to make the non-Scheduled Castes much more sensitive to the ideas of deprivation. People are keen that the protectionist policy should not be there. They think that such preferential discrimination is the antithesis of democracy.

The Government machinery by itself is inadequate and too slow to move even under emergent conditions. So when clashes occur, it is the weaker sections who are put to plight and often relieved of everything including life. Their womenfolk are wilfully subjected to ill treatment. Their modesty is meddled with. Denuding, raping and murdering women of all ages to frighten the aspiring Scheduled Castes is one of the techniques evolved in recent years, while the Scheduled Caste menfolk are harassed and often axed to death for alleged theft or molestation of caste Hindu women.

Even if an army stands by, it is doubtful that such cases can be curbed in the immediate future. The awakening which has come about in certain pockets of the Scheduled Castes population, more particularly among the educated, not only resist caste Hindu assaults but are trying to organize the weaker sections to meet the eventualities. This is just making a beginning and they may not be a match to well organized, rich, influential and powerful caste Hindus who can both inflict innumerable miseries on the Scheduled Castes, and who also seek protection for themselves by using the Government machinery often against the Scheduled Castes themselves as law-breakers. Kilvanmani incident of Tanjore district in Tamil Nadu is not an isolated event. Similar follow-up cases have been fairly widespread throughout the country.

Next to political reservations, some significant advances have been made in educational concessions. This again is causing heartburning among the non-Scheduled Castes. Reservation of seats in colleges, technical and professional courses, and other facilities given to the Scheduled Caste students are severely criticized as wilful lowering of standards, at the cost of merit. This situation causes mental torture to the Scheduled Caste students and adversely affects their educational pursuits.

Demands of social justice and achievement-oriented courses of action, although independent, can be made dependent variables. For even among the Scheduled Castes, increasing number of merited students are emerging. There is competition from among the Scheduled Castes themselves for the reserved seats. Effects of the denial of any opportunities for formal education for centuries cannot be set right overnight. What militates perhaps is the backlog of social heritage and unfavourable environmental surroundings. It is not at all correct to say that educational standards are lowering because of reservationist policy. The reasons for the lowering of standards have to be searched for elsewhere too.

Similarly reservation of jobs is said to have corroded the efficiency in administration. Barring class IV employment, in all other categories, the quota is never filled up. The Government departments themselves have paid lip service to reservation, while semi-Government and private organizations largely flout the rules. Yet by dint of hard work a class of officers among the Scheduled Castes has emerged, but they can hardly lead the Scheduled Caste masses. The official class is a small and self-contented group who can neither exploit nor help to further the cause of the Scheduled Caste masses except trying for their own chances of success—appointment, promotions—with which they are naturally concerned like everybody else.

In some ways it is only in Maharashtra, even after the exit of Ambedkar, attempts to organize the Scheduled Castes are continued. During the lifetime of Ambedkar, he tried to organize Labour Party, then the Scheduled Castes Federation and finally, the Republican Party of India. But, these organizations did not have a smooth sailing. The Republican Party factions are too well-known and the party virtually could do nothing positive for the welfare of the Scheduled Castes.

Exasperated by the internal fights and factionalism among the elderly leaders of the Republican Party, younger generation sprang up in the name of Dalit Panthers, styled after the American 'Black Panthers', in recent years. They made themselves felt by Government and others. Educated Scheduled Caste youths outside Maharashtra have also come under their influence to some extent. But in Maharashtra itself the Dalit Panthers movement was closed in from many sides. The ruling Congress Party lured some of the leaders of the Dalit Panthers and also helped to bridge the factional differences in the Republican Party. What could have become a major organization working for the welfare of the Scheduled Castes was steadily undermined by a variety of forces. Only in literary field some of them remain active today. Community-based political organizations, especially of the down-trodden, have little success. A very pathetic situation indeed.

The foresight with which Ambedkar established the educational institutions at Aurangabad and Bombay was commendable. They have played a positive role. Yet when the neo-Buddhists and Scheduled Castes of Maharashtra wanted the Marathwada University to be named after Ambedkar, one of the illustrious son of Maharashtra, there was bitter opposition from the caste Hindus. It is strange and painful to dub Ambedkar as a narrow communal leader. The downtrodden, who number several millions in the country, are as much indebted to Ambedkar for focusing the world attention on the plight of India's untouchables, as should be the Hindus for the services rendered by him.

The Government as a reform agent can achieve only limited objectives. While it has championed the cause of weaker sections, minorities and backward classes, it cannot cope up with the colossal tasks ahead. Reservations, if continued indefinitely, will convert themselves into vested interests. The political patronage will lead to social estrangement among the people and politicians as big brothers trying to increase the area of their influence have succeeded in floating and heading a plethora of communal organizations in recent years.

Whatever changes might have occurred, one thing is certain that there is very little sharing of political power between upper and lower caste politicians both in the parties and in the Government. Andhra, Bihar and Rajastan, which have had Scheduled Caste chief ministers, may be exceptions and such things could happen under exigencies and peculiar circumstances. The ameliorative measures—Constitutional provisions—under democracy will take a very long time to solve the pressing problems of the Scheduled Castes. Further structural changes, if any, cannot be simply assumed. The caste system has a notoriety about it, incorporating and absorbing everything within itself including contradictions and conflicts.

Historically caste system has withstood all attempts made to modify or destroy it. It has absorbed various shocks. Absorptions of Buddhism, Jainism, Sikhism, Christianity, Islam are but few cases proving elasticity of the system. Unless there are structural changes, values will not alter. So long as old values continue, the barriers of castes and also untouchability will continue, perhaps in different ways and shades. Government efforts are not matched by voluntary organizations in India. For bringing about large scale awakening among the Scheduled Caste and non-Scheduled Castes, it is necessary that they are made aware of the human problems. The Scheduled Castes and Scheduled Caste sympathizers can organize and exert pressure on the Government. For it is only under pressure that the Government machinery will move at some speed. Gradually Scheduled Caste problems should converge with those of other weaker sections. Equality, justice and fair play have to be achieved by mobilizing all those who are denied the same. Social mobility cannot be achieved when other groups are not willing to concede. This is exactly what is happening with new converts to Buddhism. When the secular position of the people remain unchanged, change of religion hardly matters. Lot of tensions build up when one group wishes to push itself while other groups do not concede, to its claim.

The history of the Backward Class Movements in Tamil Nadu and elsewhere highlights how the forward groups among some of the backward communities seized the opportunity to lead the movements. In this process they tried to consolidate their positions which was often detrimental to the aspirations and development of other backward classes. These lessons should provide guidelines. Both communal organizations and continued categorization and patronage extended by the Government to some caste groups will add to the existing divisive forces. Even when the Government wants to single out communities and groups for preferential treatment, the programme should be made time bound. Instead of giving doles, substantive assistance should be given to strengthen the group economically and educationally. Once certain level is achieved, the benefits should be gradually withdrawn.

In fact it is a vicious circle within which the social problems on the Scheduled Castes are revolving. Doles are given to strengthen their secular position. In this process the concerned person has to constantly declare that he comes from such and such low caste. Such public demonstration of caste status for personal benefit can never help a man to psychologically rise above narrow loyalties or to free himself from feeling constantly inferior. It is necessary' for the Government to devise measures and initiate a policy to strengthen weaker sections in general and the Schedule Castes in particular.

A number of new approaches may have to be devised. Scheduling or descheduling need not go by entire groups, but by families. Similarly the unnecessary propaganda regarding the benefits to the Scheduled Castes which adversely affects them may be stopped by the Government. Official records and discussions in the Legislative Assemblies and Parliament should serve the purpose. Economic diversification, increased educational facilities coupled with universal literacy perhaps would help to awaken the people.

Increased tensions and conflicts which the countryside witnesses today may be rightly viewed as leading to changes. Unfortunately, they may demoralize the Scheduled Castes and make them victims of circumstances. The dominant upper caste groups with landed property have emerged so strong that they influence and control policies often twisting them for their own benefits. The Government should not play itself into the hands of vested interests, but in a democracy ambition knows no scruples.

There are two ways in which the Scheduled Caste problems can be resolved. Firstly within the existing system, hoping that Constitutional benefits would continue, piecemeal development of the community will take place. This is a very slow process which is frought with internal contradictions. Public opinion, as pointed out earlier, is already against the policy which is dubbed as reverse discrimination.

Only political and educational benefits are visibly used, political reservations have catered to individual families, which in turn perhaps have helped their kith and kin. In each State there have been a monopoly of some half a dozen families. In the Centre till recently except for one person no one could continue as a minister. From the entire Scheduled Caste political leadership, apart from its being manipulated by upper caste party bosses, no one is allowed or tolerated to emerge powerful. This kind of dependency restricts their role. They always are made to play second fiddle and there is no genuine leadership as for instance, of the type provided by Ambedkar. Keeping the Scheduled Caste political leaders as showpieces, while perenially cutting at the roots to prevent them emerging strong, was not the purpose with which political reservations were given.

Political reservations should be tagged with responsibility to focus attention on the Scheduled Caste problems. Given this, the role of the Scheduled Caste politician will become more purposive and less subjective. They have to be social workers-cum-politicians and not the other way round. The handpicked Scheduled Caste politicians and the speed with which they arc lured to change party affiliation, a general malady, make a mockery of reservations. As long as this continues only individual families will benefit themselves in the name of the community. This amounts to exploiting the community for personal benefits. Can this be prevented or set right within the framework of political processes in India?

Education and white collar jobs are the well known avenues leading to achieved status. Though in the case of Scheduled Castes it is not readily happening, but over a period of time it is bound to come about amongst themselves and in relation to others. The class structure which has always coexisted with the caste structure finds a favourable milieu with the Scheduled Caste educated group. This is again a slow process and the status of the entire Scheduled Caste communities cannot be improved.

The conflict between the achieved status and ascribed status class and caste—cannot be easily resolved in the case of Scheduled Castes. What the Scheduled Castes desire is an honorable social position to the entire lot, no matter what kind of internal contradictions persist among themselves. The social hierarchy and gradation have always figured in public relation in the Indian context. So mere abolition of untouchability practices and making their observance a cognizable offence, involving the legal processes have made the situation more complex and complicated.

By and large the enlightened Hindu sympathizers of the Scheduled Castes are for reforms. They wish that the Scheduled Caste should get education, achieve economic betterment and come up in life. But when it comes to tackle traditional values, status and so forth they are not very keen or sure where it will lead. Equality of opportunity in secular life, and not achievement of social equality in absolute terms, seems to guide their thoughts and actions. They can rationalize that structural changes will come about, given the improvement in secular life. The Indian untouchable vis-à-vis the history of caste system unfortunately belies this.

The democratic form of Government cannot interfere with social lives of the people and coerce them constantly. Both in public and in private matters, the Government has to carry the wishes of the majority with it. Given the existing machinery, form of Government and policies, it will take a very long time and one can never be sure of the results. The Scheduled Caste problems will continue to persist and there will be more violence and tensions between the caste Hindus and aspiring Scheduled Castes.

If the existing system is not acceptable, then the Scheduled Castes should organize themselves and take more drastic steps. Revolutionary changes cannot occur when only a neglected section of people rise in revolt. This can be curbed with an iron hand both by the Government and public in general. The issues have to be focused internationally. By doing this once again the methodical slow process sets in. The Scheduled Caste alone cannot organize and successfully lead the movement. All the deprived and downtrodden across the castes have to come together. Caste interests need cut across class interests.

There will be more violence and bloodshed, with determined efforts to resolve the problems afflicting the Scheduled Castes. A good number of Scheduled Castes people themselves may get eliminated in this process. Though it is often generalized that Indian soil and climate are not conducive to violence and revolution, pressure tactics are paying good dividends under democracy. Pressure could be brought to bear upon the Government to use extra legal measures to resolve the problems.

So far all the efforts made by the Government and the money used in the name of the Scheduled Castes have gone down the drain. Only few have been benefited. Exploitation of the Scheduled Castes continues. Apathy of the officials and of ambitious and unscrupulous men in public life has rendered the welfare measures a source of corruption and nepotism.

Punishing the guilty is one way of containing corruption and nepotism. Instead, if the measures themselves are made such that middle men will not have a role to play, they would prove to be useful. For all economic, educational and job matters, the Government should have direct control and efficient machinery. For instance, land need not be distributed by cents and acres to individual Scheduled Caste families. Deserving Scheduled Caste and non-Scheduled Caste families can be settled on Government farms, and payment can be made on work point. Agro-industries and marketing facilities be promoted. Rights to property can be made secondary and not fundamental.

Food, shelter, clothing, a minimum standard of life have to be ensured to all. To this extent, rights to private property be limited and made secondary. Since people have never showed inclination to give up property rights voluntarily, beginning may be made with sections of people coming under direct control of the Government. Right to acquire and own only limited amount of property may be given to all people.

Awakening and organizing the Scheduled Castes, voluntary organizations taking up the cause in right earnest, the Government Machinery gearing up its actions in addition to evolving new policies and approaches, to put it modestly, can usher in changes over a period of time. There is no national consciousness with regard to the Scheduled Caste problem as is the case with religious minorities. While religious minorities can always project their image outside the country and politicize their issues, the Scheduled Castes have suffered for long, languishing for liberation. Betterment, which is coming in the form of doles that are neither sufficient nor free from foul play. The entire process is anything but short of revolutionary changes.

## Bibliography

Ambedkar, B. R. 1945. *Annihilation of caste*. Bombay: The Bharat Bhushan Printing Press.

———. 1918. The *Untouchables: Who were they and why they became untouchables*. New Delhi: Amrit Book Company.

———. 1946. *What Congress and the Gandhi have done to the untouchables*. Bombay: Thacker.

Bailey, F. G. 1957. *Caste and economic frontier*. Manchester: Manchester University Press.

Béteille, André. 1965. *Caste, class, and power*. Berkeley and Los Angeles: University of California Press.

———. 1969. *Castes, old and new*. Bombay: Asia Publishing House.

———. (ed.). 1969. *Social inequality*. Penguin.

Brass, Paul R. 1965. *Factional politics in an Indian state: The Congress party in Uttar Pradesh*. Berkeley and Los Angeles: The University of California Press.

Chitnis, Suma. 1977. 'A long way to go' (unpublished report on a survey of scheduled caste high school and college students in fifteen states of India). Surat: Centre for Social Studies.

Desan, I. P. 1976. *Untouchability in rural Gujarat*. Bombay: Popular Prakashan.

D'Souza, Victor, S. 1962. 'Changing status of scheduled castes', *Economic weekly*, 14: 1853–54.

Epstein, T. S. 1962. *Economic development and social change in south India*. Manchester: Manchester University Press.

———. 1973. *South India yesterday, today and tomorrow*. London: Macmillan.

Ghorye, G. S. 1961. *Caste, class and occupation*. Bombay: Popular.

Gough, E. Kathleen. 1955. 'The social structure of a Tanjore village', in M. Marriott (ed.): *Village India*. Chicago: University of Chicago Press.

Government of India, Dept. of Social Welfare. 1969. Report of the committee on untouchability, economic and educational development of the scheduled castes and connected documents.

Hardgrave Jr., Robert L. 1965. *The Dravidian movement.* Bombay: Popular.

Hutton, J. H. 1961. *Caste in India.* London: Oxford University Press.

Isaacs, Harold. 1965. *India's ex-untouchables.* New York: John Day and Co.

Kothari, Rajni (ed.) 1970. *Caste in Indian politics.* New Delhi: Allied.

Lynch, Owen, M. 1969. *The politics of untouchability.* New York: Columbia University Press.

Mahar, J. M. (ed.). 1969. *The untouchables in contemporary India.* Tucson: The University of Arizona Press.

Oommen, T. K. 1968. 'Strategy for social change: A study of untouchability', *Economic and political weekly* (June 22): 933–36.

Parvathamma, C. 1968. 'The case for Indian untouchables', *United Asia,* 20: 279–86.

———. 1978. *Under the impact of directed changes.* New Delhi: National Publishing House.

———. 1973. 'Ambedkar and after: The position and future of Indian scheduled caste masses and classes', *The eastern anthropologist* 26 (3, July–Sept.).

———. 1976. 'Land reforms — Problems of redistribution of surplus land', *Social and economics justice* (Feb.).

———. 1976. 'Socio-economic survey of the SCs and tribes college students in Karnataka' (unpublished report prepared for Govt. of Karnataka). Mysore: Dept. of Sociology, University of Mysore.

———. 1974. 'Scheduled caste and scheduled tribe college students in Karnataka (unpublished report prepared for ICSSR). Mysore: Dept. of Sociology, University of Mysore.

Patwardhan, Sunanda. 1973. *Change among India's harijans.* New Delhi: Orient Longmens.

Singer, Million, and Cohn Bernard (eds.). 1968. Structure and change in Indian society. Chicago: Aldine Press.

Srinivas, M.N. 1962. *Caste in modern India and other essays.* Bombay: Asia Publishing House.

———. 1966. *Social change in modern India.* Berkeley: University of California Press.

Rao, M. S. A. 1978. *Social movement and social transformation: A study backward class movements.* New Delhi: Macmillan.

# 2

# Understanding the Modern Dalit Movement

*John C. B. Webster*

The Dalit movement[1] has not received the attention it deserves from histories of modern India written a generation ago. The Dalits were treated either as marginal people without a history of their own or as objects, rather than subjects, of the history of the nation as a whole. Thomson and Garrett[2] did refer to the Dalit movement at several points but never described it (1962: 623, 631, 650). Percival Spear, in his identical revisions both of the modern section of Vincent Smith's *Oxford History of India* (1961: 835) and of P. E. Robert's *History of British India Under the Company and the Crown* (1958: 652–53), refers to Gandhi as the leader of a movement for the uplift of the Depressed Classes, but merely acknowledges Ambedkar as a 'Harijan leader' of 'outstanding' courage and ability.[3] Alone among these earlier British historians of modern India, L. S. S. O'Malley devotes a section to the Dalit movement, but portrays it as a 'movement for the uplift of the untouchables' initiated and sustained by others (1968: 374–81).[4] The latest British history of modern India, that of Judith Brown (1994), does monitor the condition of the Dalits at several points in their history, but makes no reference to any organized efforts by Dalits to improve their own lot.

The Dalit movement has not fared much better in the histories of modern India by Indian historians, who generally relegate Dalits to chapters on social reform and portray them as passive victims, recipients and beneficiaries rather than as active participants in their struggles. The one paragraph that Majumdar devotes to Dalits describes them as objects of philanthropic and social work conducted by others (1956: 959–960). R. R. Sethi refers to Dalits only in connection with the 1932 Communal Award and as objects of 'uplift' work (Dodwell 1958: 630–31, 685–86). In his later work Majumdar refers to Ambedkar and the Dalits as participants in the political bargaining of the 1930s and 1940s which ultimately led to independence (1969: 479, 494, 521, 639, 696, 731). However, in his lengthier treatment of Dalits in the book Gandhi, social reformers and the Congress are portrayed as the prime movers, while Ambedkar is cast in the role of a perceptive critic

(1969: 1000–1012, 523–525). Bipan Chandra confines his treatment of the Dalits to a three-page section on 'the struggle against caste' in his text book (1971: 231–33), though he gives them a more activist role than his predecessors. However, this cannot be said of his more recent work which describes only Gandhi's 'Harijan Uplift Movement' (1989: 291–295). Finally, Sumit Sarkar includes brief treatments of the Mahar movement but in the discussion of the 1930s decade only Gandhi's Harijan campaign is highlighted (1983: 56, 243, 328–30).

This brief survey would seem to suggest that there was no such thing as a modern Dalit movement, at least prior to India's independence. To virtually all these historians, Dalits were not movers and, even if they were, they moved not on their own but in the wake of socially concerned members of the dominant castes. Such treatment of the Dalits has been elitist and at times patronizing. Beginning with the pioneering work of Eleanor Zelliot in 1969, a growing number of historical monographs have recently offered a necessary corrective. These provide ample evidence of a Dalit movement prior to the enactment of the 1919 Constitution, growing in size and political significance through the 1920s and 1930s. Dalits may not have had a single organization parallel to the Muslim League or the Hindu Mahasabha, but they did have grassroot organizations; a recognized leadership, pre-eminent among whom was B.R. Ambedkar; and a common demand for political recognition, for their own political representation as well as for dignity, equality and justice. These demands found expression in the 1950 Constitution, of which B.R. Ambedkar was the chief drafter.

This essay provides a brief review of these monographs in the order of their date of publication.[5] Its purpose is both to indicate how the movement is currently being portrayed and to point to several important issues which any historian must face in trying to understand it. As will become apparent from the suggestions for inter-disciplinary discussion offered, historians will require the help of sociologists and other social scientists in dealing with these unavoidable issues.

Eleanor Zelliot's doctoral dissertation on B.R. Ambedkar and the Mahar movement has not yet been published, but has provided the basis for many of her frequently cited articles (1992).[6] It starts in 1890, 'the year which saw the beginning of articulate protest among the Mahars' (Zelliot 1969: 2), and concludes with an assessment of their condition following Ambedkar's death in 1956. Her history moves back and forth between developments within the Mahar caste and the movement on the one hand and, on the other, Mahars' involvement with the changing political context of the nationalist movement to which the British responded by progressively democratizing the political processes. Ambedkar, as both the acknowledged leader of the Mahars and a recognized spokesman of the Dalits, provides a continuing meeting point for these two developments. Zelliot makes considerable use of the analytical contrast between the traditional and the modern in writing this history. The early leaders of the Mahar movement, including Ambedkar, belonged to the non-traditional elite; they used modern methods of political agitation (petitions, newspapers, conferences, the Depressed Classes Institute, political parties); they also appealed to modern rather than to traditional values to press their case and further their cause. In this connection 1935 was a major turning point when Ambedkar not only gave up temple entry and renounced Hinduism, but also concentrated on using newly won political power and his own political parties to promote Dalits' interests.

While Zelliot confines her study to only the Mahar movement which had the most outstanding record of accomplishment, J.R. Kamble was the first to attempt a more comprehensive history. His *work* presents 'the saga of [how] people suffering from social, economic and political discrimination from times immemorial .... have achieved their emancipation', so that their story might become a part of modern Indian history (1979: xvii). In this narrative account, British rule provided the conditions and Hindu social reformers the changed attitudes (among caste Hindus) which made the Dalits' rise and awakening possible. Much of the history is devoted to Dalit efforts to gain political representation in the legislatures between the Montagu Declaration in 1917 and the Poona Pact in 1932. The book discusses negotiations over constitutional reform at the national level and assesses the contributions of Ambedkar and Gandhi to the Dalits' awakening, the neo-Buddhist movement. The efforts of the Government of India in promoting Dalit emancipation since independence are also evaluated. Kamble wrote as a nationalist who considered Dalit emancipation as the ongoing work of Dalits and 'all liberal and fair minded people'. He regarded Dalit emancipation as the necessary prerequisite (along with the end of caste privilege) for political stability. He was an unabashed advocate of the Dalit cause who considered their emancipation incomplete and hence requiring vigilance, continuation of the privileges conferred and organized efforts (Ibid.: 291).

By the end of the 1970s, therefore, for a historian of modern India there was not a large body of research on the modern Dalit movement to draw upon. It would be difficult to generalize from the rather exceptional Mahar case in Zelliot's study to the Dalits as a whole or to rely upon Kamble's more general work because its many large gaps and advocacy style may not inspire confidence. This situation would change in the mid-1980s.

The first monograph on the Dalit movement to appear in the 1980s is another case study, somewhat similar to Zelliot's. At the centre of Mark

Juergensmeyer's work (1982) is the Ad Dharm movement, which is traced from its origins in the 1920s to its demise in 1946 and revival in 1970. His major concern is not however with the history of one particular movement but with the role of religion in the lower caste struggles for social change. He therefore devotes one section of his book to 'competing visions', for example, the Ambedkarite (including Buddhism), the Valmiki, the Christian, the Marxist, and the Radhasoami. Thus, while much of the study is centred in and around the city of Jullundur—the headquarters of the Ad Dharmis where most of his data were gathered—it does provide insights into broader regional developments.

Following Juergensmeyer came three studies aimed at providing a more comprehensive view of the Dalit movement. The purpose of S. K. Gupta's study was to 'present a detailed and analytical account of the multifaceted struggle of the Scheduled Castes, the odyssey of their transformation from an apolitical, ostracized and indigent mass into a crucial factor in the Indian political structure' (1985: ix). He saw this transformation occurring between the last quarter of the 19th century and the Government of India Act, 1935—the precursor for Dalits to the Constitution of independent India. This transformation passed through three stages: the Dalits' initiation into politics by 1916, their establishing a political identity by 1927, and a marked change in their political status secured in the 1935 act. His account differs most significantly from Kamble's in providing considerable data on the aims and actions of Dalit political organizations at each step in the process of political change. He also saw the social reformers as playing a minimal role in initiating the Dalits into politics. Instead

> . . . political awakening among the Depressed Classes in the real sense of the term, and their introduction into the national political arena were a part of the process of their increasing importance for the various religious communities and groups that were vying with one another for increasing their strength on the one hand, and tending to decrease that of opponents on the other, in the game of 'politics of numbers' (1985: 168).

Atul Chandra Pradhan (1986) tells essentially the same story as did Gupta, but not in the same way. For one thing, his time frame is different. He considers developments prior to 1917 to be preparatory and treats them in a very summary fashion; however, he then extends his history beyond 1935 to 1947. For another, he organizes his account less around the various British-initiated announcements, missions, commissions, conferences, constitutions and elections than around the three key parties to the emergence of Depressed Classes' as a social reality and a political force to be taken increasingly seriously. These parties were the British policy-makers; Gandhi, and behind him (often far behind him in Pradhan's rendering) the Congress, the Hindu Mahasabha and other organs of Hindu religious opinion; and finally the Depressed Classes themselves, their leaders and organizations. The latter Pradhan divides into two categories: the separatists, such as B. R. Ambedkar and R. Srinivasan, and the nationalists, among whom the relative late-comer Jagjivan Ram was the most consistent.[7] Whereas the former sought recognition as a distinct minority with a separate identity and representation through separate electorates, the latter sought to become 'an unsegregated and unquarantined part of Hindu society'[8] and to work with the Congress in attaining national objectives. Pradhan's own assessment of both the identity and representation issues was closer to the nationalists' than to the separatists' position. For Pradhan, the emergence of the Depressed Classes did pose a 'problem' in national politics, second only to that posed by the Muslims, which remains not easily resolved. The concluding paragraph of his chapter on 1939–1947 provides an essentially happy ending to his story,

> With Ambedkar as the 'Father of the Indian Constitution' and the Congress as the ruling party, which under Gandhi's leadership had committed itself to the uplift of the backward sections of society, the Constitution of the Indian Union accepted the responsibility for ensuring the political representation as well as the legal, social, economic, educational and cultural development of the Scheduled Castes (1986: 313).

Trilok Nath (1987) aims to 'throw some light on the socio-political conditions which necessitated evolution of policies which made the "Depressed Classes" participation in politics a reality, however pale' (1987: vii). He concentrates primarily upon the decade from 1927 to 1937, although his treatment of the history from the end of the 19th century grows increasingly detailed as he approaches 1927. Like Gupta, he saw the communal struggle for power following the Aga Khan deputation and the 1909 Constitution as providing the Depressed Classes an opportunity for political participation. Also, like both Gupta and Pradhan, Trilok Nath not only concentrates upon politics at the All India level, which he considers to have been crucial for Dalits, but he also provides considerable information on Dalit political activities aimed at influencing policy at the Centre. His study, however, is brief. In his treatment of the 1927–1937 period, his narrative on the constitutional struggle stops with the Poona Pact instead of with the Government of India Act. He also devotes a chapter to temple entry and conversion, subjects which Pradhan treated but Gupta largely ignored. Also, like Pradhan, Trilok Nath generally pays more attention to differences between Dalit leaders and/or organizations and devotes a separate chapter comparing the contributions of Gandhi and Ambedkar.

With the publication of these three studies, there was no longer an excuse for omitting the Dalits from political histories of modern India covering the period between the two world wars. But histories of the Dalit movement since independence are yet to be published. A large number of micro-studies have, however, been conducted on reservations, social change, elites, and politics. Barbara John (1982) provides a good overview of these trends.

The number of monographs on modem Dalit history written so far in the 1990s is small. Nevertheless, it has now become apparent that there are major differences of approach to this subject which have implications for the understanding of the Dalit movement. My own study (1994) not only makes use of earlier studies, but also departs from them at three significant points. The first is that it considers Christian Dalit to be Dalits and therefore sets their history within the context of Dalit history. This point is not simply assumed but is argued in some detail at various places in the book. The result is a more inclusive and a rather more complex history. Second, I treated this history as the history of the modern Dalit movement. Of the earlier authors cited, only Zelliot and Juergensmeyer used the term 'movement'; Zelliot limited it to only one caste, while Juergensmeyer applied it to a variety of organized efforts which had anti-untouchability as a common theme. Like them, I considered the Dalits themselves to have been the major actors in their own history. Where I differed was in depicting a broader Dalit movement—of which the Mahar an Ad Dharm movements were integral and inter-connected parts—that began in the late 19th century and has continued up to the present time. This movement has gone through three stages, that is, mass conversion in the late 19th century, participation in the politics of numbers from 1917–47, and the politics of 'compensatory discrimination' since independence. Finally, I attempted a brief post-independence history of the Dalit movement. The latter proved to be a rather baffling exercise with no clear models to build upon or to critique.

Next, two disappointments should be mentioned. One is P.E. Mohan's (1993) book which is really not a history at all. In the first five chapters it provides descriptions of those organizations, agencies and individuals who were involved in elevating the Scheduled Castes. The remaining four chapters then assess the results of their efforts in *the* areas of economics, education, politics and civil rights. What is missing are the connections and dynamic interaction between the various actors in the four arenas he describes. The other disappointment is the series of *Subaltern Studies*. As Dalits certainly occupy a subaltern position in Indian society, the series could have had a significant impact upon our understanding of Dalit history. However, Dalits have been almost totally ignored, figuring occasionally as victims, even less frequently as minor perpetrators of violence, and only once as producers of a text.[9] Where they are mentioned, class categories predominate and caste is referred to only incidentally.

Jayashree Gokhale (1993) recently published a major study of the Mahar movement which not only covers a longer time span but also focuses more exclusively upon the Mahar community than does Zelliot's earlier work. She argued that 'from a depressed position at the fringes of Hindu society the Untouchable Mahars produced an autonomous political movement for their advancement and emancipation' (Ibid.: 336). This movement passed through several phases: the first from 1890–1930 was an era of self-reform characterized by a concern for social uplift and advance within the Hindu social and ideological order; in the second phase, from the First Round Table Conference until the mid-1950s, the Mahars turned their attention primarily to politics. The defeat of the Republican Party at the polls in 1952 and the mass conversion of Mahars to Buddhism mark the transition to a third phase in which they sought to establish a new identity. The rise of the Dalit Panthers and Dalit literature in the 1970s brought about the shift in the political and cultural orientation of the movement with which Gokhale concluded her study.

Two important distinctions inform Gokhale's analysis. The first is the distinction between the 'class model' and the 'caste model' of Mahar politics, each of which had its own conception of the nature of untouchability and how it is to be overcome.

> The class model was premised on the notion that Untouchability was primarily a socio-economic disability and as such, Untouchables had common interests with other members of the lower classes. Emancipation of the Untouchables could occur only through a revolution which would drastically alter the distribution of power in Indian society. In this endeavour, Untouchables had to unite with poor peasants, landless labourers, and workers; through the concerted action of all the poor and oppressed of Indian society and their incorporation within a political party, power could be wrested from the high-caste ruling class (1993: 115).
>
> The central notion behind the caste model, on the other hand, was that an irreducible gulf separated caste-Hindus from Untouchables, to the extent that political unity between the two was not possible. The hold of Hindu ideology was too pervasive to allow lower caste Hindus and Untouchables to cooperate for the realization of their common economic interests. Moreover, the problems of Untouchables were unique and could only be solved through the unity of all Untouchables, regardless of region and language. This unity of all Untouchables was to be achieved through a political organization which would operate at the national level (Ibid.: 115).

The Mahars moved back and forth between these two models during the course of their history. The other distinction informing Gokhale's analysis is that which emerged within the Mahar community itself between the urban, middle class elite, who had benefited from reservation or concessions, and the rural masses, who had not.

The most recent monograph on the Dalit movement is by Gail Omvedt (1993). Omvedt treats the Dalit movement as a part, in many ways the leading part, of a broader anti-caste movement which included non-Brahman movements as well (Ibid.: 10). This anti-caste movement was, in turn, part of a yet broader revolutionary democratic movement which included 'the national movement and communist and socialist led working class and peasant movements' as well (Ibid.: 13). Omvedt argues that the Dalit movement in particular and anti-caste movements in general should be seen as anti-systemic rather than basically reformist in nature. In so doing, she challenged the reigning Marxist view which regards class as the most important factor determining exploitation and considers the contradiction between the oppressed Indian nationality and British imperialism as the main one to be overcome and hence relegates the Dalit movement to the diversionary states of a diversionary manoeuvre (Ibid.: 13–14). Historically, the Dalit movement has questioned both the assumptions. On the one hand, it has seen caste (in both its occupational and purity-pollution dimensions) as exploitative and on the other it has questioned the meaning and identity of 'the nation' when such hierarchical divisions exist within it. Omvedt thus sets her study within a framework that is both Marxist and 'Phule- Ambedkarite' (Ibid.: 22) and concentrates on the Dalit movement in Maharashtra, Mysore, Hyderabad, and Andhra from 1920 to 1956, with a special eye to their relationship to the national movement and to other anti-caste and democratic revolutionary movements. In her analysis, which describes both 'Hinduistic' and 'autonomy' movements among Dalits, the years 1930–32 constitute a particularly significant 'defining moment' in Dalit relationship both to the Gandhian nationalists and to the Marxists. What makes her work so original is both the framework of analysis within which she sets it and her focus upon comparative regional history.

There are still no monographs on the Dalit movement in India after independence. Jogdand's *Dalit Movement in Maharashtra* (1991) does devote considerable space to what he called the post-Ambedkar era. V. T. Rajshekar Shetty's more journalistic Dalit Movement in Karnataka (1978) is also a regional study. There are synoptic accounts such as my own which focus upon protest, conflict and self-redefinition as well as Gail Omvedt's concluding chapter which described post-Ambedkar fragmentation followed by an upsurge of Dalit movement[10] in the 1970s. There have also been overviews of the current Dalit situation in India[11] (as well as theoretical analyses of Dalit movements covering the post-independence period (Oommen 1990, Ram 1995, Shah 1990). There are also numerous micro-studies on various aspects of Dalit life. However, the period from 1947 to the present remains a major chapter of Dalit history which is yet to be written.

If the ideal is a history of modern India with which large diverse groups or categories of Indians can identify, can locate themselves and their forebears in, and can claim as their own, how should the history of the Dalit movement be understood within such a history? The often conflicting understanding of the nature and dynamics of the modern Dalit movement described in this survey points to at least five unavoidable issues which historians must address to answer this question. The first of these is summed up in the question, who is a Dalit? Part of the confusion centres around the connotations of the word, 'Dalit'—the Marathi and Hindi translation of the British term, 'Depressed Classes'. Thus there is a more narrow reference which, like the original, is confined to the Scheduled Castes, as well as a broader one which includes all those (e.g., women, tribals, the poor of all castes, religious minorities) who either are similarly situated or are considered to be natural allies.

In scholarly approaches to Dalit history, those using a class analysis of Indian society subsume Dalits within categories such as peasants, agricultural labour, factory workers, students, and the like. This, however, not only fails to take account of the basic contradiction and oppression of the Dalits but also diverts attention away from them. On the other hand, those who use caste tend to adopt a communal, or what Marc Galanter has called a sacral, view of caste in their analyses.[12] Thus, only those members of the castes considered Untouchables within the Hindu sacral order who remain Hindus by religion are considered Dalits. If they convert to another religion, then they cease to be Dalits. This view is not only at serious odds with the realities uncovered by studies of caste among Christians and Muslims, but also is based upon that highly compartmentalized view of Indian society as a whole which framed the debates over the Constitution of India during the 1920s and 1930s. A more inclusive view, in which caste is seen not as an exclusively Hindu, but as an Indian phenomenon, seems called for.

The second is the conceptual issue concerning the use of 'movement' because it has either been used to refer to different realities or not used at all with reference to the Dalits. Specifically, can one speak of a Dalit movement or only of Dalit movements? Ghanshyam Shah's and Oommen's recent analyses of social movements, both of which include chapters on Dalit movements, reveal how difficult it is to come up with tight definitions or sets of characteristics which do justice to the complexities of diverse social movements in modern Indian history. Certainly, there has not been ideological or organizational unity among Dalits, if those must be the determining criteria. Yet, to borrow Oommen's terminology, there were many similarly placed primordial Dalit collectivities with similar histories of oppression simultaneously seeking to overcome similar deprivations within a common social system, albeit in different regional-linguistic areas and inspired by varying visions of their own and society's future.[13] Moreover while these movements did not have a common organization, they did not operate in isolation; they were aware of each other and did have a cumulative impact upon each other over time. Since the purpose of the historian of modern India is not to dissect such phenomena into smaller and smaller isolated bits for the sake of analytical precision, but to develop appropriate descriptive generalizations about significant continuities and changes over time, the label 'modern Dalit movement' for these many simultaneous and interconnected movements makes good sense.

Third, there has been disagreement over the background, and origins of the movement (if that is what it was). There has been a general consensus that it made its appearance on the national political scene soon after the Montagu Declaration in August 1917. What happened prior to that is treated simply as background. Those that treat it in some detail trace the sources of the movement to non-Dalit initiatives rather than to the Dalits themselves. I would argue instead that the modern Dalit movement was from its very inception a movement initiated by Dalits and for the Dalits. While there were Dalits who tried sanskritization and some who used occupational mobility to improve their lot, it was their mass conversions during the last quarter of the 19th century, especially but not exclusively to Christianity, which made their situation, identity and aspirations a matter of public concern. After the Aga Khan deputation and the 1909 Constitution, conversion acquired political overtones because it affected the communal balance of power. It was this situation which Ambedkar was able to turn to such good advantage during the 1920s and 1930s.

The fourth issue concerns the dynamics of this 'movement' not only at the 'centre' but also at the regional and local 'periphery' during the thirty years between the Montagu Declaration in 1917 and independence in 1947. The Dalit struggle during this period under the leadership of B. R. Ambedkar, M. C. Rajah and others was focused primarily upon gaining recognition, representation and power within the changing political order. On this scholars are in basic agreement. Studies of this stage of the modern Dalit movement have tended to concentrate primarily upon the constitutional struggle at the national level, as well as upon the ideology and roles of Gandhi and Ambedkar in that struggle. In fact, their thought seems to have become the major ideological resource for current reflection upon Dalit activism today. Yet part of any assessment of their ideologies would have to include a 'reality check' based upon studies of grassroots regional and/or caste movements of their day.[14] Certainly, it would be dangerous to generalize on the basis of the well-studied Mahar case alone. Additional studies of a similar nature are necessary for gaining knowledge about the foundations upon which Dalit leaders made their political claims and launched Dalit movements after independence.

Finally, amidst all the plethora of micro-studies, how is the post-independence history of the Dalit 'movement' best understood? Those who have attempted some integration and synthesis of all these studies are not agreed on what they add up to. Two approaches seem to predominate. One attempts to classify the variety of recent Dalit activity. Thus, for example, Nandu Ram differentiates the following three types of Dalit activism: movements against socio-economic exploitation and numerous types of atrocities on the Dalits; movements for better access to the opportunities and for realization of goals of equality, liberty, fraternity and justice; and movements for gaining self-respect and dignified social identity (1995: 131).

Alternatively, Barbara Joshi notes 'four alternative paths to equality' which Dalit leaders were advocating when she did her field research 'political power, economic independence, religious reform and social reform' (1982: 123). A second approach seeks an underlying unity beneath this diversity. This is the approach which both Gail Omvedt and I have adopted, albeit in different ways. In a similar manner, Rajni Kothari wrote in a recent article on the Dalits.

> The Dalit's expectation and strategy seems to be designed to challenge the dominant castes by means of education, employment and special rights, in short a struggle against the system that begins with challenging injustices within it, thinking of the struggle against imperialism and other such things as of second order importance. Or, as some of them would say, re-define the nature of imperialism in essentially social terms—both globally and locally (1994: 1592).

During the past decade an important start has been made in studying the history of what I have chosen to call the modern Dalit movement. Enough has been done now to recognize some of the major issues which all historians must face in seeking to give this movement its rightful place in modern

Indian history. In this essay I have mentioned five which seem unavoidable at present and have indicated how those issues are being framed. More issues will no doubt emerge as studies of this important subject continue. The five issues identified challenge some of the key assumptions about the nature of Indian society and the dynamics of its modern history to stimulate fresh inter-disciplinary re-visioning of the subject.

# Notes

1. This is a revision of the inaugural Ambedkar Lecture at Jawaharlal Nehru University given in November 1995. I wish to thank Professor Nandu Ram of the Centre for the Study of Social Systems for the invitation to give that lecture. A portion of it had been presented in October 1995 to the Fellows of the Indian Institute of Advanced Study in Shimla at the invitation of its Director, Professor Mrinal Miri. This revision has benefited from discussions on both occasions.
2. The work cited here is a reprint. The original edition was published in 1934 and revised following The Government of India Act of 1935.
3. Neither the Dalits nor Ambedkar find any place at all in Spear's more recent book (1973).
4. This was originally published in 1941.
5. I confine myself to monograph-length studies of the movement and do not discuss either the biographical literature, especially on B. R. Ambedkar, or the studies of the ideology of Ambedkar, Gandhi or both.
6. Many of these have been republished in her recent book *From Untouchable to Dalit* (1992).
7. In this categorization the other major Depressed Class leader, M. C. Rajah, is a rather problematic figure because he seemed to switch back and forth between the two positions. I see his shifts as basically tactical in nature; what seems to have been constant was his loyalty to Hinduism within which he wanted his people to occupy an honourable place.
8. This is Rajah's phrase.
9. This analysis is based on a survey of the first six volumes. The references above are to Gyan Pandey (1983: 60–129); Arvind N. Das, (Ibid.: 180–227); David Arnold (1984: 62–115): and Gyan Pandey (1984: 231–70).
10. This is a distillation of a much longer chapter on the anticaste movement during the post-independence period in her *Reinventing Revolution* (1993).
11. See for example, Oliver Mendelsohn and Marika Vicziany (1994). Most of this paper is devoted to poverty, discrimination and to what is being done about them. The section on Dalit activism is entitled, 'Failure of Untouchables Political Mobilization'.
12. He contrasted this with the sectarian, associational, and organic views.
13. Oommen saw these movements crystallizing first against socio-cultural oppression (especially untouchability), then for political enfranchisement, and most recently overlap but also that some movements combined the three elements (1990 256–57).
14. This is the most important thing lacking in M. S. Gore's (1993) otherwise excellent study of Ambedkar's ideology Gore relied almost exclusively on sources either by or about Ambedkar.

# References


Arnold, David. 1984. 'Famine in peasant consciousness and peasant action, Madras 1876–8', in Ranjit Guha (ed.): *Subaltern studies writings on south Asian history and society, Vol III* (62–115). Delhi: Oxford University Press.

Brown, Judith M. 1994. *Modern India: The origins of an Asian democracy* (second edition). Oxford University Press.

Chandra, Bipan 1971. *Modern India: A textbook of history for secondary schools.* New Delhi: National Council of Educational Research and Training.

Chandra, Bipan et al. 1989. *India's struggle for Independence 1857–1947.* New Delhi: Penguin Books.

Das, Arvind N. 1983. 'Agrarian change from above and below Bihar 1947–78', in Ranjit Guha (ed.): *Subaltern studies writings on south Asian history and society, Vol II* (180–227). Delhi Oxford University Press.

Dodwell, H. H. (ed.). 1958. *The Cambridge history of India: The Indian empire 1858–1918, Vol VI,* with additional chapters on 'The last phase 1919–1947' by R. R. Sethi. Delhi: S Chand & Co.

Galanter, Marc. 1968. 'Changing legal conceptions of caste' in M. Singer and B. S. Cohn (eds.): *Structure and Change in Indian society* (299–336). Chicago: Aldine Publishing Company.

Gokhale, Jayshree. 1993. *From concessions to confrontation: The politics of an Indian untouchable community.* Bombay: Popular Prakashan.

Gore, M. S. 1993. *The social context of an ideology: Ambedkar's political and social thought.* New Delhi: SAGE Publications.

Gupta, S. K. 1985. *The scheduled castes in modern Indian politics: Their emergence as a political power.* Delhi: Munshiram Manoharlal.

Jogdand, Prahlad Gangaram. 1991. *Dalit movement in Maharashtra.* New Delhi: Kanak Publications.

John, Barbara R. 1982. *Democracy in search of equality: Untouchable politics and Indian social change.* Delhi: Hindustan Publishing Corporation.

Juergensmeyer, Mark. 1982. *Religion as social vision: The movement against untouchability in 20th century Punjab.* Berkeley: University of California Press.

Kamble, J. R. 1979. *Rise and awakening of depressed classes in India.* New Delhi: National Publishing House.

Kothari, Rajni. 1994. 'Rise of the Dalits and the renewed debate on caste', *Economic and political weekly,* 25 June.

Majumdar, R. C. et al. 1956. *An advanced history of India. Modern India—Part III.* London: Macmillan & Co.

———. 1969. *The history and culture of the Indian people. Struggle for freedom.* Bombay: Bharatiya Vidya Bhavan.

Mendelsohn, Oliver and Marika Vicziany. 1994. 'The untouchables', in Oliver Mendelsohn and Upendra Baxi (eds.): *The rights of subordinated peoples* (64–116). Delhi: Oxford University Press.

Mohan, P. E. 1993. *Scheduled castes history of elevation, Tamil Nadu, 1900–1950.* Madras: New Era Publications.

Nath, Trilok. 1987. *Politics of the depressed classes.* Delhi: Deputy Publications.

O'Malley, L. S. S. 1968. 'The Hindu social systems', in L. S. S. O'Malley (ed.), *Modern India and the West: A study of the interaction of their civilizations* (354–388). London: Oxford University Press.

Oommen, T. K. 1990. *Protest and change: Studies in social movements*. New Delhi: SAGE Publications.

Omvedt, Gail. 1993. *Reinventing revolution: New social movements and the socialist tradition in India*. Armonk, New York: M. E. Sharpe.

———. 1994. *Dalits and the democratic revolution: Dr. Ambedkar and the Dalit movement in colonial India*. New Delhi: SAGE Publications.

Pandey, Gyan. 1983. 'Rallying round the cow. Sectarian strife in the Bhojpuri region, 1888–1917', in Ranjit Guha (ed.): *Subaltern studies. Writings on South Asian history and society, Vol II* (60–129). Delhi: Oxford University Press.

———. 1984. 'Encounters and calamities. The history of a north Indian Qasba in the nineteenth century' in Ranjit Guha (ed.): *Subaltern studies: Writings on south Asian history and society, Vol III* (231–70). Delhi: Oxford University Press.

Pradhan, Atul Chandra. 1986. *The emergence of the depressed classes*. Bhubaneswar: Book and International.

Ram, Nandu. 1995. *Beyond Ambedkar: Essays on Dalits in India*. New Delhi: Har Anand Publications.

Roberts, P. E. 1958. *History of British India under the company and the crown* (third edition completed by T. G. P. Spear). London: Oxford University Press.

Sarkar, Sumit. 1983. *Modern India 1885–1947*. Delhi: Macmillan.

Shah, Ghanshyam. 1990. *Social movements in India: A review of the literature*. New Delhi: SAGE Publications.

Shetty, T.V. Rajsekhar. 1978. *Dalit movement in Karnataka*. Madras: Christian Literature Society.

Smith, Vincent A. 1961. *The Oxford history of India*, 3rd edition. Edited by Percival Spear. Oxford: Clarendon Press.

Spear, Percival. 1973. *A history of India, Vol II*. Harmondsworth: Penguin Books.

Thomson, Edward and G. T. Garrett. 1962. *Rise and fulfillment of British rule in India*. Allahabad: Central Book Depot.

Webster, John C.B. 1994. *The Dalit Christians: A history*, 2nd edition. Delhi: Indian Society for the Propagation of Christian Knowledge (ISPCK).

Zelliot, Eleanor Mac. 1969. *Dr. Ambedkar and the Mahar movement*. Unpublished Ph.D. thesis, University of Pennsylvania.

———. 1992. *From Untouchables to Dalit: Essays on the Ambedkar movement*. New Delhi: Manohar Publications.

# 3

# Socio-cultural Marginality: A Theory of Urban Slums and Poverty in India*

*Victor S. D'Souza*

The poor and the slum-dwellers happen to be more or less the same people in the urban setting and therefore it is implied that one and the same theory may help to explain the problem of both poverty and slums. In many of the existing studies, the presumed causes of this problem are derived merely from a description of the problem in some society or other; one dimension or another in the description is treated as the cause. Solutions of the problem attempted on the basis of such presumed causes have rarely been successful. The present study lays emphasis on two aspects of the problem: first, the poor and the slum-dwellers occupy the lowest rungs of the social hierarchy and, second, their low status is socially inherited and perpetuated. With the help of a deductive model of propositions taken from urban studies, it is hypothesized that the problem exists because the poor and the slum-dwellers occupy marginal positions in the socio-cultural system of the community. Evidence is adduced from different towns and cities in India in support of this hypothesis. It is concluded that for a satisfactory solution of the problem in question, the poor and the slum-dwellers should be socially integrated into the community.

Slum and poverty go hand in hand in towns and cities. This situation, however, does not indicate that there are no poor people living outside the slum nor does it imply that everyone who lives in the slum is poor. For that matter, there are no clear-cut definitions of the terms 'slum' and 'the poor', and the dividing lines between the slum and the non-slum areas and between the poor and the non-poor are always arbitrary. But the fact remains that most of the poor people live in slums and most of the slum-dwellers are poor. There is no doubt that there is an intimate relationship between slums and poverty, and it is reasonable to assume that more or less the same causes underlie both the phenomena. Therefore, for the present discussion the terms 'slum-dwellers' and 'the poor', especially in the urban setting, are used interchangeably, and the slum may be regarded as the physical and socio-cultural environment of the poor.

In India, slums are found in all urban settlements, large or small, old or new, unplanned or planned. As a matter of fact, the slum problem is ubiquitous in cities all the world over, although with variable dimensions. Does it then mean that slums are a necessary concomitant of urbanization? But the mere prevalence of slums, no matter on how wide a scale, does not signify that they are inevitable in all urban communities unless it can be shown that their causes are inevitably related to some general aspect of urbanization. There are, however, some who think that slums are a by-product of industrialization which is responsible for the rapid urbanization in modern times. But slums are as much a scourge of the pre-industrial cities as of the industrial ones. The fact is that causes of slums as well as those of poverty are still not clearly understood.

Attempts at understanding slums rarely go beyond their description and, at best, beyond the formulation of their ideal types. Popular conceptions of slums emphasize three major sets of characteristics related to their physical, economic and social aspects. Slums are described as congested localities with substandard housing and insanitary surroundings accommodating poor people who follow low-paid occupations or are underemployed or unemployed, and who lead a life of crime and are morally depraved. These aspects are assumed to be interrelated and causally connected. For instance, according to a widely accepted definition, the slum is 'a residential area in which the housing is so deteriorated, so substandard and so unwholesome as to be a menace to the health, safety, morality or welfare of the occupants' (Hunter, 1968: 13). Implied in this definition is the assumption that poor housing is the cause underlying slum conditions. This line of thinking has led some to believe that the solution of the problem of slums would lie in providing the slum-dwellers with improved housing. But even the massive public-housing projects as a major effort to solve the slum problem in the United States have not yielded the desired results (Rainwater, 1974: 148–157).

There is some merit in not treating all slum-dwellers as constituting a homogeneous category. Therefore typologies of different categories of slum-dwellers, based on their characteristic differences and problems, are useful in imparting depth to our understanding of the problem. For instance, according to one typology, the slum-dwellers are classified into four ideal-types, depending upon the variables of duration of stay and the availability or unavailability of special opportunities. The ideal-types are: (1) Permanent necessitarians, (2) temporary necessitarians, (3) permanent opportunists and (4) temporary opportunists (Hunter, 1968: 17–18). Similarly, slums are also distinguished into categories such as (a) entry areas for newcomers to the city, (b) areas populated by social rejects who have not succeeded in the city and (c) places of economic opportunities insofar as they harbour some of the deviant economic activities not tolerated in the non-slum areas (Hunter, 1968: 17). Typologies such as these may help to characterize different kinds of slums and slum-dwellers, but they do not explain the existence of slums. Even as classificatory devices, they have only a limited application to the Indian setting, because slums in India cannot be divided into such neat categories.

The poor and the slum-dwellers have often been defined in terms of income. From this perspective, the solution to the problem of poverty and slums would appear to consist in raising the income of the poor people and the slum-dwellers. Indeed, such a solution has been attempted on a grand scale in the United States through the expensive programmes of the New Deal and the War on Poverty, but these programmes have only resulted in an ever greater dependence of the poor upon public welfare, without having much success in helping them to stand on their own legs Moynihan, 1973: 17–60), although the usefulness of the welfare programmes, which combine economic and with other appropriate measures for the solution of the problem, cannot be denied. Therefore better housing and economic subsidy have proved to be ineffectual in solving the problem of slums and poverty, showing thereby that the economic factor by itself is not a sufficient cause of poverty.

A much-talked-about concept concerning slums and poverty is the 'culture of poverty', formulated by Oscar Lewis. According to him, poverty, in general, and slum life, in particular, have a number of associated traits related to family structure, interpersonal relations, time orientation, value systems and spending patterns, which transcend national boundaries and which are handed down from generation to generation along family lines. To begin with, the culture of poverty comes into existence as a form of adaptation and reaction of the poor to their marginal position in a class-stratified and highly individuated capitalist society. Once this culture is formed, it perpetuates itself (Lewis, 1961). This view, although highly popular among social scientists, has been criticized on many grounds. Empirical evidence culled from various sources shows that the poor appear to be only quantitatively, rather than qualitatively, different from the people of the higher socio-economic strata (Reissman, 1973: 50). Charles Valentine considers the model of the culture of poverty to be the total picture of the culture of the lower class, as absurd and regards it as 'a middle-class intellectual rationale for blaming poverty on the poor and thus avoiding recognition of the need for radical change in our society' (Valentine, 1973: 168). Even if it can be demonstrated that the poor have a special subculture, it may, at best, be treated as a dependent variable rather than independent one.

However, even Oscar Lewis was not able to detect the 'culture of poverty' in his studies of the poor in India. This contention is further confirmed by Wiebe who, in his detailed study of the social life in a slum in Madras, has come to the conclusion that whereas the slum-dwellers are evidently poor, they do not live in a 'culture of poverty' (Wiebe, 1975). Most of the studies on Indian slums indicate that the dimension of the morally deviant behaviour, which is regarded in the popular definition as a necessary concomitant of slum life, is rarely to be found in Indian slums; the slums usually form integrated communities.

Yet another perspective suggested for an understanding of the problem of slums and poverty is to regard it as a social-class phenomenon; the poor and the slum-dwellers represent the lower-class group in society and their problems arise essentially from their living at the bottom of the social hierarchy (Rainwater, 1974: 70–76). The advantage of this perspective is that, by linking slums and poverty with the system of social stratification, it enables one to view the problem in all its complexity (Reissman, 1973: 52–57). But the authors who advocate this point of view have a restricted idea about social stratification, by which they only mean a hierarchy of status positions. Such a narrow view can help us only to describe the problem of poverty but not pinpoint its causes.

The difficulty in analysing the presumed causes of slums and poverty is that they are mostly based on the description of the problem in one part of the world or in another. In such studies, the problem with its characteristic dimensions is sought to be solved by remedying some of its dominant features. But in practice, such efforts have rarely succeeded. For a genuine understanding and solution of the problem, its true causes have to be discovered.

The new viewpoint put forward in this paper is based on deductive reasoning and verification, although it needs further scrutiny for a fuller validation. In a study published elsewhere (D'Souza, 1970: 70–74), I deduced a possible cause of slums from a set of deductively related propositions derived from urban studies. The advisability of relying on the knowledge from the field of urban studies for finding propositions in formulating a theoretical model was suggested by the fact that the intersection of slums and poverty is a ubiquitous feature of urban settlements everywhere. The line of reasoning follows somewhat like this: The slums constitute an element in the spatial or ecological structure of the city and so they represent one among the different types of land uses. This is the first proposition in my deductive model. There is an important finding of some American studies about the relationship of slums with other kinds of land uses. This relationship states that slums are usually located on marginal areas in between different types of land uses; for instance, between commercial and residential uses. In other words, the slums occupy a marginal position on the ecological structure of the community (Firey, 1963: 781–804). This is the second proposition in the deductive model.

It may be pointed out that the second proposition implies that slums tend to be located in places which are unsuitable for more profitable uses and so some of the slum conditions are inherent in the physical location itself of slums. The land values of the slum property are low not because poor people live there, but on the contrary the poor select the slum location because of the low land values already existing there. (In course of time, however, because of further changes in the ecological structure, the slum property may acquire a potentially higher value). The slums are rarely recognized as a proper mode of land use on their own right but they are included among land uses which are only marginally regular.

A third proposition, which is deductively related to the first two propositions, is that there is an intimate relationship between the ecological structure of a city and its social structure. The various theories about the physical structure of the city, such as the concentric zone theory of Park and Burgess and the sector theory of Homer Hoyt, emphasize the fact that the ecological structure of a city is a spatial representation of its social structure. For instance, the different social groups in a city tend to segregate themselves in different localities and enjoy differential advantages of their spatial locations.

From the above three propositions it may be argued that if the slums, which are an element of the ecological structure of the city, are marginal in the ecological structure and if there is an intimate relationship between the ecological structure and the social structure then it follows that the slum-dwellers also occupy a marginal position in the social structure of the community. Just as it was argued that the property in the slums has a low value because of its marginal location vis-à-vis the recognized land uses, the slum-dwellers are poor because of their marginal relationship with people who are considered to be the regular members of the community.

It can now be shown that the socio-cultural marginality of the poor and the slum-dwellers is the real cause of their poverty. The viewpoints that the poor are the people who live at the bottom of the social hierarchy and that the problem of poverty is an aspect of social inequality and stratification are of much significance. But it is necessary to stress the point that poverty is in most cases socially inherited and perpetuated. It cannot be denied that there are people who become poor in their lifetime and that under special circumstances poor people are uplifted. In a society based on the division of labour, with differential rewards and prestige attached to different positions, it is but natural that some people will live at the bottom of the social hierarchy just as the others will be placed at the middle and upper rungs. But the problem of poverty is compounded by the fact that it is the same people and the same groups who perpetually live at the bottom. Therefore the more pernicious aspect of slum is not that its residents are poor, but that they have no hope for improvement through their own efforts.

There is a naive assumption that people get positions and rewards according to their abilities and hard work; if one so chooses, one can live well by working hard. It, therefore, follows that the slum-dwellers and the poor are themselves to blame for their poverty. But the facts are different. The slum-dwellers are poor not because they are lazy or unemployed; on the contrary, they work the longest hours and perform the most arduous and unattractive tasks. The literature on slums in India does not reveal any larger extent of unemployment among the slum-dwellers than among the non-slum population. As a matter of fact, the proportion of workers among the slum-dwellers is relatively large. Therefore the only reason for the slum-dwellers to be poor is that they are paid less than a living-wage for their work. The society justifies this low payment by maintaining that the work they do is not up to the mark.

The causes of poverty and its perpetuation are much more subtle and complex than the assumption that the poor are the unsuccessful people in society. There are two views regarding the perpetuation of poverty and slum conditions. One view carries the concept of 'culture of poverty', i.e. poverty and slum conditions are self-perpetuating. I reject this view. The second view presumes that the disadvantaged condition of slum-dwellers is forced upon them by the dominant sections of the community to subserve their own interests (Valentine, 1973: 166–167). The second view, with which I agree, implies that the dominant section of the community exerts its power, although in devious ways, in forcing some people to remain perpetually in servitude. But it needs to be explained why one section is kept perpetually poor by the other. The hypothesis derived from this study gives the explanation. The slum-dwellers and the poor occupy a marginal position in the socio-cultural system of the community. It is because the poor are 'outsiders' that their degradation does not emotionally disturb the dominant sections. For the same reason we also find that in almost every society jobs considered undesirable and rejected by its own members are filled by the immigrant aliens.

However, it cannot be gainsaid that the problem of poverty and slums is related to the problem of social inequality which falls within the area of social stratification. But the existing theories of social stratification are rather too vague to throw sufficient light upon the causes of poverty. Inequality has three major dimensions: first, the social differentiation resulting from a division of labour which is necessary for an efficient functioning of society; second, the social hierarchy which is derived from the differential rewards accruing to people occupying different social positions; and third, the tendency for the social inheritance and perpetuation of the first two aspects of inequality. The theories of social stratification are too weak to explain the third aspect of social inequality and it is to this area that the explanation of poverty belongs.

The hypothesis that the poor and the slum-dwellers occupy socio-culturally marginal positions in the communities they live in may now be tested. For the time being, we may be satisfied with a descriptive analysis of some of the available evidence from various towns and cities in India. One piece of evidence, which I have already cited in an earlier paper (D'Souza, 1970) and which is repeated here, comes from a study of the slums carried out in 1969 in three cities namely Batala, Hoshiarpur and Jullundur, of the Punjab State. The information relevant to our hypothesis is presented in Table 3.1. The socio-cultural marginality is empirically defined for the present purpose in terms of two factors: (1) the position representing the lowest rungs of the caste-system i.e. structural marginality: or (2) the position representing a different culture or subculture i.e. cultural marginality, or representing both. The sample households in Table 3.1 have been classified into three categories along the dimension of caste hierarchy: non-Backward Castes, Backward Castes and the Scheduled Castes.[1] Of these categories, Backward Castes to some extent, and the Scheduled Castes, particularly, may be regarded as marginal categories in the structure of the community. Along the subcultural dimension, the sample households have been divided into the categories of displaced persons,[2] migrants from the surrounding areas and persons born in the city itself.

**Table 3.1:** The Percentage of Distribution of the Sample of Slum Households in Batala, Hoshiarpur and Jullunder on the Basis of the Caste Background and the Place of Origin

| *Place of origin/Caste background* | *Displaced persons* | *Migrants from the surrounding areas* | *Born in the city* | *Total* |
|---|---|---|---|---|
| Non-backward Castes | 10.8 | 2.8 | 0 | 6.3 |
| Backward Castes | 13.1 | 8.7 | 0 | 8.4 |
| Scheduled Castes | 76.1 | 88.5 | 100 | 85.3 |
| Total 100% | 230 | 69 | 129 | 428 |

*Source*: Victor S. D'Souza (1970).

The evidence from Table 3.1 is overwhelmingly in support of the hypothesis that the slum-dwellers are marginal in the socio-cultural system of the cities, inasmuch as 85.3 per cent of the sample households of slum-dwellers belong to the Scheduled Castes which are structurally marginal, and 53.7 per cent of the households are made up of displaced persons who are, in a sense, culturally marginal. (The enormity of the representation of the Scheduled Castes in the slums becomes evident when it is realized that according to the Census of 1971, the percentages of the Scheduled Castes in the cities, as whole including slums, were only 20.73, 12.51 and 9.50 in Jullundur, Hoshiarpur and Batala, respectively. The few heads of the households belonging to the non-Backward and Backward Castes are found only among the migrants and the displaced persons who have come to the slums for the first time in their lifetime. Among the heads of households born in the cities, all, without exception, are those belonging to the Scheduled Castes. It would thus appear that the slums serve merely as entry areas for the persons belonging to the higher castes who have their representatives in the non-slum areas and who eventually manage to move out of the slums. But the slums are the permanent habitations of the Scheduled Castes who are at the extreme end of the community's social structure.

Evidence from different cultural regions of India, besides the Punjab State, is also in conformity with our hypothesis. For instance, Table 3.2 shows the percentage distribution of the households in the city and the slums of Surat in the Gujarat State, according to their caste background. The information is taken from a study conducted in 1973 (Shah, 1975). It may be seen that whereas the higher, middle and artisan castes together comprise 54 per cent of the city's households, their share in the households of the slums is a meagre 10 per cent. On the other hand, the households of the structurally

**Table 3.2:** The Caste Background of Households in the City of Surat in the Gujarat State (N = 1964) and in Its Slums (N = 2,100)

| *Caste* | *City* | *Slum* |
|---|---|---|
| Upper castes | 14 | 3 |
| Middle castes | 27 | 3 |
| Artisan castes | 13 | 4 |
| Low castes | 8 | 8 |
| Scheduled Castes and Tribes | 15 | 44 |
| Non-Gujaratis | 8 | 22 |
| Non-Hindus | 14 | 15 |
| Others | 1 | 1 |
| Total percentage | 100 | 100 |

*Source*: Ghanshyam Shah (1975).

and culturally marginal groups, namely the Scheduled Castes and Tribes and the non-Gujaratis, are grossly underrepresented in the City (23 per cent) and are over-represented in the slums.

From a large-scale sample survey of the slums in Delhi, covering over 20,000 households, it was found that 65 per cent of the slum households were made up of low castes and the Scheduled Castes (Town and Country Planning Organization, 1975). In a more recent survey of the slums in the twin cities of Hyderabad and Secunderabad, Naidu (forthcoming) has classified the slum households into the categories shown in Table 3.3.

**Table 3.3:** The Distribution of the Slum Households in Hyderabad–Secunderabad into Ethnic Categories

| *Ethnic category* | *Total number of households* | *Percentage* |
|---|---|---|
| Caste Hindus | 3,282 | 6.73 |
| Schedules Castes and Tribes | 28,662 | 58.79 |
| Muslims | 16,799 | 34.46 |
| Others | 10 | 0.02 |
| Total | 48,753 | 100.00 |

The Muslims, like the Hindus, are also subdivided into castes of varying degrees of socio-economic status. Although this fact was not taken note of in the study, Naidu has confirmed in a personal communication that the overwhelming proportion of the Muslims in the slums belongs to castes comprising the lowest rungs of the socio-economic ladder. Thus the socio-cultural marginality of the slum-dwellers in the twin-cities is quite evident.

There are slums even in Chandigarh which is a comprehensively planned city and it is interesting to see if the slum situation in this is city is in conformity with our analysis of the slum problem. Chandigarh being a new city made up entirely of migrants, we find that there is a wider mix of caste groups in its slums. In a survey of sums conducted in 1964 (D'Souza, 1968: 252–265), it was found that 24 per cent of slum-dwellers belonged to the Scheduled Castes. This is not an impressive proportion, although compared with the proportion of the Scheduled Castes in the rest of the city, being barely 6 per cent, it was quite high. But what was more remarkable was the fact that the overwhelming percentage of the slum-dwellers came from the regions outside the former Punjab State, indicating the cultural marginality of the slum-dwellers. Whereas only 16 per cent of the population in the rest of the City was drawn from outside the Punjab, the corresponding percentage in the slums was as high as 70.

The population of Chandigarh has grown very fast and that of its slums still faster. During the 1961–71 decade, whereas its population, as a whole, grew by 146 per cent, that of its slums increased by 230 per cent. There are figures available for the proportion of the Scheduled Castes in the population. As against 24 per cent in 1961, the population of the Scheduled Castes in the slums in 1971 rose to 38.6 per cent and a few years later, i.e. in 1974, a sample survey of slum-dwellers revealed that the Backward Castes and the Scheduled Castes together constituted 57 per cent of total population of the slums (Sarin, 1975). These figures are not strictly comparable, but they certainly indicate a growing concentration of the Scheduled Castes in the slums, and this observation supports our hypothesis.

An analysis of the internal structure of the slums also lends further evidence to our hypothesis. In the 1964 study of the slums of Chandigarh referred to above, the migrants from the home State of Punjab, representing in this case the dominant section of the City's population, were not only very much under-represented in the slums, but among the slum-dwellers, they occupied a relatively privileged position. Occupationally and incomewise, they were better off than their fellow slum-dwellers coming from regions outside the Punjab. Their residences, considering slum standards, were of a better finish as compared with those of other categories which are mostly of an inferior finish; 90 per cent of the slum-dwellers belonging to the home State had pucca houses as compared with 24 per cent of the rest of the slum-dwellers.

The socio-cultural and racial marginality of a group is an important factor in its integration with the larger community. Warner and his associates, who studied the integration of racial and ethnic groups in an American community, came to the conclusion that the ease with which a racial or ethnic group integrated with the larger community depended upon the degree of nearness of its racial or cultural background with that of the dominant section (Warner, 1962: 380–425). The case is similar in Chandigarh also. In an investigation aimed at studying the integration of slum-dwellers with the larger community, it has been found that the different cultural and structural segments manifest different degrees of integration with the larger community (Kamlesh Kanta, 1970). The slum-dwellers from the home State showed the highest degree of integration; those from the neighbouring States showed the next higher degree and the those from States farthest removed showed this tendency to the smallest degree. So also the higher castes showed a greater degree of integration than the castes lower down along the continuum. The people belonging to the lowest castes, e.g. the Scheduled Castes, coming from the farthest region of Tamil Nadu, being both culturally and structurally the most marginal section in respect of the main community, are least integrated with it. They are the most disadvantaged section among the slum-dwellers.

On the other hand, integration with the larger community is inversely related to integration within a slum (Kamlesh Kanta, 1970). In a slum, the residents are integrated mostly within their kinship, caste and regional circles, so that people drawn from different regions and castes from a plural society (D'Souza, 1975). Such a phenomenon, while helping the slum-dwellers not to be demoralized and alienated, renders them incapable of politically mobilizing their numerical strength for the redress of their grievances.

The treatment meted out to the slum-dwellers everywhere follows a typical pattern. Because the slum-dwellers occupy a marginal position in the community, their misery rarely rouses the compassion it deserves from the dominant section. All the same, the dominant section is concerned with the slums because of the danger which the unhygienic conditions and the ugly appearance of the slums pose to its own health and to the aesthetic beauty of the City. Thus the problem is viewed in the light of the interests of the dominant section rather than in that of the interests of the slum-dwellers. Therefore the solution of the problem is usually construed in terms of removing the slums rather than in those of rehabilitating and integrating the slum-dwellers in the community.

The Chandigarh experience has been true to type. Even in this planned city, the housing of the poorer sections, belonging mostly to the unorganized sector of the economy was not considered to be a legitimate land use to be included as a part of the general plan of the City. In the initial stages of the development of the City, the poor, particularly the construction-workers, had to squat on the available open spaces close to their place of work. With the gradual extension of construction, they had to move from place to place, with the consequent destruction of their meagre belongings and with the concomitant disruption of their economic and social life. But the worse was yet to come.

After seven or eight years of its inception, when the City began to take shape, the slums began to stand out as ugly scars against the beauty of the new City. It was then that the authorities decided that the City should be cleared of all the slums and ordered that the squatters should remove their huts at their own cost. But there was no suggestion regarding the place they were to go to. A tense situation developed and to save themselves from this impending horrible plight, the labourers struck work and even lay down in front of the bulldozers commissioned by the authorities to demolish their lowly huts. In the end, the authorities were forced to relent, but only to the extent of providing them with alternative accommodation on the outskirts of the City and that too without any fixed tenure. When the growing numbers of the poor soon outstripped this provision, howsoever unsatisfactory, no further attention was paid to the augmenting of accommodation and, therefore, again unauthorized slums sprang up alongside the authorized ones (Sarin, 1975). Thus the poor have been denied the right to live in the regularly planned part of the City. The attitude of the authorities has been one of indifference, which can only be explained by the fact that the slum-dwellers occupy a marginal position in the community. In contrast to the plight of the poor, the housing needs of the professional and other privileged sections, which are closely connected with the decision-makers, have often received solicitous attention.

The foregoing presentation of the data about the slum situation in Chandigarh as well as in some other cities of India supports the hypothesis that one of the important causes of poverty and slums is the fact that the poor and the slum-dwellers occupy a marginal position in the socio-economic life of the community. There are also non-marginal people who are poor and who live in slums; but the poor people, who are socio-culturally marginal, are faced with severer problems of integration. It is the intersection of poverty and the socio-cultural marginality which creates the special problems of the slum-dwellers and their isolation from the rest of the community.

Whereas the definition of the slum would always remain imprecise, the present analysis would imply that it can be made more useful by including in it at least three major ideas: (1) economic poverty of the residents, (2) their socio-cultural marginality and (3) the deteriorating housing and environmental conditions. This new perspective on slums and poverty would suggest that for a real solution of the problem, the poor and the slum-dwellers, besides being provided with economic help and housing facilities, need to be integrated into the community in which they live. Integration is a complex process which cannot be adequately dealt with here. But it is useful to point out that one of the key elements in integration in the present context is the creation of opportunities for occupational mobility which the poor are deprived of. Occupation does not merely mean a person's earning his livelihood but also the major activity through which he relates himself to his community and society either directly or indirectly, and thereby realizes his moral worth, which is so necessary for the fulfilment of his psychological needs. Some occupations, especially those with high prestige, provide a greater scope for satisfying these needs, whereas some others, such as those followed by the poor, may have even the opposite potential for an attack on a person's moral worth (Rainwater, 1974: 73). Thus the poor are compelled to work mainly for their livelihood and not for other kinds of satisfaction which the occupation entails. If they are provided with economic subsidy alone, without the prospects of providing them with more satisfying job opportunities, they may just withdraw from the labour force and be alienated further from the society.

## Notes

*A revised version of the paper presented at the Ninth World Congress of Sociology in Uppsala, Sweden, 1978.

Thanks are expressed to Kirsten A. Gronbjerg for her valuable comments on an earlier draft of the paper.

1. The classification of the Scheduled Castes and Backward Castes was made in conformity with the lists prepared by the Punjab State Government under the constitutional provision for giving them special concessions.
2. People who came to India from Pakistan as a result of the historic partition of the country in 1947.

## References

D'Souza, Rita Sunita. 1975. *The social integration of a multi-ethnic slum*, unpublished M. A. dissertation in sociology, submitted to the Panjab University, Chandigarh.

D'Souza, Victor S. 1968. *Social structure of a planned city: Chandigarh*. New Delhi: Orient Longmans Limited.

———. 1970. 'Slums and social structure', *Urban and rural planning thought, Vol. XIII* (1–2).

Firey, Walter. 1963. 'Ecological considerations in planning for urban fringe', in Paul K. Hatt and Albert J. Reiss Jr. (eds.): *Cities and society* (791–804). The Free Press of Glencoe, Inc.

Hunter, David R. 1968. *The slums*. New York: First Free Press Paperback Edition.

Kanta, Kamlesh. 1970. *Some aspects of integration of slum dwellers in the large community*, unpublished M. A. dissertation in Sociology, submitted to the Panjab University, Chandigarh.

Lewis, Oscar. 1961. *The children of Sanchez*. Random House, Inc.

Moynihan, Daniel P. 1973. *The politics of a guaranteed income*. New Delhi: Affiliated East-West Press Pvt. Ltd.

Naidu, Ratna. Forthcoming. 'A report on slums in Hyderabad-Secunderabad', *Indian journal of social work*.

Rainwater, Lee. 1974a. 'Poverty in the United States', in Lee Rainwater (ed.): *Social problems and public policy* (70–76). Chicago: Aldine Publishing Company.

———. 1974b. 'The slum and its problems', in Lee Rainwater (ed.): *Social problems and public policy*. Chicago: Aldine Publishing Company.

Reissman, Leonard. 1973. *Inequality in American society*. Glenview, Illinois: Scott, Foresman and Company.

Sarin, Madhu. 1975. *Planning and the urban poor: The Chandigarh experience* (mimeographed), School of Environmental Studies, University College, London.

Shah, Ghanshyam. 1975. 'City and slums in urbanization in India and Gujarat', *Seminar, Department of Sociology*, Gujarat University, Ahmedabad, pp. 83–93.

*Town and Country*. 1975. *'Jhuggi jhopri' settlements in Delhi* (mimeographed—Planning Organization). New Delhi, Ministry of Works and Housing, Government of India.

Valentine, Charles, A. 1973. 'Alternative views of poverty and the poor, present and future', in Joe R. Feagin (ed.): *The urban scene* (166–74). Random House, Inc.

Warner, W. Lloyd. 1962. *Yankee city*, one-volume abridged edition. New Haven: Yale University Press.

Wiebe, Paul D. 1975. *Social life in an Indian slum.* Delhi: Vikas Publishing House Pvt. Ltd.

# 4

# Meaning and Process of Tribal Integration in a Democratic Society

*B. K. Roy Burman*

An international instrument in the form of a convention concerning the indigenous and other tribal and semi-tribal populations in independent countries has been adopted by International Labour Organization (ILO).

Article 2 of the convention provides as follows:

1. Government shall have the primary responsibility for developing co-ordinated and systematic action for the protection of the populations concerned and their progressive integration into the life of their respective countries.
2. Such action shall include measures for:—
   (a) enabling the said populations to benefit on an equal footing from the rights and opportunities which national laws or regulations grant to the other elements of the population.
   (b) promoting the social, economic and cultural development of these populations and raising their standard of living.
   (c) creating possibilities of national integration to the exclusion of measures tending towards artificial assimilation of these populations.
3. Recourse to force or coercion as a means of promoting the integration of these populations into the national community shall be excluded.

It is to be noted that the above Article has postulated two types of goals: firstly, the goal of promoting the social, economic and cultural development of the non-integrated tribal and semitribal population and secondly, the goal of achieving their integration in the national community. The first is obviously an ethical end, which is the essence of democracy. By rating the programme as ethical, it is not intended to ignore its other implications, specially its political implication but at the same time it must not be denied that configuration of the programme of special amenities for the tribal people is definitely humanitarian, at least in the democratic countries. Even in Soviet Russia, it is very difficult to say that the programme has always followed dialectics of class-war only. Coming to the problem of integration of the tribals and semi-tribals, one however gets enmeshed into questions of altogether different category. Firstly, one may ask whether national integration is to be visualised as an end or as a means only. If national integration be looked upon as an end, does it not amount to apotheosis of the nation in an age when in the political sphere nations are more and more accepting international obligations and in the cultural sphere national cultures are being adjusted in terms of universal values? Whatever may be the merit of the question, it is necessary to admit that this is a valid line of enquiry which must not be brushed aside. The general tendency seems to be to reckon national integration teleogically; ethical quest is therefore little sensitised about the problem. But one must not forget the lesson of history that human spirit is ultimately allergic to all that is morally unconvincing. There is therefore a danger inherent in the present situation. Not only that resentment may gnaw the heart of the rising intelligentsia of the non-integrated people, but more than that, cynicism may corrode the conscience of the nation as a whole. But the question of national integration may also be viewed as a means. Nation is not a static entity but a constellation of values in constant flux. Multiple processes are involved in it, and the interrelation of such processes is determined by historical and ecological context. Broadly speaking there is always a striving not only in the nation but also in every human group to construct hierarchy of models in terms of which internal relations are tended to be organised to present a coherent whole, but again there is centrifugal tendency of the constituent elements to form autonomous units. Result of the synthesis is emergence of new models. While it will be very rash to state that such emergent synthesis always takes place at higher ethical plane, it can perhaps be claimed that the general outcome of man's experimentation with society-building at various scales, is refinement of ethical concepts and extension of the sphere of application of ethical principles. Morality is not only the instrument of sociation but also the outcome of sociation. From this point of view, nation is a vast laboratory for experimentation with moral order, ultimate measure being humanity itself. This however does not mean that all that takes place in the nation is morally appropriate. Very frequently atomistic tendencies gain upper hand not only in the national life and other scales of group life, but also in the life of individuals themselves; again very frequently atavism tends to put back the clock of history. When we speak of national integration, we must recognise this limitation of the nation itself. The problem of national integration is not therefore simply that of transmission of the ethos of national life, but it is a question of transformation of the total national life so that cluster of values may emerge in harmony with the evolving pattern of humanism itself. In other words, national integration by itself is neither moral nor immoral but to attain success in present day world it must be ethically oriented. One may however question whether in the context of the ideal of unity of mankind, it is necessary to attempt integration of the non-integrated tribals in the national life? Is it not easier to separately orient tribal institutions towards universal categories? In reply it may be pointed out that universal categories including universally accepted values and institutions cannot flourish without the framework of modern technology. As the tribals generally live interspersed with other communities, it is only the national state which can enable the tribals to make necessary advance in technology. Further no society can assimilate the universality of humanism without experience of the complex human situations that give rise to the universality. Tribal societies with their relatively simple institutions and with communication more or less limited to primary groups are totally misfit in this respect. Thus analysed, integration of tribal societies in the national polity seems to be a historical necessity for their progressive evolution. But it must also be recognised that integration by itself is not enough guarantee for progress, either of the tribals or of the nation as a whole. There may be different levels of integration and there may be different processes too. Scientific planning will require of us to construct ideal models which may however be tested and modified in actual practice. The essential requisites in this respect are:

1. Appraisal of the psychological and sociological dimensions of integration.
2. Evaluation of the techniques of integration.

It is not proposed here to make a thorough inventory of the above in this paper. Rather these will be dealt with here in a cursory way only to indicate the necessity of a new line of enquiry, specially by those applied anthropologists who have been associated with tribal welfare administration in India through the research institutes in different states.

Broadly speaking integration differs from association mainly with respect to the constituent elements. Association is grouping of individuals for a particular end. Integration on the other hand presupposes social structure. According to Wiese, integration results from interaction of social structures and it consists of the following processes:—(1) Sub and Super ordination, (2) Socialisation, (3) Uniformisation and (4) Liberation. I feel that the above analysis is characterised by what may be described as lag of philosophy. It does not take account of the fact that through empirical experiences humanity has reached a stage when it can pattern various strands of relationships free from blind fury of the impulses.[1] Theme of any social relationship based on super or subordination is power. Root of the urge for power may again be traced to primitive instinct of insecurity sustained by ignorance of the laws of nature and laws of sociation. Mastery over the facts of nature and growth of 'scientism' and 'culture studying culture'[2] is tending to free man from his primitive helplessness. In the ideatic order, power by itself is powerless to motivate man today. Undoubtedly power manoeuvre trays the national and international fields even now, but it is not without significance that always such manoeuvres are to be rationalised in the name of ideologies of various colour. Even the rationale of class war is not class domination but classless society. It is altogether different question whether the means is appropriate to the end. But that the ball has been set rolling towards attainment of great objectivity and greater sympathy can be discerned in spite of vestiges of aggression and inhibition. In any case, in the spiritual climate of the modern age it is very difficult to ignore that social relationship based on super and subordination carries in its womb the very forces that may destroy the relationship itself.

Co-ordination of social entities rather than super and subordination must therefore be the wattle of integration in any level of society today. It must however be made clear that the concept of co-ordination is not that of unhindered autonomy. Co-ordination always means self-discipline on the one hand and respect for others on the other. Use of force is clearly ruled out as *modus operandi* for co-ordination. But doubt may be expressed whether force should be ruled out even when there is attempt to violently thwart the very basis of co-ordination. In this connection it may be noted that the general tenet of sociology today is to admit the necessity of some amount of coercion against individuals or groups of individuals to safeguard the freedom of others. In group level also, some amount of force or coercion cannot perhaps be dispensed with to safeguard the achievements of mankind including the achievements in the field of social relationship. The difference between coercion with aggressive design and coercion for defensive purpose can perhaps be revealed only in the phase of reorganisation of social relationship in the post-coercion period. This however is a question which requires greater amount of scrutiny based on empirical data. Social scientists specially bear a very great responsibility for inducing clear thinking and also perhaps clean thinking about this matter.

Coming over to the second strand of integration suggested by Wiese, I feel inclined to replace the word socialisation by the word 'harmonisation of impulses'. The term socialisation tends to gloss over the process through which such socialisation is effected, with the unfortunate result that situations which are ethically unjustified and retrograde in the scale of humanism are very often emulated in the name of socialisation. It is very difficult to ignore that very frequently socialisation only means conformation to the pattern set up by the dominant group. I wonder if seen in historical perspective, the word socialisation can even be claimed to have remained nomistically neutral. Harmonisation of impulses on the other hand not only defines the process but also gives a clearer perspective of the end of the process. One may of course question as to how to effect the harmonisation of social impulses. This however is a problem of technique in social engineering but to that I shall turn later on.

The third strand according to Wiese is uniformisation which again I prefer to restate as co-variation of standardised behaviour. It is to be noted that co-variation also implies uniformisation but that is uniformity of variation as against uniformity by conformation of the internal set up of a segment or an independent entity to the internal set up of another segment or independent entity. Doubt may however be expressed as to whether variants should leave any place in an integrated order of society. The problem has been discussed by A. L. Krobber and Clyde Kluckhohn,[3] according to whom 'there is a good case for the view that any stratified or segmented culture requires balance, counter point, an antagonistic equilibrium'. Florence Kluckhohn has further elaborated the theme,

> however important it is to know what is dominant in a society at a given time, we shall not go far towards understanding of the dynamics of that society without paying careful heed to the variant orientations. That they be individuals who lived in accordance with patterns which express variant rather than the dominantly stressed orientations is, it is maintained, essential to the maintenance of the society. Variant values are, therefore, not only permitted but actually required. It has been the mistake of many in the social sciences, and of many in the field of practical affairs as well, to treat all behaviour and certain aspects of motivation which do not accord with the dominant values as deviant. It is argued that we cease to confuse the deviant who by this behaviour calls down the sanction of his group with the variant, who is accepted and very frequently required. This is especially true in a society such as ours, where beneath the surface of what has so often been called out compulsive conformity, there lies a wide range of variation.

The only point that I want to add to above analysis is that an integrated society may not only accept the variants but also may construct models regarding locii of variation. These models may be consciously planned, or may be unconsciously determined by multiple factors. In any case they furnish the unifying principle to justify the premise of covariation of variants.

Coming to the fourth strand, viz., liberation, my comment is that in democratic society, it is to be viewed not only as the goal or product of a social process but must be realised as an inherent quality of the social process itself. Speaking metaphorically, liberation is the very breath of any social process in democracy. Sociologically it means that every interaction or co-action in society must be such as to bring satisfaction to the spiritual need of the individuals concerned by way of fulfilment of their potentialities as moulded by personal history and outward environment of each, including physical and social environment.[4]

With the above clarification and elaboration of the cardinal points of integration, let us now consider the social techniques for effecting the integration.

Mannheim has included under social technique the practices and agencies in their entirety which have as their ultimate aim the moulding of human behaviour and social relationship.[5] Obviously social techniques presuppose existence of principal manipulator to serve as nexus between practices and agencies of social techniques. In totalitarian society the principal manipulator is the ruling class. In parliamentary democracy the role vests in social elites. Perhaps in archaic civilisations and in later absolute monarchies, the situation was more or less similar, for even the absolute monarchies were not technologically advanced enough to influence life of the citizens in its totality. In primitive society as well as in organised democracy the role is diffused. But there is a vital difference between the two. Speaking with some exaggerated emphasis, it may be said that in primitive society 'custom is the king', whereas in organised democracy, conduct is regulated by enlightened appreciation of the objective reality. This is of course description of the ideal configuration, which is altogether different from the actual type. In primitive society too custom was never so immutable as is frequently made out. Even then social processes included not only interaction between institutions and environment but also native aptitude of the individual as moulded by his history.[6] On the other hand, it is perhaps too naive to claim that organised democracy can altogether dispense with elements of irrationality in our nature as reflected in social transactions. But it cannot be doubted that the theme of organised democracy is rationality—freedom and distributive justice flows from it. This predetermines the nature of social technique in democratic society. But that is in a general way; in specific situations there are other ordinates which require to be taken into consideration. Here the specific situation is integration of the tribals in national community. Before discussing the problems of social technique in this specific situation, it is however necessary to clear up two fallacies in our traditional thinking. It is a fallacy to consider all tribes as primitive and it is another fallacy to consider nation as such to be democratic or undemocratic. The fallacy has arisen out of our misconception that tribe or nation is co-dimensional with tribal community or national community respectively. The common denominator between tribe and tribal community or nation and national community is name. But whereas tribe or nation exists in unique configuration of symbols, tribal community or national community exists through institutionalised rights and obligations.

The configuration of symbols may be meaningful in the consensus of a particular section or even segment of the tribe or nation; it may again exist in the consensus of outsiders only—as in the case of Naga tribes. The institutionalised rights and obligations on the other hand may have altogether different spread out. Intellectually it is quite easy to perceive that symbols of a tribe may be primitive but actual condition of its community life, including its ecological adjustment may be quite advanced. We may perhaps consider the Khasis of Assam or modern Red Indians in this category. Again, intellectually and historically too it is not difficult to perceive that modern nation with advanced technology may build up the fabric of its community life with strands of primitive irrationality. Fascist experiment to modify the community life of the nation against the whole tide of civilisation is a glaring example of this. But even then it must be realised that national symbols by themselves cannot be fascist or anti-fascist. Social order of Germany turned fascist, but not German language, dress, history and so on. The same is true of any democratic society. By historical association democracy or fascism or any other social order itself may of course become symbol of the life of a nation, but I have doubt at least with regard to democracy, whether social order of a nation may remain democratic after democracy itself turns out to be a symbol. Symbol is a prescribed representation, the linkage between the symbol and the represented being artificial.[7] When democracy is a symbol, as appears to be the case in America through apotheosis of its democratic constitution, the symbol must represent something else. What is that? Perhaps the national ego. Under such dispensation it is more likely than not that the emotional fixation of the nation will be upon the forms of democracy rather than values of democracy. And that is a far cry from democracy. We however need not consider the question in further details here. My premise was that the problem of democracy belongs to the social order of a community rather than to its symbolic order and I think in the foregoing lines I have been able to make it sufficiently clear. Now, returning to the question of tribal integration in a democratic society, we are faced with two sets of problems:—

1. effecting synthesis between tribal and national symbols in harmony with the spirit of humanism.
2. initiating organised reform in the national situation through stages so as to attain national solidarity.

As symbols are essentially emotional complexes, synthesis in symbols cannot be effected without modification of attitude and interest. The conscious purpose for synthesis is therefore required to be diffused throughout the society, so that a diffused pattern of leadership may emerge to translate the collective purpose into actual action. But this also presupposes existence of elites at the national level of construct models of synthesis, and to skilfully manipulate mass psychology in terms of such models. Social scientists may perhaps play the role of national elites to some extent; but they by themselves are unlikely to be much effective; if not for anything else, at least for the reason that they will not have the vast machinery at their disposal to manipulate mass society.

Social scientists in close alliance with voluntary associations and enlightened bureaucracy will have to take the new responsibility of social engineering. It will be possible to discover the right basis of such alliance, only after a great deal of trial and error, orientation and reorientation. In this connection there should be greater appreciation of the role of modern bureaucracy. As pointed out by Mannheim, in our age 'a civil servant is steadily developing into a social servant'.[8] This does not however mean that modern bureaucracy has adequate grasp of the technique of social service. There should be arrangement for training of personnel, change in method of recruitment, method of organisation and so on. These matters however are not exclusive to the problem under consideration, and as such, it is not necessary to make more than a passing reference to them in the present context. Let us now consider the process through which the synthesis may be effected. In the words of Hobhouse, synthesis 'proceeds by liberation of elements originally in conflict, the building up of structures of varying degrees of plasticity and coherence'. As noted earlier, in totalitarian society the conflict is resolved by subduing the elements to conform to a pattern which serves the purpose of the ruling class but in democratic society it is to be revealed by rational understanding of the intrinsic properties of the elements concerned. This understanding consists of objective knowledge and subjective reflection resulting in new type of response to be stimulus of the conflicting elements. Very frequently the conflicting elements may be models of comparison to one another in the scale of humanism and synthesis may mean greater refinement and coherence of each set of elements, in terms of universal values, without losing its unique configuration. In any case, there is always the likelihood of eclectical acceptance of rationally valued elements from different systems. Synthesis in ideal condition of freedom and rationality should therefore mean nothing more than sublimation of units in adjustment with physical and social environment but maintaining their unitary character. The word 'should' has been deliberately used in this context, to indicate that the process as described cannot take place automatically, but that it is to be realised through conscious planning. One may question whether planning should go to the extent of remoulding emotional complexes of societies and also, even if it be desirable, whether it is feasible. In reply it may be pointed out that alternative to planning in present-day mass society is not freedom but chaos and ultimate destruction of the very conditions of freedom. And as regards feasibility, the successful implementation of social techniques, towards modification of mass behaviour in totalitarian societies may only be remembered. Democracy will definitely abhor many of the techniques of totalitarian society, but it should not be denied that the experiments of latter have revealed new possibilities of human organisation. There is no reason why democracy should exhibit pusillanimity in tackling the problems of social dynamics.[9]

There is another aspect of the problem of synthesis about which a passing reference has already been made but which requires a little elaboration. The necessity of diffusion of the conscious purpose of synthesis has been pointed out earlier, but what will be the process of such diffusion? Following the classification of social techniques by Mannheim, it may be stated that this may be done both by direct and indirect methods.[10] The direct method of influencing human behaviour is based on personal influence and is effective in primary purpose. Indirect method on the other hand, 'works from afar, and the control originally springs, not from close at hand, but from distant sources'. On ultimate analysis however every social technique is combination of both direct and indirect methods with varying degrees of emphasis. As in most cases, it is the primary group, including family, clan, village community or adjoining territories, which is significant for the tribals, more emphasis should be given upon influencing their behaviour through direct method. This means that the national elites should take care to train up local elites of integration, among the tribals specially.[11] A very great priority should be given to this task, as this is perhaps the anchor-sheet of the whole programme of integration of the tribals. For re-orientation of the outlook of the whole nation, indirect method of education will be more effective. Modern techniques of social education through audio-visual aid should be fully utilised for the purposes. Films depicting significant aspects of tribal life may be prepared in cooperation with the social scientists, and widely displayed both in rural and urban areas. This will go a long way to clear up chaffs of naive ideas about the tribals, widespread throughout the world. Joint cultural functions of tribals and others on the basis of equality and mutual respect may be another important step. These are however questions of detailed programme and have been mentioned here only for the sake of illustration.

The second task of initiating organised reform in the national situation is primarily concerned with economic and cultural development of the different segments of the people, but this also is a task of re-orientation. Economic and cultural developments by themselves do not lead to solidarity, these may, by rousing ambition, create a situation of mutual distrust and competition as well. Therefore programme of economic and cultural development should be supplemented by other programmes. It will require great skill and greater understanding to correctly appreciate inter-relation of different items of the total programme and introduce them by phases. It will again require great foresight to understand the problems of transitional stages and develop right type of machinery to grapple with such problems. As the range of economic, social and cultural development of the tribals have been discussed in great details in recent years, even in public forums, I do not propose to discuss them here. I should however take up the structural relationships that are to be reckoned with while introducing the welfare programmes and also those that may be brought about through introduction of such programmes. Nadel[12] has discussed the different forms in which the inter-relation may appear. The first form is simple co-existence in which the tribes and other segments of the nation

> may be relatively self-contained though such segments may in fact 'combine' to form the society at large, they could exist without each other and in any number; one could add to or subtract from it without affecting the working either of each segment or of the embracing group.

Undoubtedly the diagnosis above fits in with the position of the tribals vis à vis the national community in many parts of the world. There is however another facet of this coexistence which should receive our attention. I would call it inhibited co-existence: my explanation follows. Though the prevailing stereotype about the tribals in India and other parts of the world is that they are segregated from the main current of the national life, it will on scrutiny be revealed that very frequently they live not only closely interspersed with others, but culturally and socially also there is very close approximation between them and others. If even then stereotype of being 'different' continues, both among the tribals and non-tribals, it must be due to some inhibition to accept the objective fact of co-existence. This inhibition may be fossilised emotion of some historical situation of the past. A study of the distribution of the tribes in relation to the adjoining civilisations and also of the nature and history of such civilisations may perhaps throw some light on the problem. In the caste-ridden civilisation of India, for instance, there was a vested interest to maintain the social distance vis-à-vis the tribals. History will show that tribal population in India has served as a reserve pool of backwardness, to maintain the superior position of others. The process has not perhaps totally stopped even now, as will be evident from a very recent development in a West Bengal village reported by Jyotimayee Sarma[13] I quote her in toto,

> castes at the bottom make conscious efforts to move up, and their desire for a change of status is recognised by the rest of the community. The first step towards this change is the giving up of occupations thought to be unclean. For instance, the muchis who used to work in leather and hides gave up the traditional calling two generations ago for agriculture. They will not now even touch a dead animal. Their change of occupation leaves a gap in the village division of labour, as when a cow or bull dies, some people must carry the dead animal to the place set apart for it and if possible, skin it. Santhals and Oraons now step into the breach and do this work. Although they have not taken to leather work completely, whenever a cow or bull dies, they clear the dead and take the hide.

The illustration needs no comment. Only point that I want to add is that move of the muchis for gaining in social status by change of caste occupation would not have so smooth sailing had there not existed the ungraded Santhals and Oraons in the village. They would have to face stiff opposition; there is quite a good number of such evidences from different parts of India. It is only because a serious jolt to the hierarchy of caste structure could be avoided by stepping in of the tribal Santhals and Oraons that the society acquiesced to the ambition of the muchis. Similar process must have taken place innumerable times with respect to other tribes of India too. It is not without significance that many of the untouchable castes can be traced to have remained in aboriginal condition even in the recent past. In the face of this evidence of history it will be short-sighted to develop any programme of integration of the tribals without tackling the social mechanism of inhibition.

This problem discussed with special reference to India may have its bearing in other parts of world too. But there may be other factors also for perpetuating the inhibition. It is noteworthy that tribal population in different parts of the world is mainly composed of Negroid, Mongoloid and Proto-Australoid racial types and their sub-types. There has of course been some intermingling with other racial types too. But for practical purposes we may ignore them. While there is no conclusive evidence that there is significant difference in innate capacities of different racial types, it cannot also be claimed that different racial types are equally valued in social scale. Rather it appears that notions of beauty, ideal-physique etc. have tended to be associated with particular racial types. The extent to which such psychological factors have contributed to what I have described as inhibitive co-existence may also be examined. If such investigations help in no other way, their findings may rouse the civilised conscience of our age to shatter the area of inhibition.

To come to the desirable social situations, Nadel has described three processes, viz., consociation, symbiosis and transfer of loyalties.[14] Consociation is the process of alliance between potentially hostile yet interdependent communities or political factions within the same community. Symbiosis, on the other hand, is 'subjectively absolute and unalterable interdependence which causes every section, as section to assume specific duties (religious, political etc.) on behalf of the community at large i.e. on behalf of every other section'. In other words while in consociation interdependence is based on recognition of specific interests, in symbiosis inter-dependence is based on an attitude of one-ness. It appears that Nadel is of the view that potential hostilities of consociation may be finally corroded by suggestion (or simulation) of a symbolic relationship that would absorb the sectional conflicts. In this connection he has approvingly mentioned Plato's concept of 'noble falsehood'. The conceptual framework for this line of approach seems to be that of organic society, based on division of labour. But it should not be ignored that the concept of organic character of society has failed to resolve the problem of inequality and injustice in society. In the history of India specially, there is reason to suspect that the organic concept of society has tended to clamp social mobility and thus perpetuate the pattern of social relationship based on domination of one section of people by another. Taking a long-term view I feel that symbiotic relationship in society actually means subordination of interest by interest on the one hand and successful camouflage of the reality on the other hand. Only great illusion differentiates symbiosis from consociation and therefore there is nothing to choose between the two. The third alternative suggested by Nadel is transfer of loyalties, i.e.,

> loyalties formed between individuals in the narrow group remaining effective in the wider group. Thus people who have passed through the same age-sets, who are bound together by kinship ties, or belong to the same religious congregation or the same social class, will preserve loyalties fostered there when acting as members of the embracing group.

The transfer of loyalties described is only application of the model of a narrower field to the wider field. Even if the psychological process involved can be correctly described by the word 'transfer', I do not think that it covers the whole of the social situation. Preserving the loyalties of the narrower group, when acting as member of the wider group, should rather be described as parochialism. Certainly it is not an integrative force. But even then we may perhaps gain real insight into the social process if we reconstruct Nadel's concept in a slightly different way and term it as expansion of loyalties. The model of this concept is that loyalties formed at narrower groups may be organised for nisus towards wider groups.

The nisus, however, has been assumed here and unless proved through determination of its sociological and psychological mechanism, the concept is nothing more than pure speculation. Frankly speaking I feel myself in an intellectual blind-alley at this stage. This may be reflection of a social dilemma or it may be my own inadequacy. In any case the only conclusion that I feel entitled to draw through my above analysis is that the structural relation between the tribals and non-tribals in an ideally integrated society cannot conform to any rigid pattern. It must be rationally determined in specific contexts, keeping in view nature and history of the civilisation in immediate proximity of the tribals on one hand, and the extent of mastery achieved by the tribals over economic and social techniques as well as type of leadership available in the tribal societies on the other.

# Notes

1. Cf. Hobhouse, *Self-directed humanity*.
2. *Man in contemporary society*, p. 210.
3. *Man in contemporary society*, Vol. 1, pp. 201–03.
4. Cf. M. Ginsberg, *On the diversity of morals*, p. 170.
5. Karl Mannheim, *Man and society*, p. 247.
6. M. Ginsberg, *Essays on sociology and social philosophy*, Vol. 1, p. 110.
7. Nadel, *The foundation of social anthropology*, p. 67.
8. Karl Mannheim, *Man and society*, p. 324.
9. Hobhouse, Development and purpose.
10. Cf. Mannheim,

    It is quite probable that the citizens of some well-planned future age will regard our anxiety over the problem of intellectual mastery of our social destiny and our reluctance to create new forms of social organisations as the last vestiges of an obsolete frame of mind.

    (*Man and society*, p. 240).

11. Karl Mannheim, *Man and society*, Part V.
12. Cf. Pareto's 'theory of circulation of elites'—the different types of social structure and civilization are determined by the proportions in which certain types of individuals are found in the population.
13. *Foundations of social anthropology*, Chapter VII.
14. *India's villages*, p. 167, published by Development Department, Govt. of West Bengal.
15. *The foundation of social anthropology*, p. 187.

# References

Columbia University. 1955. *Man in contemporary society: A source book*, Volume: I (203–206, 210). New York: Columbia University Press.

Ginsberg, Morris. 1953. 'On the diversity of morals', *Journal of the royal anthropological institute of Great Britain and Ireland*, 83 (2, Jul–Dec): 117–135.

———. 1968. *Essays in sociology and social philosophy*, Volume I. Harmondsworth: Penguin.

Mannheim, Karl. 1940. *Man and society in an age of reconstruction: Studies in modern social structures* (247). London: Routledge & Kegan Paul.

Srinivas, M. N. 1955. *India's villages*. Bombay: Asia Publishing House.

# 5

# *Homecoming:* Ho Women, Work, and Land Rights in Jharkhand

*Ritambhara Hebbar*

## Introduction

The Jharkhand state, as we know it today, is a truncated form of the originally proposed state. The Jharkhand movement had demanded a state comprising of the tribal districts within the states of Bihar, Madhya Pradesh, Orissa and West Bengal. However, the present state includes only the eighteen tribal districts within Bihar. The originally proposed state also corresponded to the topographical division of the Chotanagpur plateau, known for its ecological and cultural diversity, both for its forest and mineral resources and for the different tribes that inhabit the area. The area has been exploited for its forest and mineral resources, which has depleted its natural resources and marginalised its people. For long, the movement resisted these processes of exploitation by demonstrating that ecological degradation and the simultaneous erosion of tribal rights on land and forests were not coincidental, and that there is an intrinsic relationship of tribes with their natural environment. It maintained that the ecology could not be restored without respecting tribal beliefs and practices around land and forests, which presented a more humble and egalitarian alternative relationship with nature as against the one pursued by the state (see Sinha 1988; Lorduswamy 1997).

The Jharkhand movement's claim acquires authenticity from the lives and work of the forest-dwellers in the area, and which includes women's contribution. However, most leaders within the movement have expressed reservations about giving land rights to Ho women. The fear is that such a move would lead to the disintegration of Ho society. I argue that in not considering women as rightful heirs in sustaining and practicing routine life activities around the forest, the movement is serving a losing battle. Denying women's rights on land inadvertently undermines the knowledge systems and practices integral to women's work around forest and land, which forms the bases for the struggle towards the establishment of a more humane and symbiotic relationship with nature.

Here, I reconstruct the daily routine of women of Mirra village in order to elucidate the role of women in sustaining the alternative relationship with the natural environment made known by the movement as its own.[1] Presented below is the case study of a Ho woman, Suru, her daily life, work and social relationships. In this context, two additional cases are cited, which are of her two daughters—one of them is married and the other, a spinster. These cases elaborate the complex interplay between personal emotions and social values in coping with crises in her life. The intention thereby is not only to strengthen Suru's case study, but also to show the precariousness of the divide between the individual and the collective spheres of community life.

Suru is a wife of a *khuntkattidar*. I concentrate on the *khuntkattidars*, as it is this category that primarily holds large plots of land and the proposed legislation will directly affect their interests than those of the others, who are not privileged in terms of either the acreage of land they hold or enjoying the protection by law. The case studies are not representative of the experiences of all Ho women. The purpose is not to generalise Ho women's experience of subjugation or accomplishment, but to arrive at the larger argument that granting land rights to women is not detrimental to the Jharkhandi struggle for self-rule and will only strengthen their cause. The claim for self-rule has been closely associated with their struggle to retain control over their land and forests and concomitantly to preserve their culture, which is kept alive through everyday practice around land and forests. I try to demonstrate how women's work and labour are integral to quotidian practices among the Ho, and how Ho knowledge system and social life are reinstated in the course of everyday life of women.[2]

## Mirra and Its People

There are 400 households in Mirra dispersed over its nine *sai* (hamlets) situated at a distance from each other. A Government Protected Forest surrounds Mirra. The forests are divided into Government Protected Forests (PF) called *marang buru* (big forest) and *huding buru* (small forests), commonly termed as *tungri* (hillock). Agricultural land is unevenly distributed in the village; most of the land is held by the descendents of the original settlers of the village. The Ho land system is founded on the *khuntkatti* system. The word *khunt,* which stands for the patrilineal descent group, is originally Munda, adopted by the British for administrative purposes. *Kati* has two meanings in Ho: 'a sharp blade', usually attached to the natural spurs of a cock for fighting, and 'to put something horizontal'. The term '*khuntkatti*' is a conjunction of these two words, '*khunt* and '*kati*' which translates in English as the 'the patrilineal descent group' and 'to clear land' respectively.

Among the Ho, pre-eminence is given to the patrilineage whose ancestor was the first clearer of land and who was responsible for establishing the village. In 1920, with the Tuckey settlement, the British extended the Chotanagpur Tenancy Act (1908) to Singhbhum and among the Ho. With this, the privileged social status of the *khuntkattidars* (the descendents of the first clearer of land) was converted into a legal one and patriliny was consolidated. Like in all other Ho villages, a particular patrilineal descent group (*killi*) dominates in Mirra. Mirra was settled by the Sinku *killi.* Over time, other *killi* members were invited to the village to work for the Sinku *killi.* Almost every village among the Ho has Gopes and Tantis, the castes of cattle-tenders and cloth-weavers respectively. In Mirra, the Gopes are the second largest group.

## Women: Work and Life

*Maghe Parab* is the most important festival of the Ho, marking the completion of an agricultural cycle. It is celebrated between the months of January and March. For Suru, it is more than a conclusion of all her hard work through the year and a preparation for another. It is a feeling of 'homecoming'. It is not only a realisation of her labour, but also an assertion of her sense of self, a reassurance of her existence. It is a celebration of all that she nurtured and reproduced: the hearth and the community; land and forests; the world of humans and the spirits. She has worked hard to secure her place in the universe. Her journey to this state of confidence and self-assuredness has not been an easy one. It is in this sense that she feels at home.

Suru came to the village after marriage. Although she had married her mother's brother's son, she was new to the village and the family she had married into. She was very young when her mother died and her father remarried. Her stepmother brought her up. As a young girl, she would often visit her uncle. However, it is very different to reside with her uncle's family for life. Soon after marriage, Suru realised that all was not well with the family and that there was tremendous antagonism between Birsa, her husband, and his elder brother. Her uncle, who is now also her father-in-law, could not cope with the daily tensions within the family, and divided the property before his death. He asked the sons to cultivate their respective plots of land. Birsa's younger brother decided to keep his plot joint with the eldest brother. Suru and Birsa set up a separate house soon after their marriage. The first house that they constructed was too close to the jungle and was unsafe, especially during the rainy season. It was about five years back that they constructed the house they presently live in. The responsibility of constructing the house was entirely on Suru: the organising of labour along with providing her own; supervising their work, paying them in kind (serving them *diyang* or rice beer) and cash; procuring wood for the doors, windows and fixing the roof; and preparing bricks for the walls and smelting iron for making door latches and bolts.

Although the event of constructing a separate house was an affirmation of rebellion, conflict and independence, for Birsa and Suru, it also reflected a renewed confidence in fulfilling all the responsibilities entailed in making a home. Ho houses vary in size and shape, but not in structure. The most important part of any Ho house is *mandi owa* or its kitchen (*mandi* in Ho means cooked rice or food and *owa* refers to a room or a house). It is the nucleus of the house; it is located in the interior of the house. The kitchen is also a sacred place as it houses the *ading.* The term *ading* is used interchangeably to refer to the kitchen and to the fireplace where all the spirits of the dead ancestors reside. The spirits are believed not only to protect and guard the family members from any evil that may befall upon them, but also protect them from the evil spirits that roam in the open and in the jungle. In this sense, it is a *home* within a home and, therefore, twice as much secure. No one except the members of the house and the lineage can enter the *ading.* However, the *ading* is also *mandi owa* and, as long as the fireplace is in use and burning, the *ading* is sheltered and venerated. To keep the kitchen fire burning involves hard work through the year in the fields and forest. It also entails keeping the village spirits content by worshipping them in all seasons and keeping the evil spirits that roam from one jungle to another at bay.

Suru took on the responsibility of a new house soon after marriage. It was clear to her that her life before marriage was no different; in fact, it was a preparation for her life after marriage. With passing years, Suru had earned the reputation of being very hard working. Birsa, who is known to be short-tempered and egoistic, is considered fortunate to get a wife like Suru, particularly since Birsa married a third time in the desire of having a son. Suru is Birsa's second wife. Birsa's first wife expired of some illness after two years of marriage. It is then that he asked Suru to marry him.

Birsa has a job with the railways as lineman in Dungwaposi, a village which is about 4 km away from Mirra. He leaves every morning by nine only to return by six or seven in the evening. Sometimes, he is required to stay back in the railway station in case there is extra work. There is another reason as to why he often stays back in Dungwaposi: his third wife is also employed in the railways in Dungwaposi. Suru has four children through Birsa, three daughters and one son. Her eldest daughter is now married, and Suru hopes to find a suitable boy for her second daughter who is about 24 years old. Her third daughter is studying in a middle school at the Block. Her son, who will be appearing for the secondary school examination soon, was born after the birth of her two girls. Paradoxically, both Birsa's wives conceived at the same time, and Suru gave birth to a baby boy a few days before his third wife, who also delivered a male child. During those days, Birsa used to spend more time with his third wife. Suru was alone in the village with her three children; there was no one to give her postnatal care. Since then, she has been complaining of stomach ache, which the doctors say, and even Birsa confesses, is a result of negligence during her pregnancy and post-pregnancy stage.

Suru manages the house and the fields single-handedly. In all, Birsa has three plots of land: one is farther away from the house, in front of the primary school in the village; and the other two are near the jungle, a short walk from the house. Birsa has sublet the plot near the school to a *deva* (shaman) in the village, a close relative of his. Ever since they moved out on their own, one of their plots has been lying fallow. However, this year, Suru managed to cultivate it. For all these years, this piece of land was a reminder of a task undone, reminiscent of the testing times both Suru and Birsa faced right after the division of the ancestral property. They were unable to build a decent house for themselves, let alone cultivate the plots of land that accrued to them on the partition of the ancestral property. Thus, the cultivation of this land was commemorative of their trying times in securing a home.

The celebration of *Maghe Parab* in the village for the year 1997 was fixed for 15 March. There is no fixed date for its celebration; it varies from year to year and from village to village. There is a general air of do and festivity around when the entire village is preparing for the celebration. Suru has a number of tasks on hand. The house, as it does every year, requires repairs. The roof needs new *kecho* (tiles); the floors and walls have to be repainted. Suru plans to ask the potter from the neighbouring village to make them this year instead of buying it from the weekly *haat* (market), though fixing it on the roof will have to be done by her. The paint on the floor and walls acts as a disinfectant and a check against pests and poisonous insects. The floors are swept with a solution made of the bark of the *hatna daru* (tree), by boiling the latter in water with a set quantity of washing soda. She also has to collect seeds of the *baru* (kusum) tree to make *sunum* (oil), which would be used as a part of the rituals in *Maghe Parab*. As the year passes by, she would do the same with *karanjia* (karanj), *nim* (neem), *dola* (mohua), *ramtiya* (a yellow flower, seeds of which are pressed to obtain oil for cooking) and *bindi* (papaya) seeds. These oils have medicinal properties and they are used for curing various skin ailments and wounds.

Besides the preparations for *Maghe Parab*, Suru maintains her daily routine of work. She gets up at the crack of dawn. Her day begins by cleaning the whole house. She mops the floors clean and then collects the refuse and dumps it in the pit near the house. The pit is a store for manure, compost, which will be transferred to the field once the preparation for cultivation begins. Soon it is time for her to let off the sheep, goats and oxen, as the cattle herder is at the door to take them for herding. She places containers of water on the way for the animals to drink. After the livestock is sent off for herding, Suru cleans the room in which they are kept. She collects all the dung and scattered silage in a basket and throws them into the pit. She then feeds the hens, cocks, chickens, ducks and pigeons by scattering grain in the courtyard. The daily upkeep of these birds is important, as they have a prominent place in Ho social feasts and ritual sacrifices.

Once in two days, Suru cleans the cemented floor of one of the rooms with water and the rest of the house with a solution of cow dung mixed with water. According to her, this is the only way to get rid of the dust that accumulates in the house. The nearest source of water is a hand pump constructed by the government some four years back. This pump, however, needs periodic repairs; her second daughter Meena has to make a number of trips to the Block to get a plumber. When it usually dries up in summer, they have to depend on the nearest *jagda* (permanent source of water), which is in the jungle, about 2 km away. Suru also replenishes the store of water for purposes other than drinking in the house and washes the dirty dishes kept away after dinner the night before. She uses the stored drinking water left over from the previous day for watering the pots of plants hanging in the courtyard.

Birsa is ready to leave for work by eight in the morning and has to be served food. Ever since Meena dropped out of school and moved to the village from her hostel at the Block, Suru finds a helping hand in her. She has taken over the responsibility of cooking in the morning. Quite often, Meena plucks vegetables from their garden; sometimes she sets off to collect spinach, which grows in the small jungle. The jungle has a wide variety of green leaves that sustain the villagers all through the year.[3] Like many others in the village who grow vegetables in the upland or in their backyards, Birsa and Suru have also maintained a small garden behind their house. In summer, it has to be watered every day, sometimes even twice a day, which is in addition to the work on the fields that begins by the end of April.

By the time Birsa leaves for work, the three people Suru hired for repairing the roof arrive. Suru serves them rice-beer before they begin work. Just then, an old Gope lady comes to visit Suru in the hope of having some rice beer. She visits Suru often as she stays all by herself in the village. In fact, Suru is one of the very few people she visits. She has a daughter, who has married a person working in the Noamundi mines. Her husband died when her daughter was very young. She has no relations to speak of. After her daughter's marriage, she is alone and lonely. Suru tries to cheer her up by sharing details of various goings-on in the village. There have been quite a few betrothals and marriages in the village lately. All the marriages have been cases of elope. Two days back, Shibu, whose mother and sister are helping Suru with the repairs of the roof, got a girl home. His mother recounts the entire incident for the benefit of the old lady.

The marriage rituals are to be held in the night accompanied by dance and drinks. Suru will make her contribution of providing one pot of rice beer towards the social function organised by any family in the village in keeping with the rule set by the villagers for some years now. Since Birsa is not around for most part of the day and, also given his egotistical temperament, Suru has to take on the responsibility of fulfilling social obligations. The main offering in all festivals to the *bongo ko* (spirits) and guests amongst the Ho is *diyang* (rice-beer).[4] Suru is very proud of the fact that the rice beer prepared by her is always fresh and sweet, unlike the stale and sour rice beer contributed by the other women in the village. It is no wonder that the rice beer prepared by her is sold off in the market before noon by her daughter and son-in-law. Preparing rice-beer takes up a lot of her time, and she is forced to send Meena out to the market every second day to purchase rice.

Although she does it for her daughter Padma, she has not reconciled with the way she got married. It still hurts to think of how she had walked away from the house disregarding her parents' wishes and at the behest of her lover. It hurts even more to know that she is not happy, having had her way. For Padma, her situation seems irreconcilable. On the one hand, she is shamefaced for having married against their will and turning to them for financial support. Her father has made arrangements for their stay in the railway quarters allotted to him near the station. She is disappointed with her spouse for not being able to support her and their child. He has a bad drinking problem and ends up drinking more on the days she chooses to nag him for the same. On the other hand, she gets extremely upset when her husband is insulted and ridiculed by her father on not being able to support his daughter and granddaughter. Her husband had been asked to leave his house by his stepmother and his father refuses to part with his share of the property. Her husband finds working as a daily wage labourer demeaning and shies away at the thought of it. This exasperates Birsa who sees no harm in manual labour of any kind to earn one's living. Given these circumstances, she feels obligated to her parents to the extent that she would not even eat properly on her visits to their place. She gives up her reticence in the face of taunts heaped on her by her mother and sister that the disrespect for the food offered may be on account of hidden wealth.

Suru's complaint against her daughter is that she is secretive and does not share her tensions and apprehensions with her. Initially, Meena had been successful in breaking Padma's silence, but now even she finds it difficult to communicate with Padma. Padma did not appreciate that Meena had divulged the details of their conversations about her marriage to their mother. In fact, it is only then that Suru came to know that Padma was not happy in her marriage and needed help. Padma considers herself lucky to have caring parents, as she knows of a number of *judi* (friends) who have lost all touch with their natal homes owing to a lack of initiative by the latter. However, she has squirmed each time her father has brought this up in front of her. It has burdened her to be told time and again of how privileged she is and to realise that she is incapable of paying back in the least.

For Meena, her sister's situation serves as a living example of what may become of her if she went against her parents' wishes and followed her heart's desire. It is only in the past three to four years that Meena has been living in the village. Earlier, she was staying in the girl's hostel at Jagannathpur, the block headquarters. She decided to come back home after she failed to qualify the matriculation examination. In Jagannathpur, she used to like one of her classmates, Mongol. He liked her, too. He tried to contact her even after she came back to the village. He got a job in the police services right after matriculation. He had proposed marriage to Meena then and another time, after two years. The first time he had asked her to come to the Block, from where he intended to take her home. He waited for an entire day, but Meena did not have the courage to walk out of the house. A month later, he opted for an arranged match on the insistence of his mother, though he told Meena that he still loved her. However, his wife died of an illness the following year. He contacted Meena again asking her to marry him. This time he planned to come to her house to take her with him. He decided to visit her house on *Baa Parab,* the festival that marks the blossoming of the *saal* (Shorea Robusta) flowers celebrated around the end of March or early April. Meena was anxious about his visit. Though she was waiting for him, she was also nervous about how she would tell her parents regarding Mongol. She was scared as to how her parents would react a second time to a situation. Mongol came with a friend around dusk. After exchanging greetings and pleasantries with her parents and her uncle, he looked at her to see if she was ready to leave with him. Just then, Meena turned around and went into the house. She was upset that he came late and that too with a friend whom she did not recognise at all. She knew that had she walked out with him, she would have had to cross the jungle at night to go to his village. Mongol left without her.

For Meena, as for the villagers, the jungle is the abode of spirits and wild animals. Meena has often heard her parents say that, if it were not for the knowledge that they have of the forest and the care they took in pleasing the spirits, they would never have been able to settle a village and have a home. They would not have had the security of a home. The insecurity of leaving home was accompanied by the fear of the jungle. The jungle was not a figure of speech for Meena of the difficult times ahead. The fear was real, as she knew what was entailed in making a home in the forest; the hard work involved on an everyday basis. She had seen her mother and other women in the village work relentlessly day and night to sustain a home. *Maghe Parab* would commence the whole process of restoring the home in the forest to protect them from the dangerous spirits and wild animals. The spirits would never let them settle in one place if they are not careful. Out of all the spirits, the most dangerous and malevolent are those that have no home and float through villages from west to east. These spirits are of various types and have different names. They reside in the forest, mostly in trees. Quite often, they enter the village by following a person. For as long as they stay in the forest, they inflict illnesses on to the villagers. Her uncle, who had lived in the town for some years, had told her that his life there was easy; one could be cured of any illness by going to the doctor. However, in the village, the spirits would destroy them if they were not particular about pacifying them from time to time. The spirits would never allow them access to the knowledge in the forest, about the diverse kinds of medicines and remedies to illnesses that afflict them regularly. Without the same, they would have been driven out of any village that they settled: they would have been homeless.

March is also the time when the *mohua* flowers are bright yellow and ripe with nectar. Unable to bear their weight, *mohua* flowers drop on the forest floor constantly giving the feel of a yellow carpet. The forest echoes with the sound of its falling and reeks of its sweet smell. Birsa owns a few *mohua* trees in the village like other *khuntkattidars* and a few privileged *non-khuntkattidars.* It is common to spot wife/wives and children of the owners collecting *mohua* flowers off the ground. Having decided to remain at home, that is, of deciding against giving up its security for the person she loved, Meena took to the routine the next day as if nothing had happened the day before.

Both Suru and Meena got up early that day so as to finish all housework and leave the house to collect *mohua* flowers. They wanted to collect as much of it as possible before noon, to avoid the afternoon sun. They resumed work in the early evening and worked till sunset. Having collected *mohua* flowers, Suru spread them out in the courtyard for drying. Till they dry, the daily routine is to put them to dry in the sun. This is done all through the year with tamarind, seasonal vegetables like cauliflower and mushrooms. In the case of tamarind, which bears fruit in April–May, it is collected from the trees and most of it is sold off in the market, with only a part of it is stored for consumption. It forms an important ingredient of their *ud* (mushroom) diet during the monsoons, between the months of June and September. For that, the skin of the tamarind is peeled off, mixed with salt and dried in the sun. The seasonal vegetables are cut into small pieces and washed thoroughly before they are put out in the sun for drying. *Mohua* flowers are used for various purposes. It is used in medicinal preparations and for making liquor. Suru, as in other years, keeps some of it at home for medicinal requirements and sells the rest in the market.

In the end of April and first week of May approximately, the manure from the compost pit is transferred to the fields. The last year, it had rained heavily in April. Suru hoped to transfer all the dried manure from the pit to the field before the rains. The work on the fields begins in April after the celebration of *Hermut Parab,* also known as *Baba Parab.* The term *her* means 'to sow; to sprinkle something dry' and *mut* is used as an affix with the latter to mean the start of the act of sprinkling seeds on the field. The practice is to call on *Desauli Mahaburu* (the residing spirit of the sacred grove; also the spirit of the village) to oversee the agricultural work and protect the crops from the wrath of the evil spirits and ill-timed weather changes. A cock and a sheep are sacrificed as a part of the ritual. There are three kinds of paddy that are cultivated: *goda baba,* or the paddy grown on upland; *pee baba,* light paddy grown on the field which cannot retain water for long; *beda baba,* heavy paddy grown on land that retains water for the longest period of time.

The field is prepared before sowing, a task that is usually understood to be done by men, as women are not allowed to plough the land. Suru manages most of the work on her own, but depends on hired labour to carry out the task of ploughing. The preparation of the field involves removing the weeds and shrubs that have taken root all over it. The earth in Ho is called *ote.* An un worked field is *paadiye ote* and a new field is *nama ote.* The worked-on field is termed as *sal,* and in some instances, it is also called *sal ote.* The term *sala* means to choose or select. *Sal* is thus field in the lowland, which is most suitable for cultivation and thereby select and special. It is also the field that is transformed from *nama ote* or *paadiye ote* to *sal,* that is, from un-worked earth to a fertile field established through labour and ritual. *Hermut* marks the beginning of this cycle of regeneration and transformation.

Suru participates as well as supervises all the work associated with agriculture, from the time of sowing the grains to the process of transplanting and harvesting the crops. In July, *Heroh Parab* is celebrated in which Desauli Mahaburu is propitiated to 'send rain from the west and air from the east and to look kindly upon the family and its livestock'. Women mostly carry out the activity of transplanting the saplings of paddy into the water-filled earth. After transplantation, the task is to ensure that grass and other weeds do not thwart the growth of paddy. A ritual called *jomnama* succeeds the harvesting of paddy grown in the upland in September. The freshly cut paddy is offered to the spirits before it is used for daily consumption. The harvesting of the light paddy follows soon after this. There are various kinds of pulses that are grown in the upland such as, *biri* or *ramba, balja ramba, kuduti, kansari, maasuri and jayti.*

Finally, by November, it is time to harvest the paddy grown on the *beda* land; then begins the task of threshing and cleaning the paddy. The hay is collected and is brought to use in various ways. It is used to make *bode* (long ropes), which are used to make *baandi* or the pouches to store paddy. The hay that is used to make *bode* is called *pual* or *babasingh.* It is also kept aside as regular feed for cattle through the year as well as used for covering the roof of the house and is called *loto.* This activity continues through *makar,* a festival celebrated by the Gopes to mark the New Year, and till *Maghe Parab.* Rituals performed by the villagers in their houses precede the main collective function of *Maghe Parab.*

The yearly calendar of the villagers, which charts out the changes in nature along with the work, festivities and rituals that accompany it, is presented in Table 5.1. The four months of *Makar, Maghe, Baa* and *Guruii Dupul* are non-agricultural months during which the villagers undertake activities such as construction and repair of houses, pressing oil from *kusum, karanj* and *neem* seeds, collection of fuel-wood from the forest, visiting relatives and fixing betrothals and marriages. *Mohua* and tamarind are also collected and stored in these months. It is during these months that vegetables are grown and stored for consumption in the months characterised by heavy work in the fields. It is a break from the work in the fields, but is characterised by work in the forest and on the house. Thus, work and rest are relative terms, in that a rest in relation to work in the field characterises work in the forest. However, these are also months, during which the villagers prepare and equip themselves for the monsoons and months of laborious work in the field. The calendar then is illustrative of the interconnectedness of nature with culture as well as how both are integrated into a way of life, wherein it is difficult to elucidate the role of one in their lives without giving details of the other.

**Table 5.1:** The 12-Monthly Calendar

| *Chandu* (Month) | Nature/Culture |
|---|---|
| *Maghe Chandu* | The month known by the most popular festival of the Ho, namely, *Maghe Parab*. It marks the beginning of a new year of work in the fields and repairs, renewals and construction of houses in the village. |
| *Baa Chandu* | *Baa* means a flower and it is in this month that *Baa Parab* or the festival of flowers is celebrated to mark the blossoming of *Sal*. *Mohua* also flowers in this month and the villagers get busy in collecting *mohua* from the forest bed. |
| *Guruii Dupil Chandu* | *Guruii* translates in Ho as cow dung. *Dupil* means 'to carry on the head'. In this month, most of the villagers transfer cow dung, stored over months in the pits near their houses, to the fields as manure. This marks the beginning of the preparation of the fields for cultivation. Tamarind also ripens in this month and the villagers collect and dry it in the sun for use during the monsoons. Some of the villagers also sell it in the local market. |
| *Baba Her Chandu* | *Baba* refers to paddy and *her* is 'to sow or sprinkle'. It is in *Baba Her Chandu* that paddy cultivation begins and it is marked by *Baba Hermutu* festival, in which a sacrifice is made to the spirits for a good monsoon before sowing the main crop. |
| *Kanail Chandu* | This month marks the arrival of the monsoons in its entirety. *Nail* is the Ho word for a plough and it is in this month that the ploughing of land is undertaken. The staples of the villagers through the rainy months are mushrooms that sprout all over the fields and forests. |
| *Rowa Chandu* | *Rowa* means 'to transplant, to plant in to water filled earth with the hand'. The villagers transplant paddy into the field during this period. A ritual called *hero parab* is performed to the spirits once the sowing is completed. |
| *Hey Chandu* | *Hey* in Ho means to puck whole leaves; it also refers to the chaff or husks of grains. The villagers remove grass, chaff and weeds that grow in the field that thwart the growth of paddy during this month. |
| *Jomnama Chandu* | This month is named after the festival celebrated before the first fruits of harvest of the crop grown in the upland are eaten. The festival is a form of thanksgiving to the spirits for allowing them to cultivate and harvest the crop without any hindrance. |
| *Pee Baba Ir Chandu* | *Pee Baba* is the paddy grown in the upland, *ir* is 'to cut'. It is in this month, after the celebration of *jomnama*, that the paddy of the upland is harvested. |
| *Beda Baba Ir Chandu* | During this month, the paddy of the *beda* land is harvested. |
| *Busu u Kuta Chandu* | *Busu* translates as straw; *kuta* means 'the foot'. In this month, the husked paddy is beaten and worked on by the oxen in the threshing floor known as *kolom*. |
| *Makar Chandu* | *Makar Sankranti* is the festival of Gopes and marks the beginning of the new year of the Oriya community. The month is known by this festival. This also marks the beginning of the winter months when the villagers maintain gardens and grow seasonal vegetables, which is then dried in the sun and stored for consumption in the rainy months. |

## A Place of One's Own: Women's Work and the Home

The reference to the term 'home' in the paper does not imply a four-walled structure alone, it stands for a human being's address or a place in the world she inhabits. For women, home is not permanent; it is a transitory category. They are raised with the knowledge that the home they care for day after day is not theirs. After marriage, they are strangers to the house they move into and therein they begin a whole new process of embracing new surroundings, people and a way of life. They don't inherit homes; they make them. They invest their labour and their emotional and mental resources in its creation. The value of a home, therefore, is that much more for a woman in as much as it is also a source of insecurity. This reality of women's life of impermanence in the context of a home is what can be termed as a form of 'crossing', which is an opening rather than a closure through which women experience the world.[5]

On marriage, Suru moved out of a home that no longer belonged to her; she moved into a home that was alien to her and ridden with conflict and dissension. This too, she realises, is not rightfully hers as her husband can claim it any day to get his third wife to stay with him. Yet, what indeed belongs to her is the capacity to build a home through her hard work and that alone provides her with a sense of self-worth and respect. Padma, much as she might like to, cannot rightfully return to the 'security' of her parents' home. She cannot rid herself of the feelings of gratitude and obligation that haunt her each time her parents help her. Meena also knew that had she walked out of her home the day her lover came to take her with him, she could never return to its warm enfold.

Similarly, homecoming is not a return of a person, who goes astray, wanders off a forbidden path. This definition assumes an omnipresent home, a place of comfort and rescue. Homecoming, as understood here, is not a return to a presupposed sense of certitude or security associated with the 'home'. Homecoming, then, is never a return to an omnipresent home, but a process of establishing a home and working towards its renewal and restoration. In this sense, women are not delimited by the confines of a home or by the supposed 'security' it offers. Its contours are set by women through their work and labour in order to secure their place in society. Homecoming is the culmination of the process of establishing a 'home' in the forest year after year and thereby securing a place in the community for themselves.

In the context of the village too, homecoming is not a return to certitude, but the act of building a 'home' in the forest. Homecoming, as is commonly understood, would imply a return to the uncertainty and insecurity of the forest for the villagers. It would entail betraying and abandoning the ancestors to the mercy of the evil spirits that roam the jungle and putting the present and the future generations in danger. This would also amount to a breach of faith towards the spirit world, in traversing the boundary between humans and the spirits. Homecoming is the celebration of the process by which the forest, an otherwise uninhabitable space, is transformed into an inhabitable one. It is a celebration of the success in building a 'home' in the forest. *Maghe Parab* is a collective commemoration of homecoming in the forest. It celebrates the success in sustaining and reproducing the home in the forest as well as restates its resilience to restore the 'home' in the following year.

Women's work is fundamental in establishing and renewing the special relationship to land and forests in the village, wherein it is difficult to separate economic labour from the symbolic capital that goes into maintaining a home and the community. How could, then, homecoming be complete without recognising the persons responsible for maintaining a home? Meena, Padma and Suru's fears are inconsistent with their role in building a home. Land rights to women would help in overcoming this ambiguity in women's lives and also reinforce the grounds for homecoming in the forest. Concomitantly, the campaign for land rights for women should redress the popular notion of the home, in which the latter is not seen merely as a site of oppression but also of self-determination.

Land and forest are not held in esteem only for their material worth. The term 'belonging' takes on a larger meaning. Land and forests are the media through which the villagers relate to the phenomena of life and death and deliberate on who they are and what is to become of them. It is this that sets it apart from the scientific, modern management of forests. Thus, the issue is not only about how much labour women put in on land and in the home, but also the kind of labour involved. There is a particular kind of relationship set with humans, land and the forests, wherein the boundary of each is maintained.

In securing a home, Suru restores the sacred and the mundane of everyday life and consequently provides the basis of community life itself. Not only are the duties with regard to the spirits and ancestors fulfilled, but also those towards relatives in other villages, the villagers and family. She carries out the responsibility of socialising her daughters and son to the community life and living. She reaches out to her daughter Padma at her time of crises and difficulty. Her attempt at securing a home and a sense of self, therefore, includes the family and community life and is not set apart from it. It is inclusive and all embracing. The home, therefore, cannot be set against the world, as a closure and in opposition to the ways of the world.

## Ho Women and Land Rights: The Crossfire

The issue of women's rights on land among the Ho came up before the formation of Jharkhand, at a time when the movement was trying to strengthen its base by forging a collective identity within tribes and of all tribes in the area. A woman activist, who filed a case in the Supreme Court demanding land rights for Ho women, brought it up for debate.[6] This sparked off tensions in the area, and lent itself to a long-standing debate over the intention behind it.[7] Conferences, debates and discussions were organised to clarify reservations to an issue that, in principle, seemed proper and just. Presented here are the main arguments for and against granting land rights to women.[8]

A main reservation with the Bill was that it would lead to the disintegration of the community. Since the Ho are patrilineal and virilocal, and women are constantly on the move through marriage, the argument is that land rights to women would be meaningless as they would not stay at a place in order to cultivate the land they claim. On the other hand, if women do decide to stay back to exercise this right, it would lead to confusion in the existing system of marriage and descent and lead to the break-up of the patrilineage, on the basis of which all Ho villages have been settled. The existing pattern of landholding, it is argued, encourages social ties of the patrilineage (*killi*) whereas the proposed bill would undermine it. The latter would lead to fragmentation of land and the disintegration of the family as a unit.

About a Rajasthan village, Rajni Palriwala (1999) has observed that, with the growing demand for labour due to the out migration of men, there has been a demographic shift in the village and changes in kinship practices. More and more married women return to their natal homes to assist during the agricultural season and that there has been a reduction of the distance between women's natal and conjugal residence over the years. This questions the assumption that once married, women are fixed residents of their conjugal homes, and allays the fear that property rights to women and their consequent mobility for managing agricultural work on land will lead to the disintegration of the family as a unit.

The experience of villages in West Singhbhum is similar in that many *khuntkattidar* men have taken up jobs in the railways and the numerous mines that have mushroomed all over the district. Many of them prefer to stay at their place of work than commute long for work everyday. The responsibility of agricultural work then falls primarily on women. The case presented in this paper then is not an exception to the rule, but illustrates the norm. In such a scenario, women's regular presence is what sustains work on land and the domestic unit within the village. In fact, it is men's mobility that threatens the survival of the domestic unit and agricultural work. In many households in the village, young unmarried daughters as well as married daughters supervise agricultural work and contribute their labour towards their natal home.

Those arguing against the bill assume that women, in all probability, would claim land if they were provided with the right through law. This need not necessarily be the case, though the fear over the same suggests the ludicrousness of not exercising the right on land if women are provided with it. There are several arguments posited as reasons for women's restraint in exercising the right to property; fear of ostracism from the community is one of them. Such explanations fall short of analysing the women's point of view, as they only engage in an analysis of the consequences that might accrue in exercising the right to property by women. Similarly, arguments in favour of land rights for women are garbed in the same vocabulary, which present similar rationalisations to make a case for women's financial and economic independence (see Kishwar 1987). For instance, property rights for widows and unattached women are justified on the ground that they lack the support of a man in their lives. Here, property is a substitute for man, and, in this sense, both land and man are in conflict over maintaining women. Women are 'objects' in relation to man and property. Property is seen as that which would enable women to seek economic, social and political independence, as against women facilitating the proper utilisation of property by exercising their rights on land.

Gender inequalities are built into inheritance laws in India. This is especially apparent in inheritance laws of agricultural land (Agarwal 1999). The Government of India Act of 1935 has vested all legislative powers regarding agricultural land to state legislatures. With independence, this power was more or less restored; with the restriction that any subject falling within the Concurrent List of the Constitution and that which has already been passed by the Parliament cannot be passed in the state legislature without the consent of the President of India. This, for one, accounts for the regional disparity on laws over women's inheritance of agricultural land. But, most significantly, it has deterred state legislatures from amending Hindu Succession Law for owned agricultural land, thereby preventing state legislatures from passing a bill against women's inheritance of agricultural property (for example, the 1969 Punjab Assembly decision and the 1979 Haryana Assembly resolution) Even though favourable laws for women's accession to agricultural property exist in certain states, women are very low down on the list of inheritors. In states where such laws exist, they are qualified by restrictions wherein a woman loses rights on agricultural property on remarriage, a failure to cultivate the land over a specified period of time and upon her death such that her legal heirs have no rights on the property and it is transferred to the heirs of the last male landowner.

This clearly reflects biases in the legal definition of the 'family' which discriminates against women and treats them as appendages rather than rightful partners in the composition of a family. The legal rights that accrue to them, therefore, seem more like concessions and privileges than a legal recognition and acknowledgement of women's work on land. It repudiates women's work on land, an aspect that resets gender inequality through law.

The campaign for granting property rights to Ho women partakes of similar perceptions of women in relation to family and work, thus failing to challenge what lies at the core of women's empowerment. Unless the fundamental bases for discrimination against women are not addressed in the campaign for granting property rights to Ho women, that is, devaluation of women's work and their position in the family, the demand for property rights to Ho women would be misconstrued as an attempt to weaken the Jharkhand movement by promoting disunity between Ho men and women over the issue of land rights.

This also raises issues of theoretical and methodological significance in connection with women land rights. The terms 'family' and 'household' have been regularly examined as units of sociological analyses, especially in the context of devaluation of women's work as well as the non-recognition of women's labour in the household (Shah 1973 and 1998; Saradamoni 1992). On the one hand, the term 'family' has been dissociated from the term 'household' in that the household is the residential unit or the living arrangement of the family (Shah 1973). On the other hand, the census operations have not paid much attention to the two terms and have restricted its utility to data collection for population surveys (Rao 1992). The two terms have been used interchangeably.

Either way, the conceptual differences have not contributed favourably towards recognition of women and women's work. The separation of the term household and family might have helped in recognising and documenting the various changes in the constitution of a household in or over a region, caste and community, but has retained the patriarchal definition of a family thereby reducing the former as a deviation vis-à-vis the latter. The household as a practical variant of the category 'family' poses no threat through its findings to the structural definition of the family, as a patrilineal, patrilocal unit, under a patriarchal head with all ritual, social and economic rights vested in the male members. 'The law is concerned primarily with the constitution of the property holding group and with the persons having rights of maintenance from the property-holding group, and not with the constitution of the household group' (*Ibid.*: 55).

Another fear of the Ho is that their women, who are illiterates and as a consequence 'naive', are easily susceptible to the connivance of the 'non-Ho' men. The 'non-Ho' men may lure Ho women into marrying them with the intention of usurping land. This would aggravate the tensions between Ho and the non-Ho and lead to the exploitation of Ho women. The non-Ho men may harass Ho women for land and later abandon them, once they get control over land. The non-Ho may even indulge in bride burning to get their way. However, the question that remains unanswered is as to what keeps Ho women 'true' or 'loyal' to their community even though they have no legal rights. If the answer is the financial and social insecurity of moving away, then the granting of land rights to women might even strengthen women's 'loyalty' to the community.

These arguments are, however, flawed in their very core. The naiveté associated with women is also reflective of the way the home is conceived. The home is set against the public sphere or community life, and women as its key inhabitants are supposedly cut off from exchanges beyond its confines. These arguments are also based on the principle of mistrust, and they construct Ho women as the 'homogenous' other with respect to the community. The community here refers to the men as against women; it is exclusive and not inclusive of women. An understanding that fails to break away from this essentially asymmetrical and marginalising relationship between men and women cannot in any way represent women's voices and positions on the matter. At the root of it is a denial of the power of discretion in women, and an assumption that they are incapable of thinking for themselves.

## Conclusion

This paper has presented another way of addressing the issue of land rights for women which breaks away from the stalemate presented by the arguments discussed in the previous section. The attempt was to make a case for women's right on land by describing the practice of everyday life, work and ritual in a Ho village through a case study. The intention was to show women's role in sustaining the knowledge systems and the way of life, which establishes a more humble relationship with nature. Women's work on land and forests helps bear form to the alternative that the movement so vociferously defends and celebrates. However, the debate over land rights to Ho women does not adequately recognise this contribution of women, nor does it realise the consequences of the same. The denial of land rights to women is premised on the under evaluation of women's skills on land and forests. This *ipso facto* undermines the practices around land and forests, which forms the grounds for homecoming in the forest and is the fundamental rally point of the Jharkhand movement. Consequently the assertion of self-rule or the reinstatement of the claim of the movement of possessing a more humble and egalitarian relationship with nature as against that of the modern, scientific one cannot begin without acknowledging the role of women in its creation.

The self-determination of women is, thus, simultaneously a claim of possessing a more humble and a humane relationship with nature and an assertion of self-rule. Therefore, the fear that granting land rights to women will lead to the disintegration of the community is misplaced. It would redefine gender relations and readjust social relations in favour of women; a phenomenon that will only strengthen the 'home' by recognising women's effort and labour in building it. It is crucial that women are included as important contributors in this endeavour, failing which the dissent and resistance of the Jharkhandis would end up as another orthodoxy-in-the-making.

# Notes

I am thankful to Professor Virginius Xaxa, my doctoral supervisor, for his guidance and observations on the earlier draft of this paper; the anonymous referee for her/his prompt response and detailed comments on the paper; and Ms Alpana Thadani for her help in typing the paper.

1. The most characteristic feature of everyday life as explicated by sociologists such as Edmund Husserl and Alfred Schutz is that it is experienced as an inter-subjective world. It is a world of shared meanings, 'known and knowable in common with others' (Zimmerman and Pollner 1971: 84). According to Don H. Zimmerman and Melvin Pollner, 'everyday activities and their perceived connected features present themselves with the promise that they may be understood and acted upon in practically sufficient ways by competent employment of appropriate proverbs, paradigms, motives, organisational charts, and the like' (*Ibid.:* 85). Thus, the practice of everyday life fundamentally relies on this shared knowledge, which allows for suspension of doubt or a taken-for-grantedness in everyday interactions and dealings. In explicating women's everyday life in the forest, the attempt is not only to give details of the shared system of meanings and practices around life and work in the forest, but also to demonstrate the process through which this shared system of knowledge and meanings help constitute a 'home' in the forest, thereby reassuring continuity and permanence of the everyday life (see Schutz 1964).

2. The use of 'substantive facts about another culture' to 'probe into the specific facts about the subject of criticism at home' dates back to the works of Margaret Mead (Marcuse and Fischer 1986: 138). However, I would like to distinguish between ethnocentrism, an extension of the self in the study of the 'other' and the pursuit of a research question, which concerns the self as much as the 'other'. The issue is no longer of 'cultural juxtapositioning' or detailing similarities and differences between cultures (*Ibid.*), but how the study of the 'other' helps us in achieving greater understanding of common concerns of environmental degradation, self-rule and gender equity.
3. Interestingly, the general criteria of classification for the wide variety of green leaves, mushrooms, vegetables, etc. found in the jungle and the village are based on resemblances and analogy as well as on its use in daily life, thereby reiterating the important role of women in sustaining the process through which such knowledge has been accumulated and preserved. To quote Michel Foucault, '...in every culture, between the use of what one might call the ordering codes and reflections upon order itself, there is the pure experience of order and of its mode of being' (1973: xxi). Thus, the everyday experience of nature is intricately tied to the question of origins and the creation of the universe. The substance and form of classification or the ability to judge and decide what resembles and is a resemblance of in nature are based on the learning and knowledge of nature. Among the Ho, this relatedness of things in nature is therefore not only reflective of their observation of nature, but also of their understanding of Creation itself. Women, therefore, are not only the custodians of this knowledge, but also of the order that encases this knowledge.
4. The preparation of rice-beer takes three days. The rice is first cooked and then spread out on a *jaati* (mat) to cool. The mat is made of a special grass found in the jungle and is also an important article in Ho marriages.
5. The reference here is to the feminist divide between the private and the public domain, the home and the community/market, wherein the private and the home are seen as the sites of oppression or nurturance by radical and ecofeminists respectively. The attempt here is to move beyond these dichotomous understanding of the home, which forecloses a diversity of experiences, besides presenting the category 'home' as a ubiquitous and a preset category. The 'home' is a site through which women experience the world; both the so-called private and public domains of life, and it is both a source of security and shelter, on the one hand, and of vulnerability and difficulty, on the other.
6. See Ahuja (1997: 211–14) for details of the Public Interest Litigation filed by Madhu Kishwar against the State of Bihar challenging Sections, 7, 8 and 76 of the CNT Act of 1908, which determines land holding pattern in the area.
7. Many in the area viewed this move as an attempt to weaken the movement at a time when alliances were being sought across class, tribe and gender. This raises the sensitive question as how to address issues of exploitation and injustice in marginalised communities or 'other' cultures without alienating them and their cause further. Then again, how does one present a case for property rights to Ho women with a view to strengthen the claim of the Jharkhand movement of possessing an alternative to the exploitative forms of modern ecological management? The question is as much a methodological one as it is political.
8. The arguments against the bill have been largely drawn from my interactions with social activists and intellectuals in Jharkhand. I also summarise the observations of some of the speakers in a two-day seminar on whether Ho women should be given property rights in Kolhan held in Tata College, Chaibasa on 20–21 December 1996.

# References


Agarwal, Bina. 1999. *Gender and legal rights in landed property in India.* Delhi: Kali for Women.

Ahuja, Sangeeta. 1997. *People, law and justice-casebook on public interest litigation (Vol. I).* Delhi: Orient Longman.

Deeney, J., S. J. 1978. *Ho grammar and vocabulary.* Chaibasa: Xavier Ho Publications, St. Xavier's High School.

Foucault, Michel. 1973. *The order of things. An archaeology of the human sciences.* New York: Vintage Books.

Kishwar, Madhu. 1987. 'Toiling without rights: Ho women of Singhbhum', *Economic and political weekly*, 22 (3, 4 & 5): 95–101, 149–55, and 194–200.

Lorduswamy, Stan. 1997. *Jharkhandi's claim for self-rule.* Delhi: Indian Social Institute and BIRSA.

Marcuse, George. E. and Michael M. J. Fischer. 1986. *Anthropology as a critique. An experimental moment in the human sciences.* Chicago: The University of Chicago Press.

Palriwala, Rajni. 1996. 'Negotiating patriliny: Intra-household consumption and authority in northwest India', in Rajni Palriwala and Carla Risseeuw (eds.): *Shifting circles of support: Contextualising gender and kinship in south Asia and sub-Saharan Africa* (190–218). New Delhi: Sage Publications.

———. 1999. 'Transitory residents, invisible workers: rethinking locality and incorporation in a Rajasthan village', in Kumkum Sangari and Uma Chakravarti (eds.): *From myths to markets: Essays on gender* (237–73). Shimla: IIAS and Delhi: Manohar Publications.

Rao, Usha N. J. 1992. 'Gaps in definitions and analysis: a sociological perspective', in K. Saradamoni (ed.): *Finding the household: Conceptual and methodological issues* (31–74). New Delhi: Sage Publications.

Saradamoni, K. (ed.). 1992. *Finding the household: Conceptual and methodological issues.* New Delhi: Sage Publications.

Schutz, Alfred. 1964. 'The homecomer', in his *Studies in social theory: Collected papers II* (106–119). The Hague: Martinus Nijhoff.

Sinha, Amarjeet. 1988. 'From popular protest to people's participation: Towards evolution of a participative people's programme for tribals and forests of Singhbhum district, Bihar' (Unpublished) [This paper summarises the main issues that were raised in a two-day participative seminar on *Tribals and Forests in Singhbhum* involving 307 villagers from all over the district held in Chaibasa].

Shah, A. M. 1973. *The household dimension of the family in India.* Delhi: Orient Longman.

———. 1998. *The family in India: Critical essays.* Delhi: Orient Longman.

Zimmerman, Don H. and Melvin Pollner. 1971. 'The everyday world of the phenomenon', in Jack D. Douglas (ed.): *Understanding everyday life: Towards the reconstruction of sociological knowledge* (80–103). London: Routledge and Kegan Paul.

# PART II

# The Working Class

# 6

# The Field of Labour*

*N. R. Sheth*

Thank you, M. N. Srinivas Endowment Committee, for asking me to deliver the third memorial lecture. Thank you, Indian Sociological Society, for organising the lecture as a part of the conference programme. You have honoured me with a prized opportunity to pay tribute to my teacher and mentor in more senses than one. I was among Professor Srinivas's inaugural students at Baroda. Having him as a teacher was a rare gift of providence. His concern for us extended well beyond the academic regime to cover our physical, social and human well-being. His notes on our assignments carried not only subject insights but also lasting lessons in communication. We witnessed his struggles and achievements as he tried to get recognition for sociology and the fieldwork method in academic establishment, public affairs and governance. His uncanny wit and wryly potent humour often made waves of delightful unintended learning.

Srinivas's intellectual interest during the later part of his life and career was characterised by a growing concern about human implications of social change in India and the global society. He was optimistic about integration among unequal caste ranks by way of emergence of an expansive middle class. However, he was concerned about the escalating force of selfishness, greed, consumerism and violence in society at large. He was perturbed about the growing failure of the conventional modes of socioeconomic development to contain the destructive forces. He continued to look for culturally meaningful measures to fight this disease. His prescription included the possibility of the humanist element in Indian spirituality and religious faith being invoked as an antidote to extravagant consumerism and individualism. This is indeed a far cry from the structure-function paradigm which Srinivas is widely believed to have followed relentlessly.

## Changing Outlook

I intend in this presentation to scan some landmarks and directions in the area of labour from a sociological vantage point. I was easily persuaded by

Srinivas to explore, for my doctoral work, the web of social relations and institutions in an urban-industrial population. I settled down to the study of a single factory. My initial perspective was guided by the structure-function paradigm and the degree of persistence of Indian tradition in its fusion with modern technology and ideas. The product of my research deviated only mildly from this perspective. Such an outcome would not have surprised sociologists of my generation. However, scholarship in studies of labour and industry has moved way beyond structure, function and tradition. This movement is in tune with changing theoretical outlook in the social sciences. Today, our sociological imagination is not constrained by organic models of states of existence and change. Today, our examination and assessment of specific groups, categories, classes and societies are not necessarily informed by models of rationality and modernity that once appeared to demand universal endorsement from analysts of social change and development. There is a sense in which this departure in our scientific outlook is related to recent upheavals in society.

The current capabilities and future prospects of modern science and technology have launched us on an apparently endless path of material progress and access to commodities and facilities. This path leads us into a vicious circle of arousal and fulfilment of personal and social needs. We are invited to live with the hope of a progressively happier and more prosperous world. This is our perfumed garden of economic and social development. The constantly visible availability of newer and smarter goods and services at all levels of social hierarchy is not a small invitation to desire, hope and euphoria.

Alas. We cannot overlook the flip side of this enchanting scenario. The visible availability of coveted goods and services is truly globalised, thanks to the omnipotent penetration of craft of publicity through media of instant communication. However, our ability to get what we crave continues to be unequal. Disparities of wealth and income between the rich and the poor have been growing everywhere. Many of us cannot afford to enjoy the new products of civilisation. Inaccessibility to objects of our desire produces a sense of deprivation in our social consciousness. Deprivation in an environment of continuous exposure to goods enhances the urge to possess. This drives us into an ideology of greed, temptation, acquisitiveness and individualism. Ethical and moral codes of conduct have been losing their value for us. We show increasing insensitivity to the needs and sensibilities of fellow human beings. Our institutions, from family to state, are going through turbulence of all sorts. Thus, our material progress and the bright prospects it presents for human happiness do not appear to be matched by human capabilities and tendencies necessary for a symbiotic global social order. It may be worthwhile here to remember that a similar mismatch between industrial civilisation and contemporary human and social reality was underscored at the beginning of the twentieth century by western social scientists.[1] We have probably been running fast to stay where we stand!

In this background, we should welcome the growing liberalisation in social science from the old tenets of objectivity and structuralism. The new sociological imagination warrants acceptance of social conditions described by terms such as equality, freedom, justice, dignity, participation and empowerment to serve as benchmarks for comprehension and interpretation of social reality. The concept of human development has lately been offered as a holistic articulator of the social order of our global dream. Distinguished scholars like Mahbub ul Haq and Amartya Sen have moulded the concept of human development with ideas of enrichment of human life and human freedom to choose a way of life.[2] Human development is generally discussed in terms of the socioeconomic conditions of the poor and disadvantaged sections of a population. Poverty implies denial of choice. Those who are denied choice deserve special attention in development discourse. This aspect of development can be covered under the title quality of life. But it is perhaps necessary to add a new dimension to the concept of human development from the vantage point of the rich and the powerful for whom the material quality of life is not an issue of social deprivation. For people in this class, ideas of human freedom, dignity, equity and empowerment may provide ground for arrogance of excessive individuality and power at the cost of fellow human beings. None of us can be unaware of how often people in high places invoke ideas of freedom and justice to claim exemption from legal or social accountability. Human development, in this context, should mean regulation of social conduct to check abuse of social standing. This can perhaps be called the social character aspect of human development. Our sociological imagination deserves a composite frame for a comprehensive view of human development.

## Labour and Society

This new direction of goal in social science has brought us a full circle from Marxian sociology of labour.[3] Karl Marx saw society as nearly divided into two classes. He wanted to liberate human spirit and labour power from the coercive superimposition of the capitalist class. He wanted the wielder of labour to achieve control over nature and society for meaningful social existence. His historical wisdom compelled him to project the future of the contemporary class-ridden world from his perceived scenario of exploitation and expropriation of labour power. He envisioned social transformation through the stages of class conflict, working-class revolution, reign of the proletariat and, finally, a classless social order where human freedom and supremacy of labour power would become a reality. Marxian hopes and projections have been deconstructed and reconstructed a million times. However, an important unfinished agenda of social development is to recognise human labour as the principal stakeholder in economic enterprises.

Visionaries of the ilk of Marx and Max Weber had ruled out societies such as India in their diagnosis and prognosis of the Industrial Revolution and its consequences. Their knowledge and understanding of non-Western societies should have made them wonder how India's baggage of primitive village communities and irrational religious culture could ever raise the capital-proletariat combination and confrontation so indispensable for the modernity of the machine age. Today we know how the *gurus* were wrong in this part of their vision. Machines and *moolah* sooner or later embraced virtually all societies around the world and created local cocktails of capital, labour, market and class relations. Local socioeconomic conditions had a lot to do with the form of evolution and progress of labour in each culture. However, this process has borne two common characteristics: (i) conditions of labour in terms of human development have remained sub-optimal, and (ii) there have been continuing efforts in some form or other to alter these conditions towards a higher degree or quality of human development. It is, therefore, possible to visualise the process of industrialisation as an engine for a concurrent process of human development or humanisation in the field of labour.

I should digress here for a moment. The field of labour for social science should ideally be coterminous with all types of work that involve construction and continuity of socioeconomic interdependence. Presidents and policemen, ministers and mafia agents, bonded workers, wives, children and all others who work for living are members of a labour force. Conventionally, however, labour has been defined within the contours of what economists recognise as labour market. This leaves out some socially significant categories of labour. The value of the labour of a spouse or child of a householder is full of economic riddles. The socioeconomic significance of a mighty labour market of drug peddlers, bootleggers, contract killers, etc. remains in our area of darkness. Our social historians seem to be cool about the labour dimension of our ancient and medieval social fabric. We need to know the way massive labour forces were recruited and sustained to meet large constructions and craft enterprises. Who knows, we may discover streaks of human development in labour relations in pre-industrial times. For now, I would like to present my reflections along the conventional categorisation of labour into the organised and the unorganised sectors.

## Organised Sector

The modern process of progressive humanisation began at the dawn of industrialisation in the West (see Webb and Webb 1897). It involved radical changes at various levels in society. The socioeconomic reality of labour conditions in industry and in community was documented by sensitive scholars. Stark pictures of poverty, deprivation and exploitation served to raise public concern. The collective consciousness of suffering and exploitation among workers and rising public awareness of the plight of labour forced governments to assume responsibility for the welfare of and justice for employees. Trade unions were recognised to enable labour to promote its interests. Bilateral negotiations and bargaining were institutionalised to provide order and stability in employment relations. Laws were made to impose economic and managerial obligations on employers in the interest of equity, justice, human rights and social welfare for labour. In short, capital-labour relations were structured in the image of the democratic framework of the society at large.

The development of industrial labour force in India has gone through similar signposts of humanisation since its inception in the nineteenth century (see Sharma 1962; Punekar and Varickayil 1989). Industrial proletariat was mainly drawn from pauperised rural population; they suffered poverty and alienation in urban slums. Liberalised middle-class social reformers pressured the government to study conditions of labour and then to impose legal obligations on employers to improve those conditions. This was followed by the rise of trade unions in the wake of working-class consciousness and the nationalist movement. The initial connection of trade unionism with nationalist politics has left a lasting legacy of fission and fusion in the union movement to follow episodes of unity and division among political overlords. In addition, employment relations in India have been closely monitored and controlled by government by legal authority and political power. Hence, the overall effectiveness of trade unions in achieving justice and equity for labour has been modest and uneven. The role of unions in serving the cause of human development of labour has depended on their political equations with people and groups in power.

Meanwhile, questions were raised about low productivity of labour in societies like India. British social scientists and administrators easily concluded that attachment of Indian workers to primordial institutions (like family, caste, village, and religion) prevented development of adequate commitment to industrial jobs and way of life. Such lack of commitment was, in fact, projected as a major hurdle in industrialisation and economic development. However, grounded historical and sociological studies soon revealed that workers' loyalty to primordial institutions was not necessarily or even primarily responsible for lack of commitment to industry. The problem of commitment was seeded more in the behaviour of employers in terms of employment conditions and quality of life. We now have a good deal of research-based information to say that a worker's social behaviour and attitudes are based on choices he/she draws from the multiplicity of social, economic and political forces governing his/her life (see Holmstrom 1976; Uma Ramaswamy 1983). This kind of awareness brings us closer to the view of labour as an important partner in industry.

## Modes of Humanisation

The status of labour as stakeholder in industry steadily gained acceptance after independence under the influence of our democratic-socialistic polity and commitment to modern industrialism (see National Commission on Labour 1969). With the growth of unions in blue-collar as well as white-collar segments of workers, employers and the government yielded concessions in economic returns, working conditions, welfare and fairness and justice in labour relations. Public sector enterprises promoted the role of government as a model employer, which meant liberal and often indiscriminate commitment for creation of jobs and welfare measures for employees and their families. Affluent and liberal employers and union militancy from time to time led to better economic and social deals for employees. Some segments of workers, especially those in government and the public sector, could clinch relatively larger gains and prerogatives with their union power. They invited in the public eye the caricature of a labour aristocracy.

These forces of humanisation of industrial labour have been supplemented here and there by efforts to introduce democratic patterns of management in labour relations at the workplace. These efforts are guided by the human relations school in management science which emphasises the value of a person's psychological, social and economic needs and obligations as a vital factor in his behaviour and performance as an employee. Various types of experiments have been made in industry to develop institutions of consultative and participative management in the areas of employee welfare, motivation, efficiency and productivity. Successive attempts have been made at national, state and industry levels to raise employee satisfaction, labour-management harmony, quality and productivity through joint managerial committees and quality circles. There have been attempts to redesign the content and rhythm of production process to make work more interesting and socially rewarding for employees. Stray attempts have also been made to promote labour participation in management and equity on the basis of Gandhian ideas of trusteeship. These democratic-humanistic experiments have largely proved short lived and remained confined to selected enterprises. However, they seem to have generated public awareness and interest in the human side of enterprise.

## Liberalisation and Labour

Labour relations began to face phases of turbulence about two decades ago with the rise of global competitiveness, economic crisis and the impact of information technology (see E.A. Ramaswamy 1988; Sheth) Employers were pushed to the wall to cut costs under threats of healthy survival. Technology created compulsions to project labour as a dispensable factor. Trade unions lost their leverage to stand up and defend their constituents. Government faced its own compulsions to adopt a soft approach to the problems of industry and compromise its long-standing policies of equity and fairness on employment-related matters such as closure, retrenchment and casualisation of the workforce. Helplessness of trade unions made union leadership powerless and alienated workers from union bonds. A view increasingly shared by workers, employers and popular opinion was that unions had outlived their value for workers and society; they should modify their roles or exit.

At the same time, the process of humanisation of labour at the work-place has continued and assumed new forms (E. Ramaswamy 19976). A new set of ideas and functions in the management of people has evolved under the titles human resource management (HRM) and human resource development (HRD). In this approach, management carries the onus for the well-being and development of workers in a comprehensive manner in coordination with the well-being and development of the enterprise. Considerable emphasis is placed on democratic management concepts such as mutuality, trust, holistic development, training, participation and empowerment. Workers and unions are projected as being treated as partners in this integrated managerial process. Unions are exhorted to abandon their adversarial role and collaborate in the march to progress. Ironically, these noble experiments in human development are often pursued along with determined plans to cut down labour costs by technological upgradations, outsourcing of production and reduction of employment. HRM-HRD executives find themselves being charged with the responsibility to deal with human development issues of employees, on the one hand, and to monitor plans for premature retirement or retrenchment, on the other. It would be interesting to learn how such potentially conflicting roles affect a manager's personal and social sensibilities. In the corporate world, the ability of an enterprise to reduce employment has become an important factor in judgements on its health and viability. Meanwhile, social globe-watchers in the West have already begun to draw scenarios of a society where goods and services will be produced entirely or predominantly without human inputs (see Kelly 2000).

Let us look at the downside of the corporate *mantra* of employment downsizing (see Breman 2003). Increasing casualisation of labour has generated irregularities and uncertainties of income and raised levels of immediate and long-term insecurity for workers and their families. Concurrently, measures such as voluntary retirement, layoff and closure of enterprise have created a large population of ex-workers in blue-collar and white-collar categories. They face various kinds of unintended consequences of separation from employment in the midst of a career. Many of those who are pushed out by closure of industry are suddenly pauperised. Their families join them in suffering diminished ability to fulfil social obligations and diminished self and social esteem. Such people are often forced into dehumanising or antisocial callings for livelihood. Those who fall into premature retirement with what is known as a 'golden handshake' may not necessarily face economic hurdles. However, many of them go through experiences of psychological and social alienation in their status as workers and citizens.

Meanwhile, the new tribe of knowledge workers tied to the new mass media of information, communication, entertainment, education and the like is growing rapidly everywhere. These people work as individuals with distinctly individualistic equations with their work-technology and organisation. They enjoy economic affluence with a relatively high social status and recognition. Their ideas and concerns regarding job security and career growth are likely to be different from those of other categories of labour.

They may develop little collective consciousness as employees and distance themselves from trade unionism. This category of labour constitutes an area of special interest for social science.

We should also take note of a special segment of our labour force. I refer to the relatively rich, affluent and powerful workers–technocrats, bureaucrats, professionals and such types of self-employed and salaried workers. They constitute labour aristocracy living on high-income islands. They tend to follow the dictum 'the more I have, the more I need'. They wield collective strength through unions or union-like combinations. Many of them are associated with services that are essential or crucial for the citizenry. This gives them added strength to put pressures on employers. Here, we can often see or suffer conventional union power in its socially damaging form. The distance between this condition and human development needs to be examined in terms of degrees of excessive freedom, justice and individualism and the ways of regulating the excesses.

We should also remember that abuse of freedom and justice has ceased to be the monopoly of the upper rungs of social hierarchy. Economic opportunities are increasingly becoming available to small segments of population even among the poorest. A large part of these opportunities arises from the needs for subcontractors and workers in the legal and not-so-legal enterprises commanded by political and business bosses of the underworld. We know that people all over the socio-economic strata partake of big incomes and political power as a part of the workforce in the parallel economy. With pots of money and tons of raw power in their hands, they easily get into a quagmire of commodities and crime. This underbelly of the field of labour constitutes a significant potential area of attention for social science.

## Unorganised Sector

The unorganised or informal sector of labour constitutes about 90 percent of the total workforce and covers divergent states of socioeconomic activities in rural and urban areas (Singh 1991; Breman 2003). Agriculture, construction, cottage industry, vending, wayside business, self-employed workers, domestic services and many other types of labour fall within this category. Here, employees or workers are either not protected by any labour law or exploited by employers who violate laws with the help of bureaucracy. Recruitment is usually based on primordial loyalties such as kinship, caste and language. It is widely known that the norms of minimum wages prescribed by government for various categories of workers are disregarded by employers who possess political power and capacity to buy off official intervention. They also have social and economic leverage over workers who are bound to them by indebtedness or patronage. Workers, on their part, suffer from lack of collective consciousness and political power. They are also divided in terms of caste or caste combinations in perennial conflict with one another. Conventional trade unions have usually distanced themselves from this category of workers. At many places, voluntary service organisations have been engaged in serving the unorganised workers. They combine the role of trade unions with their other major responsibilities. These efforts have served to raise workers' consciousness about their conditions and rights. Some of these organisations have acquired strength and resources to undertake comprehensive human development work for their constituents. Their programmes include skill development, finance, marketing and roles within family and society. Some of these ventures are known to have achieved exemplary success in human development.

Women have been entering the labour force in increasing proportions (see Carr *et al.* 1996). This trend is likely to continue as a result of the rise in female literacy and changing status of the woman in family as well as in the society at large. The new consumerist culture has generated new needs for income at all levels, which may also push women into the labour force. Increasing employment of women may help the process of liberalisation in ideas of female rights and gender equity. However, female workers in today's society may have to grapple with various types of harassment and exploitation. Male dominance is likely to oppress women at home and at work for a long time. This condition is often reinforced by willing acceptance of women of their inferior status and subordinate role in family regardless of the actual support their income may lend to the family.

Child labour is a major social problem of our society. Children are employed and exploited in all types of jobs in the informal sector (see Chaudhri 1996). They work limitlessly for their bosses. They are paid ridiculously low wages. They have little freedom or ability to protest. They bring coveted incomes to parents. Denial of individual freedom and opportunity for minimum personal and social development is the obvious price paid by child workers. Government legislation against employment of children is largely ineffective due to perceived compulsions of greedy employers and impoverished families. In fact, this is an area of labour where everybody seems to show social consciousness about criticality of a social evil and urgency to deal with it but unable to obtain results. Across nations and regions, we point fingers at others, but cannot set our own house in order.

We have a large mass of people in the labour force who are totally unemployed or seasonally employed or employed marginally with unpredictable or irregular chances of petty jobs. Insofar as these people are the main breadwinners for their families, they lead pauperised existence and a sense of alienation in self-respect, dignity and social worth. Governments have been sensitive to the problems of this category and, over the decades, launched schemes and plans for exigent employment and social security. However, these efforts have yielded only marginal results (see Hirway and Terhal 1990). The field of labour bears a massive force of tailenders, who work, earn and consume in fits and starts and manage somehow to keep their body and soul together. One wonders if they dream of any mentionable trickle-in from the benefits earned by 'India Incorporated' in pursuit of our collective dream of emergence as a global power.

## Emerging Patterns

I should now try to collect the main signals in the field of labour emerging from the broad-brush picture I have presented. The social construct of labour is ideally coterminous with the construct of work. The chief executive of an enterprise is its first worker. Proximity to capital or entrepreneurship does not exclude a person or position from the cohort of labour. An important task of social science today in studies of labour is to learn where a given position, group or category stands on the path of human development. The goal on this path should be viewed in two dimensions: *quality of life* (in terms of standards of nutrition, health, education, equity, justice, empowerment, etc.) and *social character* (in terms of control over individualism, greed, acquisitiveness, insensitivity to others' needs, etc.).

The field of labour is complex, uneven and stratified. At the upper end, we meet the affluent, privileged and powerful aristocracy of labour. They face no shortages in achieving high standards in quality of life. In fact, their existing resources of wealth and power fuel a tendency to multiply the assets. They possess considerable union power to promote their ideas and demands. Their clubs and combinations can generate as much pressure on society as any militant trade union can wield. Concurrently, they have the means to participate aggressively in the world of consumerism and individualism. This may place them far short of the goal in the social character dimension of development.

People on the lower rungs of hierarchy survive at various distances, but mostly far away, from the goals of quality of life. Their social existence is dominated by degrees of poverty, deprivation, indignity and powerlessness. Growing social awareness of the developmental needs of these categories has led to widespread action by government, voluntary organisations and civil society in general for improvement of their material conditions, social esteem, self-dependence and skills of governance. These efforts have yielded and will continue to yield reassuring dividends. However, the huge magnitude of the task of development of the poor warrants no more than a modest vision of people leisurely inching towards the goal. The path is laden with other roadblocks too. First, the material and human resources earmarked for development frequently get diverted to satisfy vicarious needs of the greedy and the powerful. Second, exercises in empowerment of the powerless often end in yielding greater real power to the powerful behind the façade of power formally attributed to the less privileged. Third, the poor and the deprived who gain material benefits in the labour market may fall in the trap of consumerism and remain as distant from the development goals as ever. This makes for a double whammy: material gains are offset by fall in quality of life as well as in social character.

The layers of labour between the two ends of hierarchy would cover a wide span of material conditions, benefits of labour laws and unionisation. Legal entitlements on emoluments, working conditions, job security, welfare and union rights place workers on a high ground in quality of life. Progressive management practices in employee motivation and workplace democracy enhance the gains in quality of life. However, the existence of congenial institutions and conventions for enrichment of quality of life does not uniformly lead to progress in human development. The institutional base of trade unions, labour laws, bargaining and dispute-settling devices and participative management have constantly been used, misused or abused by various stakeholders for sectional political or economic ends. Now the new power of global market and technology seems to pose a major challenge to the status of labour in industry.[4] One notices a gradual erosion in the significance of labour. In the world of technology, market and capital, labour is increasingly regarded as a commodity. Curiously, this trend grows along with growth of new models for humanisation of management of people in enterprise. I have earlier indicated the human consequences of commodification of labour. However, we are just beginning to feel the tremors of this transformation. Social science needs to monitor future events as a vital going concern.

The new wave in labour relations has also led to erosion in the role of trade unions. Unions are admonished to shed their adversarial posture and play the game of partnership with management in human resource development for the growth of industry. An alternative suggestion is for unions to expand their scope and become agencies for integrated human development of workers including their work environment and work relations. The question we need to raise is: why do unions play an adversarial role? Our unions have often played adversarial roles for political reasons. However, the logic of adversarial role is embedded in the social reality of unfair, unjust or illegal treatment received by labour at the hands of employers and others. Trade unions are necessary and relevant as long as unfairness and injustice remain in employment relations. The logic of trade unionism, which has never been a closed issue in social science, has just got more widely open. The future of a precious, but much-maligned, modern institution seems to be in the dock for judgement on its worth in the upcoming knowledge society.

## Notes

* This is the revised version of the text of the M.N. Srinivas Memorial Lecture 2003, delivered at XXIX All India Sociological Conference, Maharana Pratap University of Agriculture and Technology, Udaipur, 21–23 December 2003.

1. An appealing expression of such humanist concern is contained in Elton Mayo (1946).
2. A comprehensive treatment of the concept of human development and its application is available in S. Fukuda-Parr and A. K. Shiva Kumar (2003).
3. My main source of information for statements made here is T.B. Bottomore and Maximilien Rubel (1973).
4. For perspectives on the future of labour and trade unions, see Peter Ackers (2002), Navin Chandra (2002), and Deepak Nayyar (2003).

## References

Ackers, Peter. 2002. 'Reframing employment relations: The case for neo-pluralism', *Industrial relations journal*, 33 (1): 2–18.

Bottomore, T.B. and Maximilien Rubel (eds.). 1973. *Karl Marx: Selected writings in sociology and social philosophy*. Harmondsworth, Middlesex: Penguin Books.

Breman, Jan. 2003. *The labouring poor in India: Patterns of exploitation, subordination and exclusion*. New Delhi: Oxford University Press.

Carr, M., C. Martha and R. Jhabvala (eds.). 1996. *Speaking out: Women's economic empowerment in South Asia*. New Delhi: Vistaar Publications.

Chandra, Navin. 2002. 'Organising labour: The question of form and content', *Indian journal of labour economics*, 45 (4): 1330–37.

Chaudhri, D. P. 1996. *A dynamic profile of child labour in India—1951–91.* New Delhi: Child Labour Action and Support Project.

Fukuda-Parr, S. and A. K. Shiva Kumar. 2003. *Readings in human development.* New Delhi: Oxford University Press.

Hirway, Indira and P. Terhal. 1990. *Towards right to work in India: Indian and international experiences in rural works programmes.* New Delhi and The Hague: ICSSR and IMWOO.

Holmstrom, Mark. 1976. *South Indian factory workers.* Cambridge: Cambridge University Press.

Kelly, G. M. 2000. 'Employment and concepts of work in the new global economy', *International labour review,* 139 (1): 5–32.

Mayo, Elton. 1946. *The Human problems of an industrial civilisation.* Boston: Harvard University.

National Commission on Labour. 1969. *Report.* New Delhi: Ministry of Labour.

Nayyar, Deepak. 2003. 'Work, livelihoods and rights', *Indian journal and labour economics,* 46 (1): 3–13.

Punekar, S. D. and R. Varickayil (eds.). 1989. *Labour movement in India (Vols. I and II).* Delhi: Indian Council for Historical Research.

Ramaswamy, E. A. 1988. *Worker consciousness and trade union response.* New Delhi: Oxford University Press.

———. 1997. *Question of balance: Labour-management relations in practice.* New Delhi: Oxford University Press.

Ramaswamy, Uma. 1983. *Work, union and community.* New Delhi: Oxford University Press.

Sharma, G. K. 1962. *Labour movement in India: Its past and present.* Jaipur: University of Rajasthan.

Sheth, N. R. 1996. 'We, the trade unions', *Indian journal of industrial relations,* 32 (1): 1–20.

Singh, Manjit. 1991. *Labour process in the unorganised industry.* New Delhi: Manohar.

Webb, Sidney and Beatrice Webb. 1897. *Industrial democracy.* New York: Reprints of Economic Classics.

# 7

# Rajasthani Contract Labour in Delhi: A Case Study of the Relationship between Company, Middleman and Worker

*Maren Bellwinkel*

## Introduction

The fieldwork for this study was undertaken between September–December, 1970, on a worksite in New Delhi.[1] The initial aim was to collect data on the socio-economic conditions of unskilled Rajasthani workers. Access to the site was made possible by a well-known voluntary organization which provided basic education and nutrition to the children of these workers. Both men and women Rajasthanis were employed, and consequently no adult looked after the children during the working hours. On this particular work site the voluntary organization had opened a school-cum-crèche. With its active support all the 53 interviews, covering 37 per cent of the 141 unskilled labourers' households, could be conducted in the school.

Contract labour had a much more important role to play at the start of Indian industrialization than it does today. In the past, middlemen recruited labourers for the tea gardens in Assam and Ceylon, the Bombay textile mills, the P.W.D. and the Chota Nagpur coal mines. Concerning the reasons for the development of contract labour in India, there is something of a controversy. Mukerjee (1945: 70) and the Royal Commission on Labour (1931: 22) take it for granted that contract labour developed as a result of the initial shortage of labour in industry. This argument holds true for the development of plantation contract labour. Jain (1970: 199) and Jayaraman (1997: 326) make the point that South Indian contract labour went to Malaya and Ceylon because there was no local labour willing to accept the ill paid job of plantation coolie. Myrdal (1968) has shown that during the colonial period labour supply was only discussed from the employer's point of view. He was the one who dictated the terms on which wage labour was employed, and consequently experienced a shortage of labour which was overcome by recruiting labourers from distant regions. The ideological background of what Myrdal calls the 'Colonial Market Approach' (1968: 980). was the assumption that natives prefer idleness, that social and environmental factors make them unfit for work, and ultimately that they are racially inferior.

The second set of theories which Myrdal calls the 'Modern Approach' is equally ethnocentric. It assumes 'rationalistic attitudes, standardized working conditions, and fluidity of markets—assumptions that for Western countries are highly realistic' (Myrdal 1968: 993)—in discussing the employment prospect in South Asia. Leaving social, cultural and environmental factors out of consideration, this set of theories regards 'idle labour there as a reserve of unemployed constituting a readily available labour supply which could be tapped primarily by enlarging the scope of work opportunities' (Myrdal 1968: 993). Morris (1965) can be considered to be an advocate of the second set of theories. Contradicting the Royal Commission, Morris (1965: 6) says that there was never a shortage of labour in the nineteenth century when the Bombay textile industry began its development. He also rejects the theory that contract labour developed as a result of the socio-lingual barriers between management and workers. He feels that the middleman was needed neither as a liaison between management and labour nor as a recruiting agent. He was needed in his capacity as a foreman because he was skilled enough to supervise the labour force (Morris 1965: 131).

The shortcoming of Morris' argument is that he completely overlooks the middleman's function as a catalyst in the supply of labour. The argument advanced in this paper is that the middleman does not have to recruit labourers constantly. He only has to initiate the recruitment process and a constant labour supply follows, as Morris has shown. This is possible only because the middleman and the recruits belong to the same community, caste and kin group. The workers are willing to take up urban employment only with the middleman who is bound by locally accepted caste and kinship obligations. The reason why there was never a labour shortage in Bombay's textile industry was not that there was a 'readily available labour supply', as Morris' reasoning would suggest, but that the middleman facilitated the labour supply.

In different regions the middleman is called *jobber* (in Bombay), *mukkadam, mistri, jamadar* (in North India) and *kangani* (in South India). He has two different functions: that of foreman of his gang and that of recruiting agent. The middleman is given an advance by the firm to recruit workers. In some cases this advance is to be refunded on completion of the task (Jain 1970: 201), whereas in others this is considered as payment to the middleman (Jayaraman 1967: 327). Frequently the middleman receives head money for each recruited labourer (Morris 1965: 134; Mukerjee 1945: 19). Sometimes he is paid a commission by the employer which is deductable from the labourer's wages.

It is the usual practice of the middleman to give an advance to the labourers. Jain (1970: 199) and Jayaraman (1967: 355) report that this advance was given at the time of employment, which led the workers consequently into debt-bondage. In contrast, with this view Vaid (1968: 155–170) maintains that an advance was only given to workers who were well-known to the middleman. The advance was given interest-free and was considered by the workers as a proof that they were accepted as permanent members of the gang. The workers were in no hurry to repay it, because as long as they remained in debt their place in the labour gang was ensured.

Today, as Vaid (1968) and Pandey (1969) show, contract labour is found predominantly in the construction industry. This is, on the one hand, due to the fact that an urban labour force has developed and, on the other, to the built-in disabilities of construction work which make it necessary for the employer to recruit rural labour. Construction work is of a seasonal character. In the rainy season certain kinds of work cannot be done and at least a part of the labour force is idle. Construction work also demands geographical mobility on the part of the labour force, since after completion of a contract the workers are shifted to a new site. The employer cannot offer permanent employment. Nor does he compensate for losses arising out of periods of unemployment.

This set of conditions leads to the perpetuation of contract labour in the construction industry. The urban labour force is not willing to take up an ill-paid job under miserable working conditions, whereas, under certain conditions, a rural labour force is. The employer has to make use of a middleman because the rural labour force has no knowledge of the supply and demand situation in the urban labour market and is not acquainted with the working conditions as such. The middleman fills this communication gap and is also, in the eyes of the workers, trustworthy enough to ensure their employment.

Although the studies referred to above contain data about the recruitment pattern, payment of wages and the moneylender function of the middleman, there is no account yet of the relationship between employer, middleman and worker. There are statements, as for example by Johri (1969: 445), describing the middleman as 'creditor, helper, supervisor and tormentor' of his workers, but no full assessment of his role. This paper is an attempt to bridge this gap.[2] The statistical data presented here are primarily meant to illustrate the qualitative aspect of this problem.

## The Worksite and the Construction Company

The worksite is situated in South Delhi on the outskirts of the city. It consists of three multi-storeyed buildings under construction and a *jhuggi* colony with a total of 182 households. At the premises of the worksite are a brick-factory, water-tank, sand-storage place, and the school. *This jhuggi* colony is meant to house mainly the unskilled Rajasthani workers. At the beginning of construction the company gave damaged bricks and other building material with which the workers could build their houses. These one-room huts are the workers' sleeping place and storage for their belongings. The company has also installed a water tap but there is no electricity nor latrines. There are three functionaries and seven shops at the premises of the worksite: barber, shoemaker, tailor, cigarette shop, ration shop, two vegetable shops and three tea stalls. For the main shopping the men go to the weekly market in a near-by village. With the city as such the workers have little connection. They do not go to cinemas, and in case they need things from Delhi itself, they send the middleman for shopping.

The construction company is a well-known company in Delhi, specializing in multi-storeyed buildings. It is a family firm and all important positions in the company are filled by relatives. Whenever the company gets a new contract a relative is appointed as in-charge of the worksite. The financial transactions with the client are carried on by the head office of the company. Bills and wages are paid directly by the head office. The worksite-in-charge is responsible for the procurement of building materials and labour, but he does not have any financial autonomy. Table 7.1 gives the break-down of employees on the worksite into the different occupational categories. The worksite-in-charge gives orders directly to each occupational category. There is a gradation of authority from engineer to work *mistri*. Work *mistri* and supervisor have complementary functions and occupy the same rank in the hierarchy on the work-site. Mainly they give orders to the various categories of workers. With the exception of the unskilled workers, all other occupational groups on the worksite are directly called upon to fulfil orders. The unskilled workers interact with the other occupational groups on the worksite only through their middlemen.

Unfortunately, I have no information on the earnings of supervisory and technical staff and skilled and semi-skilled workers. Only the unskilled workers' wage rates are known. Table 7.1 shows that the unskilled workers are the most numerous occupational category on the worksite. The particular

**Table 7.1:** Distribution of Employees on the Worksite by Occupational Category

| *Occupational category* | *No.* |
|---|---|
| Supervisory and technical staff | |
| Worksite-in-charge | 1 |
| Engineer | 4 |
| Overseer | 4 |
| Civil foreman | 2 |
| Supervisor | 15 |
| Work *mistri* | 6 |
| *Jamadar* | 3 |
| *Total* | 35 |
| Skilled worker | |
| Mason | 25 |
| Carpenter | 21 |
| Electrician | 3 |
| Blacksmith | 3 |
| Mechanic | 17 |
| *Total* | 69 |
| Semi-skilled worker | |
| Driver | 2 |
| Tile polisher | 8 |
| Mechanic helper | 7 |
| Peon | 2 |
| Watchman | 4 |
| Cutter | 10 |
| *Total* | 33 |
| Unskilled worker | |
| Water carrier | 20 |
| Scaffolder | 18 |
| Male coolie | 134 |
| Female coolie | 164 |
| Boy coolie | 10 |
| *Total* | 346 |
| *Grand Total* | 483 |

feature of construction work is that within the category of unskilled labourers, men, woman and children—boys above the age of 13—are employed. Within the group of unskilled labourers we find a gradation of skills and wages. Water carriers get Rs. 3.50 a day, scaffolders Rs. 3.25, male coolies Rs. 3.00, boy coolies Rs. 2.50 and female coolies Rs. 2.75. There is not much difference in the work between male, female and boy coolie, but their different physical strength is remunerated differently.

## Social Characteristics of the Middleman

On the worksite there are three *jamadars*, as the middleman is called in the Delhi region. *Bhola jamadar* is between 65 and 70 years of age. He is a Berwa—Untouchable—from a village in Sewai Madhopur district in Eastern Rajasthan. He started his middle-man business thirty years ago and has been employed by the company for the last fifteen years. He has an average of 178 workers in his labour gang, and earns Rs. 1135 per month as commission. Bhola has a monthly expenditure of about Rs. 100.

A great deal of his everyday work is delegated to his son, Mangru. But Bhola is still called upon in all important matters concerning the management of the gang. He is still the person who exercises authority. Bhola lives in two huts in the *jhuggi* colony with his wife, son, son's wife and their two children. A total of 13 persons constitutes the group of Bhola's relatives working in the gang. They are mostly affinally related to him.

*Ramlal jamadar*, also a Berwa, is 35 years old and belongs to a village in Eastern Rajasthan. He has been a middleman for already ten years and has been working with the company for the last seven years. His work gang is 79 workers strong. Ramlal earns Rs. 503 a month as commission and spends Rs. 100. Although Ramlal can read and write, he has employed a *munshi*. In case a middleman employs a *munshi*, he gets paid the unskilled labourer's wage for supervision. The *munshi* is expected to help Ramlal in the supervision of the gang. Interestingly enough, it is not the *munshi*, but his wife Chotey who is called upon by the company when Ramlal is absent. Chotey is considered to be Ramlal's adopted sister. She belongs to Ramlal's *gotra* and her children will inherit from Ramlal because he does not have any children. Ramlal lives in the *jhuggi* colony with his wife and father. His father is not employed by the company, and has no authority in business matters. Ramlal's group of relatives in the employ of the company consists of the two brothers of his wife and Onkar, Chotey's father. Three other persons claim to be related to Ramlal but the nature of the relationship is not clear.

Nathu *jamadar*, forty-five years old, is a Rajput from a village in Western Rajasthan. Although Nathu became a middleman only two years ago, he has already got a work group of 89 members. He gets Rs. 567 a month as commission. He says that he spends only Rs. 60 because he is alone. He is the eldest of three brothers, all of whom are working for the company. His youngest brother is employed as driver by the head of the firm. The other brother is working as a *mistri*. All the three brothers live in the servant's quarters of the contractor's house. Nathu has been given employment as a middleman because his two younger brothers have proved their loyalty to the contractor.

Nathu has no relatives working in his gang. When he started his business he first worked together with another middleman to get his labourers recruited. Now he works on his own. Because Nathu does not live in the *jhuggi* colony he does not know his workers well. He comes only in the morning to distribute work or when he is called upon by the firm. The internal management of the gang he first left to Siriphool, a Baniya from his village, whom he recruited as *munshi*. In the meantime Siriphool got promoted as work *mistri*. Keli, a 35 year old Rajasthani woman, Berwa by caste and one of Nathu's oldest recruits, has now replaced Siriphool. She does not get any special remuneration for the work she does. Her position is comparable to that of Chotey. Whenever the worksite-in-charge or any of the supervisors or work *mistris* has to give orders to Nathu's gang while Nathu is away he gets Keli to do it. Keli, in contrast to Nathu, knows all the workers in his gang. She has a supervising, but no sanctioning function.

Middlemen can save considerable sums of money. Much of it is used to lend to the members of the gang, recruit more workers or as an insurance against slack seasons and business risks.[3] Mangru gave an example of the risk involved in the middleman business: when the construction began and the foundation was to be laid, the entire excavation work was given to Bhola's gang on the understanding that if the job was completed within the prescribed time limit, he would get Rs. 2,500. During the excavation work Bhola paid his workers out of his own pocket. But he never received the promised amount. In slack seasons, when the middleman and his gang are unemployed, the middleman must have enough capital to maintain at least a part of his gang. His success as middleman depends considerably on whether he can secure labourers as soon as he gets a contract.

Although the middleman requires a lot of capital to run his business, he can accumulate wealth. Thirty years ago Bhola was a landless labourer in his village. Now he owns sixteen hectares of land and a double-storeyed house in his village. Ramlal has acquired ten hectares of land in his village since he became a middleman ten years ago. Nathu has not yet been in business long enough to buy land, but he belongs to a landowning family with sixteen hectares of land. This shows that the middleman is economically able to improve his situation in the village with the help of urban employment.

## Social Characteristics of the Workers

All the unskilled labourers come from Eastern Rajasthan, with the exception of two households of South Indians. Ninety-eight per cent of the workers are illiterate, 50 per cent have taken up urban employment for the first time, and 81.5 per cent are Untouchables. On the average the workers are 38 years old. The labourers work 26 days a month, which gives them a monthly income of around Rs. 150. An enquiry into the expenditure and consumption of unskilled labourers' households shows that on an average 56 per cent of the total wages is spent on food and clothes and 19 per cent on items not specified by the workers, presumably alcohol and status symbols. The balance cannot be considered to be a saving because it is either consumed by the worker's family in the village or used to pay back their debt. Eighty-nine per cent of the workers are in debt, 70 per cent to village moneylenders, 17 per cent to the middlemen and 2 per cent to urban moneylenders.

There is no big difference in life-style between middleman and worker, but in life chances. The middleman is able to improve his economic situation in the village with the help of urban employment, whereas the workers are not. Fifty per cent of the respondents have no land at all, 30 per cent own below 2.5 hectares and 20 per cent own between 2.5 to 20 hectares. Seventy-seven per cent of the workers expressed a desire to improve their economic condition, either by paying back their debt or by saving up money to buy land. This is wishful thinking because most of the workers overestimate their saving capacity which is, as already stated, very low.

## Company and Middleman

Usually a company tries to build up a middleman out of one of its own employees, preferably one who is loyal to the firm and has some hold over the workers. On this particular worksite Nathu had been built up as a middleman by the contractor. The contractor has a paternalistic attitude towards his middlemen. Dugal, a contractor himself, describes his personal experience in the following terms:

> Khanga, a labour chief from Northern India, brought his men and came to work for my father about thirty years ago at the age of twenty-five. He has worked for my father continuously over the entire period on numerous jobs of all kinds. Our association with Khanga has been a pleasant one. Whenever we get a contract, Khanga and his men are the first to be employed. Fortunately, business has been good and we have been able to provide almost continuous employment for them, but I can recall one occasion when Khanga and his men spent almost a month without work because we had no work for them. But he maintained that he would rather wait a while than look for work with

> someone else. Such loyalty is one of the most valuable intangible assets which our company holds today. ... Khanga is almost like a family member now. He has seen most of us grow up and is always warmly greeted when he visits. He is very devoted to my father (1959: 175).

Dugal's statement supports the finding that the contractor-middleman relationship is modelled on the master-servant relationship in a patriarchal household. Servants are part of the household; they have minor personal rights in comparison with the kin group but both are subject to the benevolent authority of the master. Nathu's case is a good example. He and his brothers are treated as servants in the contractor's household.

In practice there is no differentiation between the role of the jamadar as a middleman of the construction company and as a servant of the contractor's family. Although these two roles are analytically separable, there is a great deal of overlap between them. The paternalistic attitude of the contractor prevents the middleman from fomenting trouble or going on strike. The quotation above makes it clear that Khanga would consider a strike inconsistent with the personal loyalty he owes to his master. Besides, it is the explicit policy of the construction company to engage more than one middleman on a construction site. This is done so that the middlemen can be played against one another in the event of a strike. The question of organizing a strike on this particular work-site does not arise because the other middlemen know that Nathu will in any case remain loyal to the contractor. This was confirmed by Mangru with whom the middlemen's attitude towards strikes was once discussed:

> There is not enough solidarity either among the workers or among the *jamadars.* Although I know all the *jamadars* in Delhi, including those working for other companies, I am sure they would never support a strike. If a strike were organized on this worksite, Nathu would definitely break it and I would be dismissed. The risk involved is too great.

The construction company expects the middleman to recruit labourers and to supervise the work group. Only when a middleman is built up by the company does he get an advance enabling him to recruit labourers. This advance, excluding the railway fare of the new recruits, has to be paid back. An old and established middleman has to even pay the railway fare of his workers. The recruitment pattern is interesting insofar as 81 per cent of those interviewed claimed to have contacted the middleman on their own initiative and not *vice versa.* Of those persons (19 per cent) who were contacted by the middleman six were contacted by Nathu who is unlike the other two middlemen in that he has been built up by the company and is new to the business. Middlemen who have been in the business for a considerable time do not need to contact the labourers for recruitment. They are sufficiently known in their local group so that workers approach them through relatives and friends.

The middleman has not only to supervise his gang but also to disburse wages. The commission is given directly to him along with the wages for the workers. This has two implications. First, the middleman does not have to collect his commission from the workers directly. Secondly, the middleman's hold over them increases psychologically because he gives them their wages.

## Middleman and Worker

The middleman has to fulfil social and economic functions for his labour gang. He settles disputes within the work group, gives advice and helps the workers in cases of hardship and illness. He is also the labour gang's money-lender. At the time of recruitment 33 per cent of the workers had borrowed money from him. At the time of investigation 17 per cent of the workers owed him an average of Rs. 520. In contrast, 69.8 per cent of the workers owed on an average Rs. 3,000 to the village moneylender. The village money-lender charges around 18 per cent as interest per month whereas the middleman charges none.

The amount of credit given depends on the working capacity of the family. Only relatives and labourers who have worked with the middleman for a long time get credit in excess of their working capacity. All the workers confirmed that the middleman does not charge any interest. Bhola gives credit for a maximum of six months while Ramlal gives it for a year. Mangru says about his money lending business:

> I give advance of Rs. 20 to Rs. 50 to any labourer and recover them on pay day. Credit above Rs. 50 is available only to those workers who are well known to me. Relatives can borrow as much as they want. I do not charge any interest.

It is evident that kins get the maximum credit, followed by caste-men. This is well recognized by the workers and is clearly reflected in the amount of credit they said they would expect from the middleman. There were only a few minor discrepancies between their expectations and the amount actually advanced. Nathu is the only middleman who has no relatives or caste fellows in his gang. Table 7.2 shows that all of Bhola's and Ramlal's relatives have got an advance of more than Rs. 100. One of Ramlal's relatives has got a credit of Rs. 1,000 and one of Bhola's relatives, Rs. 5,000.

**Table 7.2:** Amount of Credit Extended to Workers by *Jamadars*

| | *Bhola* | | | *Ramlal* | | | *Nathu* | | |
|---|---|---|---|---|---|---|---|---|---|
| *Amount in Rs.* | *Kin* | *Berwa* | *Other castes* | *Kin* | *Berwa* | *Other castes* | *Berwa* | *Other castes* | *Total* |
| 0–50 | – | 4 | 6 | – | 1 | 1 | 2 | 2 | 16 |
| 50–100 | – | 2 | 2 | – | – | 2 | – | 1 | 7 |
| 100–200 | 1 | 3 | – | 2 | 2 | – | 2 | – | 10 |
| 200–300 | 2 | 1 | – | – | – | – | – | – | 3 |
| 300–400 | 1 | 1 | – | – | – | – | – | – | 2 |
| 400–500 | – | – | – | – | – | – | 1 | 1 | 2 |
| 500–600 | 1 | 1 | 1 | – | – | – | 1 | – | 4 |
| 1,000 | – | – | – | 1 | – | – | – | – | 1 |
| 5,000 | 1 | – | – | – | – | – | – | – | 1 |
| Not known | 1 | 1 | – | – | – | – | – | – | 2 |
| *Total* | 7 | 13 | 9 | 3 | 3 | 3 | 6 | 4 | 48 |

## The *Jhuggi* Colony

With the exception of Nathu, the other two middlemen live in the *jhuggi* colony with their workers. The *jhuggi* colony consists of 182 households of which 141 belong to the occupational category of unskilled workers. Five households are those of *mistris*, twelve of skilled workers, fourteen of semi-skilled workers and ten of shopkeepers and functionaries. If we analyze the settlement pattern of the *jhuggi* colony it is possible to distinguish between four house clusters, as shown in Table 7.3.

In *this jhuggi* colony status in the work hierarchy is not important for residential segregation. This is particularly visible in Cluster D where skilled

**Table 7.3:** Distribution of Households in House Clusters by Occupational Category

| | *No. of households* | | | | |
|---|---|---|---|---|---|
| *Occupational category* | *Cluster A* | *Cluster B* | *Cluster C* | *Cluster D* | *Total* |
| Work *mistri* | – | 3 | 2 | – | 5 |
| Skilled worker | – | – | – | 12 | 12 |
| Semi-skilled worker | 1 | 4 | 1 | 8 | 14 |
| Shopkeeper and functionary | 2 | – | 1 | 7 | 10 |
| Ramlal's unskilled workers | 29 | – | – | – | 29 |
| Bhola's unskilled workers | – | 80 | – | 2 | 82 |
| Nathu's unskilled workers | – | – | 27 | 3 | 30 |
| *Total* | 32 | 87 | 31 | 32 | 182 |

workers, semi-skilled workers, unskilled workers, shopkeepers and functionaries live together. It is membership in the labour gang which determines the place of residence. Cluster A consists predominantly of Ramlal's workers, Cluster B of Bhola's and Cluster C of Nathu's workers. The hierarchical order of the different occupational categories in the functional context of the worksite does not influence the community pattern. The only residential segregation is between the work gangs of the three middlemen. The labour gangs are segmentary insofar as they occupy the same rank in the work hierarchy. In the *jhuggi* colony social interaction is not determined by the caste of the workers, their place of origin or their position in the occupational hierarchy. Workers from the same caste belonging to different work groups may not even know one another. Even within the labour gang few workers know everyone. The main link within the group as well as between work groups is provided by the middleman.

More than half of the households in the *jhuggi* colony belong to the Berwa caste. This is not so merely because Bhola and Ramlal, being Berwas, have recruited their castemen and kin. Most of Nathu's workers, although he himself is a Rajput, are also Berwas. With a few exceptions, all the inhabitants of the *jhuggi* colony are from Eastern Rajasthan.

The respondents were asked to arrange the castes in the colony in a hierarchical order, which is given in Table 7.4 (pp. 92–93). This hierarchy is more or less in conformity with the caste hierarchy which Sharma (1969: 34) reports as being socially accepted in six Rajasthan villages. There are two exceptions. In our hierarchy the Mehnas rank higher which might be due to the fact that in Eastern Rajasthan most of them are landowners. Second, the Berwas claim a rank just below the Mehnas, but distinctively above the artisan and Untouchable castes. Simmons (1971: 71) shows that the Berwas are the former Balais—weavers—and are still referred to as Chamars in Rajasthan villages. Since 1862, a famine year, they have left their villages and taken up construction work in Delhi. She also reports that many Berwas have cut off their links with the native village and settled in Delhi for good. This is not, however, true of our respondents. Many of the Berwas have gained wealth as middle men in the construction industry, and have consequently tried to improve their social status. The sanskritizing efforts of the Berwa caste date back to the 1930s, when the Balais gave up their traditional duties as Chamar and, by changing their caste name to Berwa, claimed Kshatriya status (Simmons 1971: 120).

In Table 7.4 the Berwas are not ranked according to their claim. This is due to the fact that, although the Berwa caste leaders claimed a higher ritual status,

**Table 7.4:** Hierarchy of Castes in the *Jhuggi* Colony

| *Trad. occup.* | | *Shopkeeper & Functionary* | *Work* mistri | *Skilled worker* | *Semi-skilled worker* | *Unskilled worker* | | | *Total* |
|---|---|---|---|---|---|---|---|---|---|
| | | | | | | *Bhola* | *Ramlal* | *Nathu* | |
| *Upper castes* | | | | | | | | | |
| Brahmin | priest | – | – | – | – | – | – | 2 | 2 |
| Baniya | shopkeeper | 3 | – | – | – | – | – | 1 | 4 |
| Rajput | warrior | – | – | 1 | 1 | – | 1 | – | 3 |
| Thakur | landlord | – | – | – | 1 | 1 | – | 1 | 3 |
| *Middle castes* | | | | | | | | | |
| Gujar | cowherd | – | 1 | – | 1 | 1 | – | – | 3 |
| Mehna | cultivator | – | – | 1 | 2 | 5 | 1 | 1 | 10 |
| Mali | gardener | 2 | – | – | – | 1 | – | – | 3 |
| *Artisan castes* | | | | | | | | | |
| Kohli | weaver | – | – | 1 | – | 2 | – | – | 3 |
| Kumhar | potter | 1 | – | 1 | 1 | – | – | – | 3 |
| Khatik | basketmaker | – | – | – | – | 1 | 1 | 1 | 3 |
| Lohar | blacksmith | – | – | 3 | – | – | – | – | 3 |
| Nai | barber | 1 | – | – | – | – | – | – | 3 |
| *Untouchables* | | | | | | | | | |
| Berwa | scavenger | – | 4 | – | 6 | 60 | 18 | 19 | 107 |
| Regar | working with hides | – | – | 2 | – | – | 7 | 1 | 10 |
| Jatav | shoemaker | 1 | – | 3 | – | 1 | – | – | 5 |
| Bhangi | sweeper | – | – | – | – | 8 | – | 1 | 9 |
| *Others* | | | | | | | | | |
| Bhil | | – | – | – | – | – | 1 | – | 1 |
| Muslim | | 2 | – | – | 2 | 2 | – | 1 | 7 |
| Misc. | | – | – | – | – | – | – | 2 | 2 |
| *Total* | | 10 | 5 | 12 | 14 | 82 | 29 | 30 | 182 |

they also tried to improve the caste's status in the political and administrative domain by getting themselves listed as a Scheduled Caste separately from the Balais. They succeeded in this in Rajasthan, but not in Delhi.

With the exception of the Bhangis and Muslims, the different castes in the *jhuggi* colony live together. The Bhangis live in one row of houses in Cluster B. Two other households, one of Muslim and one of Berwa, also live in the same row. It appears likely that the Bhangis live separately not so much because of the pressure brought on them by the other castes as because of their sense of caste identity. A similar case are the Muslims. There are seven Muslim households in the *jhuggi* colony of which six are to be found in Cluster D. One Muslim belongs to Bhola's labour gang and one to Nathu's gang. In these two cases religious solidarity is stronger than solidarity with the work group. There is only one Muslim who lives with his labour gang. He has been working for Bhola for quite some time and is from the same village.

The workers do not strictly observe certain norms of caste segregation in the *jhuggi* colony. People of different castes live in houses adjacent to each other. On the worksite they sit and smoke together. The Bhangis are allowed to draw water from the tap whenever they want without having to wait. But there is still no commensality between the different castes. The question whether people of different castes participate in common functions in the *jhuggi* colony does not arise because all important social and religious festivals are celebrated in the village. The workers consider their life in the *jhuggi* colony to be of a transitory character even though some of them have been living there for several years. The general attitude is reflected in the often repeated statement: 'Here in the town we are not strict but he would never do that in the village.' This attitude is described by Gould as 'compartmentalization of behaviour' (Gould 1965: 30). Within the confines of the family and the village caste norms are strictly observed while in the town and the work situation people are more lenient. This leniency is a result of adaptation to the work situation and the congested living conditions. It does not mean that a fundamental change in social values, institutions and behaviour has occurred.

## The Middleman's Role

The social and economic importance of the middleman arises from the fact that he is able to secure work for people belonging to his community and caste group. Although this analysis has shown that he does not contact his recruits, but is contacted by them, he nevertheless secures labour. The middleman is a labour recruiter insofar as he stimulates labour supply from his community. Unless he offers employment these workers from Eastern Rajasthan may not be prepared to move to urban and metropolitan areas in search of employment. They constitute a 'readily available labour supply' only under the condition that they can work for the middleman. To put it in Myrdal's words: 'Even those of working age who are prepared to work for an employer may be available only locally or only in the service of a particular kind of employer, or only for certain types of tasks' (1968: 1015). The same applies to the supervising function of the middleman. The workers are only willing to work for the company as long as the middleman provides a link between them and the employer. The middleman enables them to get acquainted with the work situation as well as with life in town.

The Rajasthani workers are employed by the company because only rural migrants are willing to work and live under conditions which prevail in the construction industry. They do not fight for their rights such as fair wages, proper housing and education for their children to which they are entitled under the Contract Labour Regulation and Abolition Act of 1970. The trade unions, as Pandey (1969: 310) and Johri (1969: 442) show, do not consider an agitation among construction workers to be politically rewarding due to the temporary character of the work and the constant fluctuations in their composition. Only the voluntary organization on the worksite seems to have taken up their cause. It has made the contractor erect a shed with water connection for the school and pay the salaries of the six school teachers and helpers. Fortunately, this contractor proved to be cooperative and aware of the problems of working women and their children, so that he could be persuaded to help. It would have been outside the voluntary organization's range of action to enforce the workers' rights, as for example a trade union or the government could.

The middleman is neither willing nor able to ensure fair treatment to the workers. As Mangru put it, 'A strike is the workers' business. A wage hike would mean a great deal to the workers, but the enhanced commission accruing from this would not make much difference to me.' This statement clearly brings out the disparity between the economic interests of the middleman and workers. The middleman represents the company's interests although his commission is less than one half per cent of the cost of construction, a trifle compared to the enormous profits made by the company.

Unlike the industrial worker, the construction worker is exploited by the company as well as the middleman. The middleman is an exploiter in the Marxian sense, but he does not take undue advantage of his position although he could. For instance, the middleman does not charge any interest from the members of his work gang. Certainly, one reason for this is that he does not need to bind his workers to the job by placing them in debt bondage. There is no shortage of workers in his community willing to work for him. But an equally significant reason is that the relation between the middleman and the work gang is mediated by kinship and caste norms of help and assistance. These norms are extended to non-kin as well as to members of other castes in the work gang. The personal relationship which the middleman has with the workers calls for similar obligations as to a relative. As Freedman (1957: 88) points out, '... the real distinction is not between family and non-family, but between personal and impersonal. Kin-ship may be the personal relationship par excellence but is not the only one of its kind'.

Personal norms which govern the interpersonal relationship outside the kinship context are modelled after kinship norms. The special feature of the relationship between middleman and worker is that it is a personal relationship, although in a functional context, governed by norms of help and assistance which are derived from the kinship context. Kinship norms developed in a peasant society are maintained in the industrial system insofar as they become the model for all other interpersonal relationships. They have proved to be functional for the profit maximization of the construction company and the middlemen. In summary, kinship and caste norms have changed their context but not their content, and help regulate the interaction between middleman and worker in a personal manner.

# Notes

1. Thanks are due to Meera Mahadevan and Mridula Sharma for help and assistance in fieldwork.
2. I would like to thank Dr. Anandalakshmy, Dr. André Béteille, Dr. P. C. Joshi and specially Dr. E. A. Ramaswamy for comments on an earlier draft of this paper.
3. It is likely that the middleman charges interest for loans given to his workers in slack seasons. This point was discussed with Dr. S. M. Pandey, who did field work among construction workers in Delhi in 1968. Pandey reported that at the time of fieldwork there was a slack season in the building industry, and that the middleman was charging interest. This con-tradiction between Pandey's findings and mine may be explained by the boom in the industry when I did fieldwork in 1970.

# References


Dugal, Brijinder Singh. 1959. 'The village chief in construction industry', *Human organization*, 18: 174–76.

Freedman, Maurice. 1957. *Chinese family and marriage in Singapore.* London: Her Majesty's Stationery Office.

Gould, Harold A. 1965. 'Lucknow rickshawallas: The social organization of an occupational category', *International journal of comparative sociology*, 6: 24–47.

Jain, Ravindra K. 1970. *South Indians on the plantation frontier in Malaya.* New Haven and London: Yale University Press.

Jayaraman, R. 1967. 'Indian emigration to Ceylon: Some aspects of the historical and social background of the emigrants', *The Indian economic and social history review*, 4: 319–59.

Johri, C. K. and S. M. Pandey. 1969. 'Employment relationship in the building industry', *Indian journal of industrial relations*, 4: 433–61.

Morris, Morris D. *1965. The emergence of an industrial labour force in India: A study of the Bombay cotton mills 1854–1957.* Berkeley and Los Angeles: University of California Press.

Mukerjee, Radhakamal. 1945. *The Indian working class.* Bombay: Hind Kitabs.

Myrdal, Gunnar. 1968. *Asian drama: An inquiry into the poverty of nations*, volume II. London: Allen Lane, The Penguin Press.

Pandey, S. M and C. M. Vikram. 1969. 'Trade unionism in Delhi's building industry', *Indian journal of industrial relations*, 4: 289–321.

Royal Commission on Labour in India. 1931. *Report.* Calcutta: Royal Commission on Labour in India.

Sharma, K. L. 1969. 'Pattern of occupational mobility: A study of six villages in Rajasthan', *Indian journal of social work*, 30: 34–43.

Simmons-Schafer, Ruth. 1971. *The Berwas of Delhi: Social and political mobility in a caste of ex-untouchables.* Unpublished Ph.D. dissertation, University of California, Berkeley.

Vaid, K. N. 1968. *The new worker: A study in Kota.* New York and Bombay: Asia Publishing House.

# 8

# Organising Unorganised Workers: The Case of Bindery Workers in Calcutta[1]

*Biswajit Ghosh*

This paper focuses on the problems and prospects of mobilising workers in the 'unorganised sector' of Indian industry. Till recently, it used to be considered difficult, if not impossible, for trade unions to mobilise workers in the 'unorganised sector' for collective action. The small size of industrial units, intimate and informal work relationships, dispersal of industrial units over, a large area and workers' low level of education were considered to be some of the major obstacles to trade union activity. This view now needs to be revised in the light of numerous reports of successful trade union activities in the bidi (Basu, 1977; Avachat, 1978; Mohandas, 1980), coir (Issac, 1982) and construction (Johri and Pandey, 1972) industries. These reports point to the crucial role played by cadre-based political parties in launching strikes and demonstrations. But now there is a need for undertaking deeper studies to assess the long term viability of such trade union activities and their social implications. It is with this intention that an attempt is made here to grasp the problems and prospects of mobilising workers in the binderies of central Calcutta.

To begin with, a few conceptual clarifications are necessary. The pairs of terms, 'organised' and 'unorganised' sector or 'formal' and 'informal' sector, may give a misleading view of the socio-economic structure of industry in India as consisting of autonomous, if not autarkic circuits of economic activities. Following such a view, an inference may be made regarding the qualitative distinctions in regard to labour problems, and hence of trade unions, between the 'organised' and 'unorganised' sectors. It is the contention of this paper that unless the socio-economic linkages that connect the 'unorganised sector' to the 'organised sector' and to the political system are taken into account, it is not possible to appreciate the constraints on trade union activities in the 'unorganised sector'. Further, the nature of the working class can be properly understood only when such interconnections are taken into account.

## Growth of Book Binding Industry in Calcutta

Though printing in Calcutta has a long history, book binding as a distinct cottage industry emerged only in the beginning of the present century. Earlier, book binding used to be done in the printing presses. With the growth of Calcutta university and several colleges, demand for books increased. To cope with the increased demand, printers started encouraging bindery workers to establish their own binderies. Several binderies sprang up around important printing presses and publishing firms in central Calcutta. The area in which the binderies were concentrated came to be known as the *Daftari Para*.[2] Book binding became a household industry. Initially the binders were Muslims drawn from Dhaka and Mymensing districts of erstwhile East Bengal (Guha Thakurta, 1984: 3). From 1930 onwards, however, Hindu migrants from East Bengal also took to book binding. After the communal riots of 1946 and the partition of India, the social composition of binders and bindery workers changed drastically. Muslim binders migrated to Pakistan and Hindu refugees from East Bengal took over their abandoned binderies. It is estimated that today a majority of the bindery workers and binders in Calcutta belong to Hindu refugee families from East Bengal.

After independence, the book binding industry received a big impetus with the opening of numerous schools and colleges and the consequent increase in the demand for text books. The official data available on bindery units in Calcutta, however, mask the growth of book binding industry because they refer mainly to units registered under the Factories Act. Over the 1974–77 period, the number of such units went down from 11 to 8 (Government of West Bengal, 1977). This decline is more than compensated by the growth of small bindery units which have not registered themselves with the government agencies. Representatives of employers' associations and of trade unions estimate that including units which are engaged in the making of envelopes and cartons and packaging and labelling, binding industry in Calcutta comprises of around 2000 units. Of these, about 500 units together employing 6000 workers are considered to be engaged exclusively in book binding. During the busy season stretching from November to March when the demand for binding school text books and diaries goes up, the number of workers employed is believed to go up to 8,000. According to these estimates there are 15 large binderies each engaging more than 20 workers. In recent years, the demand for the products of book binding and allied industries is increasing and spreading itself out over the whole year. As a result, the industry is losing its seasonal nature. To cope with the steadily increasing demand, binderies are now coming up in far flung localities of the city such as Goabagan, Sobhabazar, China Bazar, Tallygunge and Barrackpore. Yet nearly 400 binderies employing 4,000 workers are supposed to be concentrated in the *Daftari Para* area making this the focal point of binding industry in West Bengal.

Binderies are constituents of the printing and publishing trade in Calcutta. They depend on printing press and publishing firms who put out binding jobs at fixed rates. The established practice is that publishing firms enter into informal agreements with the binders and ask them to directly lift from the printers the required printed materials. Now-a-days, with the takeover of the production of primary school text books by the state government, a few large printing presses get bulk orders for producing books from the government. They, in turn, put out binding jobs to several skilled bindery workers who undertake the work in their own houses.

The binders are in a dependent, subordinate position *vis-à-vis* printers and publishing firms. This is because there is keen competition among binders and because there is such great demand for books that the publishers can ignore the quality of binding. Hence, rates for binding are low. Binders are expected to meet the cost of transporting printed material from the printing presses to their binderies. The publishers get their printing done in bulk but ask the binders to bind books in small batches to adjust the supply of books to the fluctuating demand in the market. This means that the binders have to store printed material at their own expense for an extended period till the stock is exhausted by staggered orders for binding.

The recent trend of printers directly subcontracting binding jobs has further weakened established binderies with long-standing reputations. They have now been forced to reduce their work force drastically. In the face of such adversity, the established binders in Calcutta have formed as association called *Bangiya Pusthak Granthan Byabosaee Samiti* (Bengal Book Binders Association, henceforth referred to as Samiti) to put pressure on the state government to distribute orders for binding directly with the established binderies and to deal with trade union pressures.

## Work Relationships in Binding Industry

The dependent, subordinate relationship that the binders have with publishers and printers provide the setting for recruitment practices, working conditions and work relationships that obtain in the binderies. To a certain extent, recent attempts to organise bindery workers have succeeded thereby altering and improving working conditions and wages, But trade union activity is itself constrained by the structure of publishing and printing industry as will be demonstrated in the following discussion.

As has already been mentioned, after Partition, Calcutta binderies have attracted Hindu refugees from East Bengal, who displaced Muslims who left for Pakistan. Today nearly 75 per cent of the workers are Hindus while the remaining are Muslims. Among the Hindus, a majority claim to belong to the Kayastha caste. Of late, several members of Scheduled Castes as well as Brahmins have taken to the book binding craft.

At present, more than 40 years after Partition, the Bengalis preponderate among the bindery workers. Out of 100 workers selected for my study only 6 hailed from outside West Bengal. Seventy four of them claimed the city of Calcutta or its hinterland district, 24 Parganas, as their place of permanent residence.

The bindery workers, possess the typical characteristics of the labour force in the unorganised sector. Only 12 of the 100 workers in my sample had studied in high school. There are 29 illiterate workers and 19 who have had only primary education.

Recruitment of the workers is mostly done through informal social networks. Most of the workers have got jobs in the binderies through kin and friends belonging to the same natal village. In the recent years the employers are showing a tendency to recruit more and more women and children, in my sample, 30 workers were women. The employers are now recruiting children also. Both women and children work as helpers and as unskilled labourers. This tendency to appoint women and children is a reaction to the growing strength of the trade union movement in the book binding industry. Women and children are not only hardworking and docile, they also keep away from trade union activity.

Bindery workers work in decrepit crowded rooms with no proper ventilation. Many of the binderies are damp and dirty. There are no proper drainage facilities in *Daftari Para* and even a small shower renders the whole locality a water-logged area. There are no proper toilet facilities even for women workers. The workers are prone to tuberculosis because they inhale paper dust. Binding is a handicraft industry in these parts, the only machine used being the cutting machine.

Thanks to union activities, workers have gained some wage and social security benefits. Earlier there were no rules governing work and employment, There was considerable variation in wage payment, workers had to work for 15 to 16 hours a day, they had no leave facilities and did not have job security.

The conditions of work and terms of employment depended on the discretion of the employers. The situation has now improved although much still remains to be done. Although the bindery sector has not yet been covered by minimum wage legislation, strong trade unionism has ensured uniform wage rates. Wage rates, however, differ according to the size of the bindery unit. In small units engaging less than twenty workers, wage rates are lower. There are three types of wage systems. There are workers who get wages on a monthly basis, daily basis and those who get piece rates. Monthly wages vary from Rs. 195 for a 'boy' or apprentice to Rs, 345 for a skilled worker. Those working in large binderies get an extra Rs. 10 per month. The monthly wage workers are also entitled to yearly increments. Daily wage and piece rate workers do not get annual increments although some of these workers are permanent. These workers, however, are paid more as compared to the monthly wage workers. Daily wage rates range from Rs. 13 to Rs. 15, and they work out to be higher than the wage rates of monthly wage workers. For piece rate workers, the rate is calculated according to the number of pages to be folded or stitched. For folding, a piece rate worker earns between Rs. 12 to Rs. 15 on an average day. Significantly, temporary piece rate workers receive higher rates for both stitching and folding operations as compared to the permanent workers. This discrepancy in rates is to compensate for the temporary workers' lack of access to ESI, Provident Fund, leave, bonus and gratuity benefits. While the employers' association under the pressure of the union has agreed to pay higher rates to temporary piece rate workers, daily wage temporary workers are not given higher wages. Some of them, however, receive bonus and enjoy 12 days leave a year. Women workers are paid on par with their male counterparts. But, piece rate women workers generally earn less than their male counterparts because they cannot work till late in the evening.

Bindery workers also earn from overtime work for which higher rates are provided. During the peak business season binderies remain open till midnight. In some big binderies, where pressure of work remains throughout the year and workers get overtime work almost throughout the year, earnings range between Rs. 1,200 to Rs. 1,500 per month.

Social security benefits such as provident fund and health insurance are provided only to permanent workers of binderies registered under the Factories Act. Workers of other binderies, even those having a permanent work status, are deprived of these facilities. Gratuity is, however, available to a majority of the permanent workers irrespective of whether they work in a registered factory or not. Leave and bonus facilities are also available to nearly 70 per cent of the permanent workers. To formalise the terms of employment, the permanent workers are now being issued appointment letters and they get to sign attendance registers.

While the bindery workers, especially the permanent ones, enjoy some benefits which are not enjoyed by their counterparts in several other industries in the unorganised sector, their position continues to be vulnerable in several respects. This is partly because the employers are continually searching for ways by which they can skirt their legal obligations and commitments to the workers. It is in part also due to the inherent contradictions generated by the trade union movement as will be discussed in the following sections.

## Trade Unionism in the Book Binding Industry

Considering that printing industry was one of the earliest in Calcutta to witness the emergence of trade unions, it is surprising that workers in the allied activity of book binding could be organised into trade unions only after Independence. Till independent binderies emerged in the *Daftari Para* during the 1940s, printing presses used to have their own bindery sections in which workers used to be hired only during certain months of the year. Seasonal nature of their employment, their marginal status in the printing presses, and their inability to maintain links with bindery workers scattered among printing presses located far apart were some of the factors inhibiting trade union activity among bindery workers. But as more and more binderies sprang up in the *Daftari Para*, the bindery workers could come together and exchange views and ideas. They also became visible as a category of workers for labour leaders and social workers to attempt to set up exclusive trade unions for them.

The first successful attempt to set up a union for the bindery workers was made by Dr. Prabavati Dasgupta, who was herself, a resident of *Daftari Para.* Before she organised the Bangiya Binding Association in 1952, she had become a prominent labour leader in Calcutta. She had successfully organised a strike of Calcutta sweepers in 1928 and had also been the President of the Bengal Jute Worker's Union in 1929. The bindery workers approached her to set up a trade union for them and lead them. In 1953 she launched a strong agitation under the aegis of the Bangiya Binding Association, demanding fixed hours of work and reduction of working hours to nine per day. The agitation succeeded but the union suffered a setback with the sudden demise of Dr. Dasgupta. There were several other attempts to organise bindery workers following the example of Bangiya Binding Association.

These attempts proved infructuous till the All India Trade Union Congress (AITUC), the trade union wing of the Communist Party of India, set up its Calcutta Book Binding Worker's Union (henceforth referred to as the Bindery Union) in 1957. The Union was headed by Mr. Govinda Rudra, a reputed 'outsider' (non-worker) leader. Under Rudra's leadership the union established its permanent office in 1957. In the initial stages, the trade union leaders relied mainly on their local party cadres to launch agitations for an eight hour working day, a uniform wage rate system applicable to all categories of workers and the abolition of arbitrary retrenchment. Not knowing the strength of the union, and fearing victimisation from the employers if they openly supported the union, the workers showed a reluctance to join the Bindery Union or be openly associated with it.

Bindery Union's first success came in 1958. It decided to organise a one day strike to press its demands for an eight-hour working-day and for a new wage system. The Union used posters and pamphlets and organised public meetings, processions and demonstrations to win over the reluctant workers. To boost the bindery workers' confidence, party cadres were recruited to join meetings and demonstrations and to approach the workers and persuade them to support the strike. To put pressure on the employers, the strike was deliberately called during the peak business season. The strike proved to be effective in mobilising even reluctant workers. The employers who knew that the Union was still not very strong, nevertheless acceded to its demands to ensure uninterrupted work during their peak business season. For the Bindery Union, employers' acceptance of its demands acted as a shot in the arm. The Union leaders could now widen their support base by enrolling a large number of bindery workers as members.

During the 1960s, Bindery Union suffered several setbacks. The first was the Chinese Aggression of 1962 which led to arrests of communist leaders, Several Bindery Union leaders went underground to evade arrests and the trade union work suffered as a result. Later, in 1967, the Bindery Union was revived because the United Front[3] in which the Left parties dominated, came to power in the state. In the same year, the Bindery Union affiliated itself with the Centre for Industrial Trade Unions formed by the CPI(Marxist) (CPI(M), henceforth) party which emerged as an alternative Communist party after the split of the CPI. The first United Front government, however, did not last long because the Central government dismissed the ministry and imposed President's rule in the state in 1968. During this time, CPI(M) workers felt too intimidated and threatened to carry on trade union activity. The United Front was returned to power once again in 1969. The Bindery Union once again made efforts to mobilise bindery workers. The Union sent an official letter to the government's labour department listing several demands such as the maintenance of attendance registers, payment of bonus, wage enhancement, provision for paid holidays and the abolition of arbitrary retrenchment. Realising that the workers had the upper hand in the changed political environment and anxious not to interrupt work during the peak business season, the Samiti took the initiative to organise a bipartite meeting, The meeting arrived at the following decisions: (a) daily attendance register would be introduced from the following year; (b) festival bonus would be given to all workers at a mutually agreed rate; and (c) employers would refrain from retrenching workers arbitrarily.

The political situation became adverse for the CPI(M) once again in 1972. The Congress came back to power. The CPI(M) leaders were chased out of *Daftari Para.* Several active members of the union who had sympathy for the CPI(M) were dismissed by their employers. The rise of Naxalite movement followed by the declaration of Emergency in the country in 1975 further eroded the Union's strength. The Congress party made a serious bid to organise bindery workers under the aegis of its labour wing, the Indian National Trade Union Congress (INTUC). The attempt succeeded only partially but the INTUC pressure prevented workers from openly aligning themselves with the Bindery Union. Hence the Bindery Union became dormant. Notwithstanding such adverse circumstances, the Bindery Union managed to get itself registered as a trade union in 1974.

The Bindery Union, managed to survive despite adverse political circumstances during the first half of the 1970s. This is partly due to the inability of the INTUC union to build a strong base among the bindery workers utilising the political advantages it enjoyed during the period, The INTUC is a loosely structured organisation lacking the support of political cadres. Hence, it was unable to systematically organise workers in the numerous binderies spread over the *Daftari Para.* It only managed to win over the sympathies of workers located in a few large binderies.

## Unionism after 1977

The political situation changed drastically once again when in 1977 the Emergency was withdrawn and the General Elections were held. The Left Front was returned to power and with it, the Bindery Union bounced back to regain control over the trade union activities in the book binding industry. Learning from experience, the Bindery Union was reorganised in 1978 so that it could be more responsive to the worker's needs. It set up Unit Committees in every workshop to attend to the day-to-day problems of workers within each bindery. The Unit Committees were placed in charge of a senior and respected worker who acted as its Convenor. To ensure coordination and co-operation among workers in scattered binderies, Zonal Committees were formed consisting of party leaders of the locality, some unit convenors, committed union volunteers[4] and representatives of bindery workers within the given zone. All the bindery workers of Calcutta were divided into four geographical zones each with its own Zonal Committee. To coordinate the Zonal Committees, a Council Committee consisting of representatives of Zonal Committees was constituted. Finally, at the apex, and Executive Committee consisting of ten members was created to supervise the work of other lower level committees. Only six members of the Executive Committee were drawn from the Zonal Committee while the remaining were important party leaders of the locality who were not members of other committees. The 'outsider' political leaders in the Union were also 'insiders' in the locality. In fact, a majority of the members of the Executive Committee (both workers and non-workers) were actually party members. The more respected of them were chosen as the President and the General Secretary of the union. The new structure allowed a judicious mix of rank and file leaders with 'outsiders'. This arrangement enabled the Union to put pressure on the employers by involving CPI(M) leaders of the locality and even the MLAs. The involvement of rank and file members ensured that the Union responded to the problems of the workers. It also ensured continuity of Union work even during periods when party leaders are forced to go underground.

After its reorganisation, the Union turned its attention to recruitment of new members. Every member of the Union was asked to use his informal networks of friendship and village links to enroll new members. Even the CPI(M) offices in villages were utilised to contact workers belonging to that particular village and influence them to join the Bindery Union. The union also used its influential Unit Convenors to gain the support of newly recruited workers. The success of the Left Front in the 1977 State Assembly election in West Bengal itself encouraged many bindery workers to join the CPI(M) led union. The strength of the Union went up from 200 to 600 members (as claimed by the leaders) in just two years. Workers in units which were earlier dominated by INTUC unions also switched over their allegiance to the Bindery Union.

To consolidate its gains, the CITU called an indefinite strike in printing and allied industries in 1978. The strike which had been initially called by the North-East Calcutta Press Workers and Employees Union was later extended to cover allied industrial units like the book binding units and ruling and exercise-book binding units, in order to create a major impact on the entire chain of book production. The Bindery Union was caught unawares by this general call. It had not even prepared a charter of demands, let alone issuing the necessary legal strike notice to the employers. Nevertheless, it joined the strike and hurriedly prepared a charter of demands for wage increase and paid holidays, for the issuance of appointment letters and for the maintenance of attendance registers. The Union leaders claimed that the entire local party unit of the CPI(M) and its cadres worked day and night for the success of the strike. Members of North-East Calcutta Press Workers and Employees Union also came forward to help the bindery workers. Not a single employer was allowed either to open his unit or to release bound books to the publishers, thanks to the cooperation extended by party volunteers and the press workers. Even workers who were not members of the Union and members of the INTUC-led union came forward to support the strike. The combined strength of the party and Union volunteers scared away even the known blacklegs. To maintain solidarity between the Hindu and Muslim workers Union volunteers organised several cultural programmes on the theme of communal harmony. The strike lasted for nineteen days till 4th January, 1979, when an agreement was reached between the Bindery Union and the employers' association. The agreement provided a wage increase of Rs 25 per month for the monthly wage workers. The daily wage and piece rate workers were provided an increase in the rate which amounted to an increase of one rupee per day (eight hours of work). A consensus was also reached on holding a bipartite or tripartite meeting within six weeks to settle other demands. The success of this general strike helped the Bindery Union secure a firm base among the workers.

The Union leaders now turned their attention to the unfulfilled demands of the bindery workers such as the issuance of appointment letters, granting of annual leave, annual increment, provident fund and gratuity facilities. Hence in November 1980 they called for another strike. The Union leaders met the then Labour Minister of the State and appraised him of the condition of workers in the industry. The Minister assured them that the government would not intervene in their 'legitimate democratic struggle' and that he would seek the union's help in resolving their problems. This boosted the workers' hopes and they resolved to stop overtime work from 25th November. A token strike was organised on 3rd December and the Union issued a notice for an indefinite strike from 15th December. Around this time a new development took place among the employers. A group of employers arose which began to openly support the Left Front government and stressed resolution of labour problems through negotiations. This group broke away from the Samiti and formed the Book Binding Traders Association under the leadership of Govind Rudra, one of the founders of the Bindery Union, who had now set up his own bindery. This association strongly supported the workers. Subversion in their own ranks and the threat of a long-drawn-out strike forced the employers to arrive at a compromise with the workers even before the expiry of the strike notice. The settlement which was worked out not only enhanced wage rates of different categories of workers but also provided for a uniform system of wage payment and annual increments. The employers agreed to issue appointment letters to the workers within a period of 15 days from the date of their joining and to maintain attendance registers and pay books for each worker from January 1, 1981. The settlement provided gratuity to all the permanent workers at the rate of 10 days' salary in a year in binderies employing less than 20 workers, and 15 days' salary in a year in binderies employing 20 or more workers. Even those workers who were not eligible for gratuity but had worked for five or more years were to get gratuity. The employers conceded to the provision of leave facilities for permanent workers. Those permanent workers engaged in binderies employing less than 20 workers would enjoy ten days festival and fifteen days casual leave as well as earned leave. Those permanent workers employed in binderies with 20 or more workers were to get 15 days festival leave and 15 days casual leave as well as earned leave. Even piece rated workers who had become permanent, became entitled to some annual leave facilities. It was agreed in principle to provide dearness allowance from January 1982 onwards. This settlement was really a spectacular achievement for the workers in the history of the book binding industry.

Reaching settlements with the employers which are favourable to the workers is one thing but to ensure that the settlements are actually implemented is another. The employers started playing a cat and mouse game with the Bindery Union. During the peak business season they would agree to the demands put up by the union but would postpone implementing them deliberately waiting for the peak season to end. During the lean season, the workers went back to their villages and the Union would not have any strength to ensure that attendance registers were maintained or appointment letters were issued. It was partly to overcome this problem that the restructuring of the Bindery Union had been undertaken. The Convenors of the Unit Committees were charged with the task of monitoring the implementation of the agreements in each bindery. This was coupled with occasional visits by representatives of the Executive Committee to binderies to ensure smooth implementation. These practices which were initiated after the 1980 agreement made it difficult for the employers to evade their commitments.

The 1980 settlement marked the beginning of revisions in 1984, 1985 and 1986 in regard to wage rates of different categories of workers. That these revisions were attained by the Bindery workers without even resorting to a call for strike is an eloquent testimony to its newly acquired strength. This success is in no small measure due to the organisational structure of the Bindery Union.

The success of the Bindery Union is also because of its alliance with the CPI(M). The alliance is so close that at the grass roots level often no distinction is made between party cadre and union members. The office room of the Union is also used by the party for its various activities. This alliance landed the Union in deep trouble several times prior to 1977. Since then however, the CPI(M) has been in power in the state and the patronage and support of the ruling party has proved beneficial to the Union in its confrontation with the employers.

Success, however, has brought several problems for the Bindery Union. Paradoxically, it has reduced the membership strength of the Union, Left sympathisers explain this paradox by saying that the workers have much faith in the Union's effectiveness and they know that they would benefit from the Union's activities, irrespective of their becoming members of the Union, The Bindery Union in accordance with its party's goals seeks to inculcate in the workers, the party ideology and a political consciousness. Towards this end the Union organises several study circles, meetings and rallies. The workers have not been enthusiastic about attending such programmes. They turn out in large numbers only for meetings and demonstrations which are called in pursuance of wage demands. The workers are indifferent even to their appalling working conditions and have not bothered to raise these issues individually or collectively with their employers.

Some of the problems facing the Bindery Union are due to the social contradictions that have been generated by its strategy. The union leaders have, of late, realised that there is a limit to the extent to which the employers can be pressurised into conceding to the demands of the workers. Most of the binders run and operate small binderies on meagre capital and wage payments bulk heavily in their costs because they use labour intensive processes. Hence, they can give better wages and other benefits to workers only if they get better rates for bindery jobs. As mentioned before, with the recent take-over of the production of primary school text books by the state government, binders are facing acute competition from several skilled bindery workers to whom big publishers and printers subcontract bindery jobs. Recognising the problem, the Bindery Union recently held a 'dharna' jointly with the Samiti, in front of the government press demanding an appropriate scheme for the distribution of bindery jobs among the established binders. Both the Samiti and the Bindery Union have now arrived at an understanding to fight jointly for higher rates for bindery jobs from the publishers to the binders. Such joint action, however, blurs class antagonisms and blunts the militancy of the Union.

The Bindery Union's success has evoked evasive responses from the employers. To reduce their overheads on labour under the pressure of wage and non-wage demands of the Union, the binders prefer to keep their binderies small by showing less than twenty workers on their rolls. By doing so, they can avoid provident fund and gratuity and health insurance payments to the workers. If in case their volume of work requires recruitment of more than twenty workers they prefer to set up on paper separate binderies in the name of other persons. Another device they resort to is to reduce the intake of 'permanent workers'. Earlier they used to do it by deliberately neglecting to keep proper written records of attendance and appointments. But now that the Bindery Union has developed ways of checking such malpractices, the binders now prefer to disperse their binderies in areas beyond *Daftari Para* where the Bindery Union is not strong. Fortunately for them, the workers also prefer the temporary status because they get higher wages than permanent workers.

## Conclusion

From this study of trade unionism in the book binding industry in Calcutta several conclusions may be drawn on the nature and scope of trade unionism in the unorganised sector. It is possible that these conclusions are not applicable to other segments of the unorganised sector. Hence systematic comparative studies of trade unionism in the various segments of the unorganised sector are needed so that advances may be made both in the theory and the practice of trade unionism in India.

One important feature of trade unionism in the book binding industry of Calcutta is the positive role played by the political party apparatus and the party leaders in mobilising workers scattered in several binderies. The organization of the CPI(M) with its units in different localities manned by local leaders proved effective in approaching workers even in their residences and their villages. The party leaders also brought to bear considerable social and political pressure on the employers to accede to the workers demands.

While recognising the positive role of the political parties, it is also important to recognise that this association with the CPI(M) has also made trade unions vulnerable to changes in the political environment. Association with the CPI(M) has not instilled working class consciousness in the workers. The workers are acutely aware of the advantages that flow to them through their membership of the trade union but they are only interested in trade union activity in so far as it helps them get higher wages. They consider wages, especially the wages they get in hand, as more important than even long term benefits such as provident fund and gratuity. Hence they prefer to be temporary workers. They are also indifferent to the physical conditions of work and have not cared to demand better conditions of work. It is perhaps this monetary orientation that also explains their indifference to ideological issues. Trade unionism is not likely to convert workers in the unorganised sector into a revolutionary proletariat—the experience of bindery workers shows that they are only oriented towards immediate monetary benefits.

The experience of organising bindery workers also highlights the peculiar problems faced by trade unions. The blurring of class lines that occurs in the unorganised sector makes it difficult for trade unions to follow a policy of sharpening class contradictions. The leaders of the Bindery Union realised after a point that they cannot regard the small binders as an antagonistic class. They realised that they have to even collaborate with the binders and ultimately join them in opposing the policy of the Left Front government itself!

Another important observation that can be made is in regard to the strategy of trade unions. It is clear that the socio-economic structure of West Bengal provides ample scope for the employers to develop strategies and devices by means of which they can bypass or skirt the implementation of agreements arrived at with the trade unions. This means that the trade unions have to show a capacity for continual improvisation in working out their tactics and strategies. Hence, it is too early to conclude that trade unionism can get institutionalised in the unorganised sector just because the Bindery Union has registered several successes since 1977.

## Notes

1. This paper is drawn from my Ph.D. thesis titled 'Organising unorganised workers: A sociological study of trade unionism in leather and book-binding industries in Calcutta' submitted to the Jawaharlal Nehru University, New Delhi, 1988. I thank my supervisor Dr. M.N. Panini of the Centre for the Study of Social Systems, Jawaharlal Nehru University for his valuable comments and guidance.

2. The term 'Daftari' in Bengali generally denotes a peon or record keeper in an office. The binders are called 'Daftaries' probably because the record-keeper of an office also used to bind these records in the past. 'Daftari Para' is the place where Daftaries live.
3. The United Front government in West Bengal in 1967 was the first non-Congress government in the State. The Front was composed of 14 parties. The major parties among them were Bengal Congress, CPI and CPI(M). See for details, P. Roy Choudhary (1984).
4. It may be possible that some of these 'union volunteers' were actually party members. It is very difficult to identify how many of these volunteers or ever, other leaders were CPI(M) members because the party keeps its membership list a secret.

# References

Avachat, Anil. 1977. 'Bidi workers of Nipani', *Economic and political weekly.* XII (29): 1203–05.

Basu, Timir. 1977. 'Beedi workers of Calcutta', *Economic and political weekly,* XII (4): 81–82.

———. 1977. 'Calcutta's sandal makers', *Economic and political weekly,* XII (3): 1262.

Government of West Bengal. 1977. *Statistical abstract, 1976–77.* Calcutta: Bureau of Applied Economics and Statistics.

Guha Thakurta, P. 1984. 'Bound to last', *The statesman,* 3 December.

Issac, Thomas T.M. 1982. 'Class struggle and structural changes-coir mat and matting industry in Kerala: 1950–80', *Economic and political weekly,* XVII (31): PE13–PE29.

Johri, C. K. and Pandey, S. M. 1972. *Employment relationship in building industry: A study in Delhi.* New Delhi: Shri Ram Centre for Industrial Relations.

Mohandas, M. 1980. 'Beedi workers in Kerala: Conditions of life and work', *Economic and political weekly,* XV (36): 1517–23.

Roy Choudhary, P. 1984. *Left experiment in West Bengal.* Delhi: Patriot Publications.

# PART III

# Marginal and Liminal Categories

# 9

# On Some Aspects of Family Structures of the Refugees of West Bengal 1947–48*

*Kanti Pakrasi*

Act of partition of undivided Bengal and subsequent forced exodus of thousands of rural and urban folk belonging to Hindu community from East Bengal (East Pakistan) may be treated as one of the important events of the decade of 1941–50. Under the spell of riotous situation leading to uprootment from homeland of regular residence the Hindus had to endure, it was obvious, in varying degree stresses in the inner organization of their respective family on their way towards different places of destination beyond East Bengal. In the back-drop of this fact it is hardly known how the immigrants behaved to be held together in individual *family* level by their inner kin-bonds immediately after their migration in West Bengal (1947–48).

To enquire into social and economic condition of the refugees the Indian Statistical Institute carried out a comprehensive survey in West Bengal from May to September, 1948. With regard to a suitable technique for sampling the procedure of stratified sampling was adopted and accordingly the whole of West Bengal was divided into three broad strata and seven sub-strata. *Stratum* I included three sub-strata of Calcutta (Corporation) area, Howrah City and Industrial suburbs of Calcutta, *Stratum* II consisted of three sub-strata of larger towns, smaller towns and townships and other towns and townships, and *Stratum* III included one sub-stratum of Rural areas not covered by the above. Refugee colonies and concentration camps were, of course, excluded from the sample survey. Moreover, variable sampling fractions were precisely adhered to to provide with suitable representation of the refugee families in different sub-strata in question. Thus, from Calcutta and Howrah city areas 5051 family units, from town areas including industrial suburbs 9950 family units, and from rural areas 2435 family units were taken into consideration.[1]

Though a sample-size of 17436 refugee families was originally within the scope of the survey, ultimately data related to 16156 families could be taken into account at the time of study. Most of the rejections were due to incomplete recordings in the schedules concerned.

In the present study an attempt has been made to examine structural characteristics of those refugee families only whose all members were displaced *directly* from East Bengal to West Bengal. In this context data[2] related to structural compositions of the families of the rural Hindu folk of undivided Bengal (1948–47) have also been utilized to make certain comparative examinations.

A careful study of the nature of migration of every member of each one of the total 16156 families reveals that in as many as 11880 families (74 per cent) the members concerned migrated due to partition directly from East Bengal to West Bengal. Place of migration-wise break-up of this 74 per cent families shows that 52 per cent and 17 per cent came directly from rural and urban areas respectively of East Bengal, while in 5 per cent cases only came those families whose members lived before migration partly in rural and partly in urban areas of East Bengal. This note deals with 11880 refugee families only.

A look into the modes of organization of kinship ties by the refugee members having face to face relationships shows that a very large number among them maintained family life in both extended (joint) and non-extended structures. Uni-member units of persons living only by themselves without any kind were found to have concentrated in 8.61 per cent cases only, the non-familial female individuals being less dominant (1.57 per cent) among the refugees in question. It is to be noted that immediately after their arrival in West Bengal (1947–48) the refugee immigrants continued to maintain family-units like conjugal, elementary and extended (joint) in 91.39 per cent cases. They formed extended (joint) units with and without 'complex'—constituents** in as many as 45.60 per cent cases (Table 9.1).

**Table 9.1:** Distribution of Family Structures Among the Refugees Migrated Directly from East Bengal to West Bengal (1947–48)

| *Family structure* (1) | *Frequency* (2) | *Percentage* (3) |
|---|---|---|
| non-familial unit (man) | 836 | 7.04 |
| non-familial unit (woman) | 186 | 1.57 |
| conjugal | 475 | 4.00 |
| elementary | 4083 | 34.36 |
| extended | 4459 | 37.53 |
| non-familial (man)-complex | 56 | 0.47 |
| non-familial (woman)-complex | 45 | 0.38 |
| conjugal-complex | 136 | 1.15 |
| elementary-complex | 645 | 5.43 |
| extended-complex | 959 | 8.07 |
| all structures | 11880 | 100.00 |

With regard to the mode of family living in *undivided* Bengal (1946–47) it has been observed that the rural Hindus organised relatively more extended (joint) families with and without 'complex'- elements (51 per cent). And eventually the norm of patrilocal–patrilineal joint family living was still paramount among the majority of the Hindus concerned. Concentration of elementary (simple) families with and without 'complex'-elements was available in 35 per cent cases only. On the other hand, it has been pointed out that just before the act of partition Bengal villages were not lacking in those persons who lived singly by themselves without any kin. Total strength of these non-familial single member units was in the order of 5.08 per cent only, female single members alone being dominant in 3 per cent cases.

As the presence of the 'complex'-constituents in a family organisation testified to a complementary process of integrative extension of one structure at the expense of disintegrative shrinkage of another, classificatory importance of familial and non-familial units with or without such complex-constituents is obvious. Analysis of the rural Hindu family organizations of undivided Bengal in terms of complex-constituents indicates that in 19 out of 100 cases occurred structural breakdowns—temporary or otherwise—of some families to which the 'complex'-constituents belonged before they were articulated with the families under consideration. Incidentally, it may be noted here that among the refugees in question articulation of complex-constituents was found to have occurred in only 16 out of 100 units studied.

Relevant findings related to the proportional occurrences of different non-familial and family structures within and between the rural Hindus of undivided Bengal (1946–47) and the displaced Hindus (1947–48) under study have been incorporated in Table 9.2.

Again, in examining the distributions of different family and non-familial structures particularly among the Hindus of rural East Bengal (1945–47) and the refugees migrating from rural East Bengal (East Pakistan) to West Bengal (1847–48) certain interesting features are available (Table 9.3).

While the rural Hindu-folk in question organised in pre-partition period extended (joint) families with and without complex-constituents in 53 per cent cases, the refugees migrating from villages of East Bengal showed such extended (joint) families with and without complex-constituents in only 45 per cent cases. On the other hand, non-familial units (males and females) concentrated in about one-twentyfifth cases among the rural Hindus of East Bengal, but among the refugees concerned such units concentrated in slightly less then one-tenth cases. That the rural refugees in question maintained, after migration, relatively more non-extended family and non-familial structures than the rural Hindus of East Bengal (1946–47) remains perhaps a significant fact of sociological interest.

**Table 9.2:** Percentage Distribution of Family Structures Among the Rural Hindus of Undivided Bengal and the Refugees of West Bengal

| | *Percentage distribution of family structures* | |
|---|---|---|
| *Family structures* | *Rural Hindus of undivided Bengal (1946–47)* | *Refugees migrating from East Bengal to West Bengal (1947–48)* |
| *(1)* | *(2)* | *(3)* |
| non-familial unit (man) | 2.06 | 7.04 |
| non-familial unit (woman) | 3.00 | 1.57 |
| conjugal | 6.36 | 4.00 |
| elementary | 30.03 | 34.36 |
| extended | 39.08 | 37.53 |
| non-familial (man)-complex | 0.40 | 0.47 |
| non-familial (woman)-complex | 0.85 | 0.38 |
| conjugal-complex | 1.39 | 1.15 |
| elementary-complex | 5.24 | 5.43 |
| extended-complex | 11.59 | 8.07 |
| all structures | 100.000 | 100.00 |
| total number of units | 2234 | 11880 |
| obtained *value of chi-square* = 169.203 *with* 9 d.f.; *probability* = less than 0.001 | | |

**Table 9.3:** Percentages Distribution of Family Structures Among the Hindus of Rural East Bengal and the Refugees Migrating from Rural East Bengal to West Bengal

| | *Percentage distribution of family structures* | |
|---|---|---|
| *Family structures* | *Rural Hindus of East Bengal (1946–47)* | *Refugees migrating from Rural East Bengal to West Bengal (1947–48)* |
| *(1)* | *(2)* | *(3)* |
| non-familial unit (man) | 2.00 | 7.06 |
| non-familial unit (woman) | 2.44 | 1.83 |
| conjugal | 5.33 | 4.34 |
| elementary | 29.56 | 34.50 |
| extended | 41.78 | 36.92 |
| non-familial (man)-complex | 0.56 | 0.47 |
| non-familial (woman)-complex | 0.56 | 0.42 |
| conjugal-complex | 1.33 | 1.21 |
| elementary–complex | 5.33 | 5.38 |
| extended-complex | 11.11 | 7.87 |
| all structures | 100.00 | 100.00 |
| total number of units | 900 | 8332 |
| obtained *value of chi-square* = 57.430 *with* 9 d.f.; *probability* = less than 0.001 | | |

Contextually, a separate examination of the distribution of different family structures as found to have occurred among the rural Hindu autochthones of West Bengal (1946–47) and the refugees migrating from rural East Bengal

(East Pakistan) to rural West Bengal (1947–48) helps to pin-point certain notable features. In contrast to the proportional occurrence of non-familial structures as found among the said Hindu autochthones (5.4 per cent) the refugees in question showed such non-familial units in 10 per cent cases. Male refugees who lived alone by themselves were especially maintaining a higher concentration. While the Hindu autochthones of pre-partition times organized extended (joint) families with and without 'complex'-constituents in as good as 49 per cent cases, the refugees showed such family structures in only 39 per cent cases. Moreover, the refugees showed those units which only had 'complex'-constituents in relatively lesser strength (Table 9.4). It is significant to note that while the refugee immigrants concerned maintained non-extended family and non-familial forms in substantial volume (61 per cent) in rural West Bengal after partition (1947–48), the Hindu autochthones of rural West Bengal (1946–47) were found to have formed such non-extended units relatively in lesser strength (51 per cent).

**Table 9.4:** Percentage Distribution of Family Structures Among the Hindus of Rural West Bengal and the Refugees Migrating from Rural East Bengal to Rural West Bengal

| | *Percentage distribution of family structures* | |
|---|---|---|
| *Family*<br>*(1)* | *Rural Hindus of West Bengal (1946–47)*<br>*(2)* | *Refugees migrating from rural East Bengal to rural West Bengal (1947–48)*<br>*(3)* |
| non-familial unit (man) | 2.10 | 7.09 |
| non-familial unit (woman) | 3.37 | 3.15 |
| conjugal | 7.05 | 6.97 |
| elementary | 30.36 | 35.40 |
| extended | 37.26 | 30.49 |
| non-familial (man)-complex | 0.30 | 0.73 |
| non-familial (woman)-complex | 1.05 | 0.30 |
| conjugal-complex | 1.42 | 2.42 |
| elementary-complex | 5.17 | 5.33 |
| extended-complex | 11.92 | 8.12 |
| all structures | 100.00 | 100.00 |
| total number of units | 1334 | 1650 |
| obtained *value of chi-square* = 80.499 *with* 9 d.f.; *probability* = less than 0.001 | | |

Lastly, an attempt has been made to examine mutual interactions of three factors related to (1) family structures—non-familial units (males and females), non-extended family units with and without complex-constituents and extended (joint) family units with and without complex-constituents; (2) areas (rural and urban) in East Bengal (East Pakistan) from where the refugees migrated; and (3) refugees' present residence or location (village/town/city areas) in West Bengal after migration and in this connection some statistical tests (chi-square) have also been made (Table 9.5A and 9.5B). It appears clearly from the features analysed that (1) occurrences of any type of family structure among the refugees concerned were independent of the influence of their modes of migration from rural or urban areas of East Bengal, but (2) occurrences of any type of family structure among the refugee immigrants in question were highly significantly associated with their post-migrational locations or residences in village or town or city areas of West Bengal, (3) In the next instance, irrespective of the over-all non-existence of association between the factors of the area in East Bengal from where a family migrated and its ultimate structure in present residence in West Bengal after migration, proportional differences in structures are observed among the refugee families of the village areas (West Bengal) according to their respective area (East Bengal) from where they migrated. The proportional differences are relatively more marked in the cases of non-familial units and extended families.

**Table 9.5A:** Percentage Distribution of Family Structures Among the Refugees Migrating from Rural and Urban Areas of East Bengal to Village/Town/City Areas of West Bengal (1947–48)

| | | *Migrated from rural areas of East Bengal with present residence in West Bengal in (1947–48)* | | | *Migrated from urban areas of East Bengal with present residence in West Bengal in (1947–48)* | | |
|---|---|---|---|---|---|---|---|
| *Family structures of the refugees after migration (1)* | *Village areas (2)* | *Town areas (3)* | *Village areas (4)* | *Town areas (5)* | *City areas (6)* | *(7)* | *City areas (8)* |
| non-familial units (males & females) | 10.24 | 7.85 | 10.63 | 4.88 | 5.37 | 11.36 | 8.54 |
| non-extended family units with and without 'complex' constituents | | | | | | | |
| extended (joint) | 51.15 | 45.15 | 45.07 | 47.56 | 48.41 | 42.39 | 46.29 |
| units with & without 'complex'-constituents | 38.61 | 47.00 | 44.30 | 47.56 | 46.22 | 46.25 | 45.17 |
| all structures | 100.00 | 100.00 | 100.00 | 100.00 | 100.00 | 100.00 | 100.00 |
| total number of units | (1650) | (4950) | (1702) | (164) | (1640) | (1012) | (11138) |

obtained *value of chi-square* = 554.469 *with* 12 d.f.; *probability* = less than 0.001

Thus, in summarising the highlights of the findings of the present study it is sociologically interesting to note two distinct structural patterns in the formation of families among the Hindu autochthones of *rural* West Bengal

**Table 9.5B:** Analysis of Component Chi-squares in Relation to the Factors in Table (9.5A)*

| *Comparison—chi-square—Probability* | | | |
|---|---|---|---|
| between M and L | 266.1180 | 2 | less than 0.001 |
| between L and F | 62.2335 | 4 | less than 0.001 |
| between M and F | 5.9099 | 2 | In between 0.05 and 0.10 |
| between M and L and F | 220.2078 | 4 | less than 0.001 |
| total | 554.4692 | 12 | less than 0.001 |

*Note*: M refers to areas in East Bengal (East Pakistan) from where migrated L refers to present residence in West Bengal after migration F refers to family structures of the refugees in West Bengal.

*Author appreciates Sri S. Bandyopadhyay. ISI, for his suggestion of the procedure of chi-square analysis.

(1946–47) and the refugees migrating from *rural* East Bengal to *rural* West Bengal (1947–48) due to partition. The refugees in question formed relatively more non-extended structures in West Bengal whereas the Hindus autochthones of rural West Bengal were found to have maintained relatively more joint (extended) families with and without 'complex'-constituents in 1946–47.

The tables (9.1–9.5A) have been appended in the paper.

(Thanks are due to Dr. R. Mukherjee, Professor of Sociology, Indian Statistical Institute, Calcutta, for his guidance in the preparation of the paper.)

# Notes

*This is a revised version of a paper contributed to the Anthropology and Archaeology Section, 50th Session, Indian Science Congress, 1963.

**Complex constituents may be female patrikins or matrikins of the head of the family/non-familial unit concerned. *Female Patrikins refer* to all married and/or widowed female agnates and affines related only through them to the 'head'. Matrikins refer to all males and females genealogically connected with some female married into the family of the 'head'.

# References

Chakravarti, N. C. 1949. *Report on the survey of refugee population* in *West Bengal.* Calcutta: Indian Statistical Institute.

Pakrasi, Kanti. 1962. 'A study of some aspects of the types of households and family organizations in rural Bengal, 1946–47', *The eastern anthropologist*, XV (3), 55–63.

# 10

# Foreigners, Refugees and Outsiders in the Indian Context

*T. K. Oommen*

All the three categories—foreigners, refugees, outsiders—are products of spatial mobility and are viewed with varying degrees of legitimacy by the people of a nation-state among whom they are present. The foreigners are alien citizens who migrate in search of better economic opportunities to another country; the refugees are those who flee from their country being victims of discrimination perpetrated against one or another of their identity—religion, language—and whose citizenship status is in dispute; the outsiders are fellow citizens who are perceived as intruders by locals from other administrative units or cultural regions within the nation-state.

It is clear then that the foreigners as such do not pose a problem if their entry and number are regulated by the host country through immigration policy, laws and procedures and of course depending upon its absorption capacity. But large scale illegal influx of foreigners is bound to create conflicts between them and the citizens of the host country particularly when the latter perceive the presence of foreigners as an economic and political threat to them. Legal instruments and administrative actions to identify and deport illegal foreigners exist in all nation-States; the foreigners become a 'problem' only when the state apparatus does not function effectively. In contrast, in terms of the Declaration of Human Rights of United Nations a government cannot refuse territorial asylum to a refugee or he cannot be returned 'in any manner whatsoever to the frontiers of territories where his life or freedom would be threatened on account of his race, religion, or membership of a particular social group or political opinion' (Collins 1971). However, if the inflow of refugees is beyond the accommodation-capacity of the host country and if they tend to become a permanent burden on its economy, conflicts between the citizens and the refugees are likely to crystallize over a period of time. The outsiders do not share the illegitimacy of foreign intruders nor are they protected by international laws or Declaration of Human Rights as refugees, yet their predicament is often comparable to that of foreigners and refugees in plural societies such as India, partly because of the complexity of the nation-state but largely because of the gap between the theory, and practice of law.

In legal-conceptual terms, then, foreigners, refugees and outsiders are distinct categories but in empirical contexts they often converge and coalesce rendering practical solutions often difficult. In order to understand the emergence of these categories in the Indian context two political events in the sub-continent—the partition of India in 1947 based on religion, and the partition of Pakistan based on language leading to the emergence of Bangladesh as a sovereign state in 1971—and an administrative action within Indian union—reorganization of Indian states based on language—are important. We will deal with each of these cases successively. But before that a few conceptual clarifications would be pertinent.

## Some Conceptual Clarifications

While the notion of refugee is understood and used without much ambiguity, the two terms, foreigners and outsiders, are frequently used interchangeably in India notwithstanding their clearly different legal meanings. While the Assam agitators of today use the term foreigner to refer to the 'illegal intruders' from other countries, the people of the erstwhile princely state of Travancore (now a part of Kerala) in their first widespread 'national' protest organized in 1891 referred to Tamil Brahmins as 'foreign' Brahmins. Similarly Bengalis were considered as foreigners in British Bihar, or in Assam. In all these cases the term foreigner was invariably used to refer to dominant groups from other cultural regions and not necessarily from a different political unit. At the same time so far as people from other cultural regions migrated into a region for lowly occupations or for agricultural colonization there was rarely any organized opposition. Usually these humble migrants learnt the local language, adopted the local style of life and got assimilated while the dominant migrants maintained their cultural exclusivism thereby persisting in their alien identity in the locale of their migration. Part of the problem arises from this cultural resilience of the dominant emigrants and their insistence on cultural identity in an alien land. Thus the problem of foreigners or outsiders is the disjuncture between their historical and cultural roots on the one hand and the territory of their origin on the other. The delinking of culture from territory, which is alien to the Indian situation is at the root of the problem of foreigners or outsiders in contemporary India.

In all Indian languages there are terms for natives or locals (*Swadeshi* or its equivalents) and for foreigners/outsiders (*pardeshi/bideshi* etc.). This implies that the territorial identity was and continues to be strong. And given the co-terminality between culture and territory, outsiders were easily identified because they were just a few, spoke a different language, differed in their style of life. Spatial mobility of individuals and groups across cultural regions was a rare phenomenon. When spatial mobility occurred on a large scale it was in the form of people of the same cultural region colonizing hitherto unoccupied land geographically contiguous areas in the process replicating and recreating the same cultural situation. This co-terminality between territory, language, culture and style of life was seriously disturbed for the first time with the onset of the colonial administration. The colonial situation provided opportunities for spatial mobility wherein people drawn from various cultural backgrounds got mixed and interacted; they gradually lost their territorial claims but retained cultural identity. Thus the Telugu speakers of Burma or Tamil speakers of Sri Lanka, came to be identified with the country of their habitation but still retained their cultural identity. This is equally applicable to all multicultural nation-states such as India.

To add to the complexity of the situation, there exists a basic divergence between the official and folk conceptions of language and region. Although the Census of India lists 1652 languages as mother tongues in India only 14 of these are listed in the VIII Schedule as official languages. The numerical strength, development and distinctiveness of the languages seem to be the basis of according official status. This situation created and perpetuates a distortion in that the underdeveloped and numerically weak languages got neglected and are facing the threat of extinction. Thus a substantial number of Indians lose their linguistic-cultural identity while for others, those whose mother tongue is one or another of the 14 official languages, their cultural identity is defined and reinforced mainly in linguistic terms. This applies not only to numerous tribal languages spoken by smaller groups but also to serveral languages which are mother tongues of vast peasant groups. Thus, Bhojpuri, Brij Bhasha, Maithili, Rajasthani, to mention but a few of these languages, are simply treated as dialects of Hindi in the official effort to show Hindi speakers as the biggest speech community and to legitimize the language as the national language of the country. However, these languages are spoken in regions which are culturally distinct and people do have distinct cognition about their region, culture and language. Several mobilizations against outsiders/foreigners within the same administrative units (such as states) testify to the disjuncture between the state and folk definitions of regions, languages and cultures.

In the final analysis, then, the referents to the notions of locals and outsiders vary substantially; the referent could be region, language or culture independently or all these simultaneously. Given such a situation the contending parties invoke the kind of label which is most advantageous as they perceive it often making solutions to problems difficult. Territory as an exclusive referent of identity is used mainly within a homogenous linguistic region e.g. Mulkies and non-Mulkies in Andhra Pradesh, Jodhpuris and Jaipuris in Rajasthan etc. Language as the referent of identity is used to distinguish a migrant community by the host community: Tamils in Bombay, Punjabis in Madras, Bengalis in Assam. But the migrants themselves press their claims based on residence in the region into which they migrated, a claim usually not acceptable to the host community. Much of the social tensions generated by mobilizations and counter-mobilizations by the sons of soil on the one hand and outsiders and foreigners on the other, then, is the resultant of the lack of congruence in definitions and labelling used by the contending collectivities.

## Partition of India and the Punjabi Refugees

Accurate estimates of refugees who came to India due to partition do not exist for a variety of reasons. First, communal tensions have started as early as 1920s and in March 1940 the All India Muslim League at its Lahore session resolved: 'the areas in which the Muslims are numerically in a majority as in North-Western and Eastern zones of India should be grouped to constitute "Independent States" in which the constituent units be autonomous and sovereign' (see, Rajendra Prasad, 1946: 199). Consequently migration to 'safer areas' have started much before partition and no clear account of these exist. Second, when the large scale influx occurred finally during 1946–47 all of them were not visible as refugees as their relatives and friends sheltered them in large numbers Third, while the influx from West Punjab almost stopped by 1951 the flight of refugees from East Bengal (Bangladesh) continues even today, the latest being the Hindu and Buddhist tribal refugees from Chittagong Hill Tracts to Tripura in 1981. Therefore, one can estimate refugees only with specific reference to certain time points.

Between 1946–51 nearly nine million Hindus and Sikhs came to India and about six million Muslims left India for Pakistan. Of the nine millions who came to India, five millions came from West Pakistan and four millions came from East Pakistan. However, according to the 1951 Census of India, only 7,295,870 were enumerated as displaced persons; 4,746,480 from West Pakistan and 2,549,390 from East Pakistan. Most of those who left India were from North India and only a limited number left from East India. Thus the influx from East Pakistan to India was not balanced by a corresponding efflux from India. The refugees from West Pakistan were absorbed much more rapidly, partly because of the vacuum created by the departure of Muslims in the eastern region there was no such vacuum and the government had been faced with a monumental task of fitting those millions of refugees into an area which was already overpopulated and saturated in terms of employment market (Government of India, 1957: 98). Apart from this, historical circumstances imparted specificity to the situation in West Pakistan and North India which rendered the process of partition more violent and the refugees more bitter. While in the pre-partition Punjab Muslims constituted 57% of the population by 1951 the Muslim population was reduced to less than 2% of the population (Moon, 1964: 29) of Punjab, including Haryana. In contrast the situation in Bengal was relatively less violent; 42% of the Hindu population in undivided Bengal was in Pakistan. The influx at the time of partition was a mere trickle considering the massive Hindu population in this sector (Rao 1967: 142–3). But by 1952 the influx started and as we have noted earlier it continues even today. It is necessary to explain the variations in the two different situations—Punjab and Bengal.

In the last decades of 19th and early 20th century canal colonies were opened by the British in West-Central Punjab. These districts were arid and unproductive and sparsely populated. The British encouraged colonization by agriculturally progressive castes, mainly Jats, who flocked to these districts from the districts of Amritsar, Gurudaspur, Jullunder, Hoshiarpur and Ludhiana of East Punjab, now in India. But families rarely moved into and it was usually the young able bodied males who migrated in the first instance. The young men alone with the retired military men who received land grants free or on concessional basis formed the backbone of canal colonies. Under the circumstances it was necessary for these immigrants to find their brides from East Punjab, as there were few eligible ones in the west at that time. When the bride went to the husband's household she was often unhappy with the frontier-like atmosphere and visited her natal village on every possible opportunity—life cycle rituals festivals. This provided the possibility of constant interaction between the west and east Punjab (Douie 1961: 132–41). Given this social-historical background, for a substantial proportion of those who came to India from West Pakistan it was often a return to their natal villages and towns home-coming to ancestral land and yet conditions which forced them to leave created bitterness and frustration and this in turn a sense of aggression and adventure.

Of the 4.7 million displaced persons from West Pakistan enumerated in 1951 census as many as 3.4 millions came from West Punjab, 7,76,000 from Sind and 5,16,000 from elsewhere in West Pakistan. The agricultural pioneers who developed the canal colonies of West Punjab districts were mainly Jat Sikh peasants. They were the worst sufferers not only because they lost the fruits of their hard work for several decades in the canal colonies but also because of their physical visibility. The Sikhs were particularly visible due to the five symbols of Khalsa enjoined as mandatory for all Sikh by Guru Gobind Singh in 1699. For them to hide or convert becomes particularly problematic and this made them vulnerable. The Muslim animosity to Sikh was more pronounced since the 1850 struggle, which led to the exile of Mohammad Bahadur Shah, the last of the Moghuls. The Lahore branch of the Muslim League offering Rs. 250/- for a, Sikh head while only Rs. 100/- for a Hindu head is to be seen against this long standing animosity between Sikh and Muslims (Keller 1975: 106). It must be recalled here that Sikhism started as a movement to reconcile Hinduism and Islam, but the intolerance of and persecution by the Moghul emperors, especially Aurangazeb, forced Sikh-Muslim animosity.

Economically frustrated and religiously persecuted Punjab refugees were willing to go anywhere and to take up any job. Although their highest concentration according to the 1951 Census was in Delhi and Punjab (397 and 231 pa thousand local population) they got dispersed almost all over the country. The Punjab–Haryana region was a food-deficient one and nearly a non-industrial area at the time of partition, but leaped to the forefront of development in India within two decades. Having deprived of the fruits of their hard work in the canal colonies in west Punjab they returned to their home districts and started hard work again; they were twice uprooted and this seems to have made them economically aggressive. Net only in Punjab but also in other areas which they colonized such as the Ganganagar district of Rajasthan and Terai legion of Uttar Pradesh or townships where they settled down such as Faridabad, Ulhasnagar, Pimpri, Govindnagar etc., have been turned economically prosperous. The other major group which came from west Pakistan namely Sindhis number about 7–8 lakhs and they were dispersed in to several towns and cities who soon responded to the business opportunities gradually becoming captains of industry, trade and commerce. The mood of the refugees from west Punjab was 'home was now where we earned our living' (Tandon 1963: 254). Thus the history of the refugees from West Pakistan is a history of quick economic success and cultural accommodation and assimilation as they tame into the midst of the people who had same religious faith, spoke the same language and had more or less the same culture and style of life. But it is important to recall here that the Hindu refugees although less prosperous economically seem to have completely assimilated culturally and do not show any indication of political disloyalty to the nation. The situation is somewhat different in the case of Sikhs, at least in the case of a section, Keshadhari Sikhs.

Having successfully fated the economic crisis and psychic damage wrought by the partition the Sikhs were eager to establish their identity as a specific community. Although Sikh history is 400 years old, Sikh consciousness crystallized only by the turn of the century, with the founding of Chief Khalsa Diwan in 1902. This was reinforced by the 1920s during Gurudwara reform movement to get rid of corrupt religious functionaries from Gurudwaras, particularly Hindu Mahants. The agitation led to the passage of the Sikh Gurudwara Act of 1925 and the formation of Shiromani Gurudwara Prabandhak Committee (SGPC) to manage the Sikh Gurudwaras and the Akali Dal its arm for political mobilization. Both SGPC and Akali Dal limited their membership to Sikhs thereby defining the boundary between Hindus and Sikhs. The Gurudwara movement was an effort to purify Sikhism of the Hindu accretion. As the movement gained strength came partition and the Muslim onslaught on Sikhs. Understandably they turned to Hindus and India for safety and security. But once the problems threw up by partition were over, the Sikhs wanted to be recognized as a specific religious community. In fact, Hindus were accused of trying to absorb Sikhs back into Hinduism religiously and the government to absorb them politically (see Gurnam Singh, I960: 10–40).

The chief carriers of Sikh identity and consciousness are the Jat Sikh peasantry and particularly the Keshdharies whose attachment to the five symbols is acute. The sense of separateness is less strong among Scheduled Caste Sikhs and Sahajdari Sikhs, who do not display the five symbols (Nayar 1966: 59–63 and 196–7). Religious sects, such as Nirankaris and Radha Soamis are difficult to classify as clearly Hindu or Sikh. Thus the core carriers of Sikh religious tradition are the Keshdhari Jat Sikh peasantry a substantial proportion of whom had experienced atrocities at the time of partition. But demanding a separate state based on religion was politically unacceptable in free India. And therefore, the demand was camouflaged on the basis of language—Punjabi. In the process Punjabi written in Gurumukhi script came to be identified with Sikhs and the Punjabi speaking Hindus started disowning their language and instead started claiming Hindi as their language. Thus the formation of Punjabi Suba—a Punjabi speaking state in form but a Sikh state in substance—was largely the resultant of the mobilization by Akali Dal the political wing of SGPC. This was a great political victory to the refugees who already are experiencing tremendous economic prosperity. The success both on economic and political fronts imparts a sense of courage and recklessness to the Sikhs, at least part of which can be traced to their refugee experience. As one of the respondents of Keller puts it (1975: 273):

> We have been through so much; what more can happen to us? No one can do anything to us that can be more terrible than has already occurred. Why should we be afraid? "Once everything was taken, from us (in partition) and we have come back from our pennylessness to prosperity. If we lose it all again we could do it once more.

There is both self-confidence and despondency, both desperation and invincibility in the above statement. Such a value-orientation is at once an asset and a liability; an asset if it is channelized for economic development and social change, a liability if it is utilized for narrow, parochial and religious-fundamentalist goals. Viewed thus, the incipient demand for a separate Sikh nation, Khalistan, is bound to weaken the social fabric of a plural society such as India.

Interestingly enough from among the refugee groups from West Pakistan only the Punjabi Sikhs, who finally have a separate homeland for themselves, pose such a threat. Other groups with specific religious identities such as Hindus got already assimilated or those with separate linguistic identities such as Sindhis got dispersed into different urban centres of India. While the Sindhis do constitute urban ethnic enclaves in several big cities and towns (Sen 1957: 6) and economically prosperous they do not seem to be mobilizing towards the formation of a home-state. Thus it seems safe to conclude that a refugee group is likely to generate conflicts in host society only if they get concentrated in a specific territory and gain political clout. Their political strength is likely to be substantial if their mobilization is done by invoking their religious sentiments.

## Partition and Bengali Refugees

We have seen that the inflow of Punjabi refugees practically stopped by early fifties, and within two decades they became an economic and political force within India. In contrast, the influx of Bengali refugees continues even today and it cannot be said conclusively that they transformed themselves into a prosperous community. The reasons for this will have to be found in the characteristics of Bengali refugees. First, 80% of the initial migrants (1946–48) from East Pakistan were middle class persons who depended on white collar occupations or medium or petty trade. Very limited number of the actual tillers of land migrated as they could not take the risk of leaving behind land because there was no guarantee of getting land in an area where man-land ratio was already adverse (Chakravarti 1948). Further, the Muslim migration from West Bengal to East Bengal was very limited and as such land vacated by them was not available to be distributed. Second, the refugees were mainly well-to-do high caste and educated persons. Their rehabilitation was much more difficult as they preferred urban white collar-professional occupations (State Statistical Bureau, West Bengal 1951). Third, according to the 1956 estimates, although the initial migrants were mainly from non-agricultural occupations later ones constituted larger percentage of agriculturists. But on the whole the Bengali refugees took to petty trade, shop-keeping etc, which meant that they scarcely contributed to the production of food or industrial products, assist in capital formation but are engaged in occupations which do not add to the wealth of the country (State Statistical Bureau, West Bengal, 1956). Fourth, even after a decade of migration 26% of the Bengalis considered themselves to be refugees. But the incidence of this phenomenon namely perceiving one's status as refugee shows a marked variation between different types of settlements. The incidence is highest in cities, the lowest in the villages, with towns coming in between. It seemed that,

> those among the displaced people who are still pursuing relatively less stable livelihood, have less security of settlement, are more burdened with familial obligation etc, tend to identify and isolate themselves from the local social milieu as "refugees". The scope of acquiring the material or economic bases and consequently the feasibility of adjustment of the displaced persons within the local social milieu, has been offered the maximum by the villages and the minimum by the cities . . . (Bandopadhyay and Chattopadhyay 1965: 508–9).

Finally, the Bengali refugees are not yet assimilated and still maintain social distinctions, not so much because they are cultural aliens but their refugee status was used to get some special economic privileges (Pakrasi 1971: 134). The refugees came from all social strata and their frame of reference was their previous status in East Bengal which left a large number of them deprived and dissatisfied, particularly the well off. Their status was defined by the government, host community and by themselves as receivers and not as givers and this has been socially degrading and stigmatizing. Where they perceived themselves as contributors rather than as receivers of charity their rehabilitation and assimilation was quicker as in the case of Punjabis (see Saxena, 1961).

## The Split of Pakistan and the Refugee Influx into India

Although pan-Indian Islamic unity and sentiment paved the way for the emergence of Pakistan, geographic discontinuity, linguistic-cultural diversity and developmental disparity between the West and East Pakistan led to the division of Pakistan leading to the emergence of two nation-states. The emergence of Bangladesh in 1971 was possible only after the defeat of Pakistani armed forces by the combined strength of Bengali soldiers, volunteer forces and the Indian army. At the initial stages almost all Bengalis, Hindus and Muslims, supported the national liberation struggle. The Bihari Muslims (an appellation used for all non-Bengali Muslims in Bangladesh) were identified as pro-Pakistani and they fell prey to the violence of national liberation groups. But soon after the establishment of martial law on 25th March 1971, the objective of flushing out the Hindus became a definite policy of the official machinery. The Bihari Muslims regained their legitimacy and played an important role in executing the official design. The propaganda that the Hindus had massacred Muslims in large numbers in the initial phase of the liberation struggle gained currency and even the Bengali Muslims believed it. Once again a regional linguistic (West Pakistan-Punjabi versus East Pakistani-Bengali) conflict was transformed into a religious (Muslim versus Hindu) confrontation. The martial law administration labelled almost the entire set of political parties and groups as disruptive elements and traitors which destroyed Pakistan. The army and civil authorities used Hindus as scapegoats, having identified them as the corrupting influence on nationalist forces. It was against this background that the Hindu migration from Bangladesh to India began in April 1971, to save themselves from the onslaught from administration, Bihari Muslims and even a section of Bengali Muslims.

According to official statistics, by December 1971 ten millions sought refuge and of these nearly seven millions were accommodated in about 850 camps and the remaining were staying with friends and relatives. Almost the whole of the refugees were Hindus. The Hindus were responding through flight only when the Muslims started showing a marked tendency towards aggression and by severing social bonds. However, the attempt was only to socially uproot them and not to physically eliminate them. The 1971 situation was radically different from the earlier ones in that it was a one-way flow and hence the burden was entirely that of the host country, namely India. But the 1971 migrants from Bangladesh were defined as a temporary group by themselves as well as by the receiving country, who would eventually return Therefore, the question of their rehabilitation or assimilation on a permanent basis did not arise; they were treated as foreign nationals right from the beginning and this was made abundantly clear in the administrative instructions issued for transit relief camps for refugees from East Bengal in 1971, by the Government of India. This policy necessitated that the refugees be kept as both physical isolates (in camps) and social parasites (on doles). Thus the refugee's in camps received food, clothing, shelter, medical care but were not allowed to engage in any economic or political activities. This marginalization was a necessary price to be paid by the refugees for the hospitality extended to them by the host country. Indeed the acceptance of this asymmetrical relationship between the refugees and the hosts was an inevitable corollary of the conditions—persecution and perhaps death—they faced in their native country. The refugees were made receivers, a status which degraded them, but about which no options were open to them.

But the degradation did not demoralize the refugees for a variety of reasons. First, when the immigration began in April 1971, the hosts welcomed them, in fact the receptions of refugees were organized often with a festive touch. Second, the instantaneous sympathy extended by the fellow Hindu Bengali often operated as a tension absorbing mechanism. Third, a substantial number of the locals were themselves ex-refugees who came from East Pakistan and this facilitated the reliving of similar experiences and establishment of primordial ties both of which facilitated crystallization of empathic relationships. Apart from these, once the camp life was established the evacuees tried to establish communication with their kinsmen, acquaintances and caste people; the Jajmani relations got established, economic exchanges began. In fact the East Pakistan community structure *was* sought to be recreated without of course its ecological base (sec Mukherjee 1974).

Within one year's time the situation in East Pakistan was stabilized, a new sovereign nation, Bangladesh, emerged and the nationalist Mukti Bahini was taking stern action against the pro-Pakistani elements such as Bihari Muslims. Initial enquiries by the refugees revealed that the conditions in their natal villages and towns were favourable for them to return and the process began. Generally speaking, the refugee suffers from a lot of psychological imbalances as he gets uprooted from his native environment and is denied his national identity. But in the case of Bengali refugee of 1971 this was not true, because he has been received by his Indian hosts with great gusto and he could recreate his community life in the camps. Although he was marginalized in that he was proscribed from participating in economic and political life, this was not an individual punishment but a collective proscription, which led to the emergence of a collectively shared identity, we-feeling and cohesion. Additionally, the marginalization of the refugees was a temporary phenomenon, in that the emergence of Bangladesh offered a new opportunity, a new symbol and a new hope. This seems to have more than compensated for the temporary misfortune the refugee has experienced.

## The Problem of Foreigners in India

Presently we will discuss the problem of foreigners, using the term in its strict legal sense, so as to avoid confusion. The North-East of India—Assam, Meghalaya, Arunachal Pradesh, Nagaland, Manipur and Mizoram—is facing the danger of massive influx of foreign nationals from Bangladesh, Nepal, Bhutan and Burma. It is claimed by the people of North East that 40 to 50 lakh foreigners from these neighbouring countries have intruded into India illegally. And in Assam alone 13 lakhs of them have enlisted themselves as voters. Among the foreign nationals those from Bangladesh are the majority followed by a substantial number of Nepalis and most of these intruders are found in Assam. Although infiltration occurs in the entire North East region, due to the existence of inner line restrictions and the Sixth Schedule restrictions of transfer of land and immovable properties and the homogenous character of population the infiltrants are easily detected in units other than Assam and Imphal valley in Manipur. Further in Assam, the erstwhile migrants from East Pakistan/Bangladesh and Nepal facilitate the entry and settling down of their fellow countrymen. They buy land, acquire voting rights and have become a threat to the local population.

Faced with such a situation the Assamese population, particularly the students, have been demanding the detection, deportation, deletion from voter's list and/or dispersal of foreigners to other states. But the provocation for the current massive mobilization began in the context of bye-election in Mangaldai parliamentary constituency which was due in March 1979. At the time of revision of electoral list objections were filed against 70,000 voters, that is they are foreign nationals and hence not eligible for voting. Of these 45,000 were declared as foreigners by competent courts. The court verdict was objected to by political parties which stood to benefit by the inclusion of these voters in the list. The chief Election Commissioner then ruled: 'A person whose name has been included shall be presumed to be a citizen of India ... scrutiny of electoral rolls can be taken up after the election is over.'

The All Assam Gana Sangram Parishad, a confederation of two local political parties and a large number of voluntary associations, was formed on 27th August 1979 at Dibrugarh. The All Assam Students Union and the AAGSP jointly lead the movement against the foreigners. The movement leaders argue that Bangladesh is deliberately pursuing a policy of driving people into Assam to grapple with the problems of high population growth and low economic development and to create a secure border between India and Bangladesh with a substantial population of Bangladeshis in Assam. They explicitly declared that the fight 'is only against non-Indians staying illegally in India and not against people from rest of India who are residing in Assam' (see Save Assam Today to Save India Tomorrow, 1980). However, the agitation is described as 'an open movement for secession, a violent movement directed against the religious and linguistic minorities' (Rammurti 1980: 1).

Part of the problem in understanding the real character of the current Assam movement arises from the fact that it follows an earlier mobilization against Bengali Hindu migrants from West Bengal and Marwari and Punjabi businessmen. Viewed in a historical sequence then, the present Assam movement against foreign nationals follows an erstwhile mobilization against fellow nationals from other parts of India. Those who support the Assamese 'nationalism' emphasize the current dimension and those who attack the Assamese 'chauvinism' go back to the earlier phase. But the fact is that the basic thrust of both mobilizations are the same, protecting the interests of local people, essentially Assamese, but the enemies under attack vary—earlier it was fellow nationals, now it is foreign nationals. To understand this transformation we must look at the historical context.

The Assamese fear and anxiety about losing their cultural autonomy dates back to 1837, when Bengali was introduced as the medium of instruction and administration in Assam. They started suspecting the possibility of converting Assam into a Muslim majority state as the Muslim League mobilization began. Assam had the first influx of Hindus in 1946–47 from East Pakistan who were linguistically different. But Muslims from East Pakistan/Bangladesh continued to migrate which they see as motivated by

(a) certain politicians in India to create vote banks in Assam in their favour,
(b) encouraged by Bengali immigrants to add to their security,

(c) economic hardships in Bangladesh and
(d) political designs by the country to create a safe border with India.

The Assamese suspicions were reinforced when demands such as the following were made by the immigrant population, (i) To incorporate the district of Goalpara to West Bengal and to establish a new state carving out territory from Assam named Purbachal, in 1953–55. (ii) Mobilization to convert Assam into a bi-lingual state in 1960 at the time of adopting Assamese as the language of Assam. (iii) Resistance to the adoption of Assamese as the medium of instruction for collegiate education in 1972. (iv) Resistance to detection and deportation of infiltrators or their dispersal to other states (see Leaflet No. 1, by Ganhati Teachers Association).

The economic threat to Assam from Bengali Muslim peasantry from East Bengal began by the beginning of the century. To face the situation the administration devised what was came to be known as the 'line system' according to which the immigrants were not allowed to settle in same villages or buy land and settle only in some parts of villages. The legal restrictions however did not bring about the desired results that C. S. Mullan, the Census Commissioner observed in 1931: 'It is sad but no means impossible that in another thirty years Sibsagar district will be the only part of Assam in which Assamese will find himself at home.' While the Assamese population continued to press the administration for regulation the migrants wanted that all restrictions be lifted. Finally, a 'line system committee' was constituted in 1937 to review the working of the system and its report was submitted in 1938. The Committee recommended the retention of immigrant restrictions. Notwithstanding this, immigration continued. Thus while the immigrant population of Assam was only 18% in 1901 it rose to 41% by 1971. Again the population growth in Assam during the period works out to be 344% (Bhuyan cited in Das, 1980: 1–20).

The major categories in Assam today are (Das 1980: 1–20):

(i) The plantation labour constituting about 10% of the population. These are tribals from Bihar, Orissa, Andhra Pradesh and Madhya Pradesh, (ii) Peasants, mainly Muslims, from East Bengal constituting about 15% of the population, (iii) Professionals and white collar workers, mainly Bengali Hindus from West Bengal constituting about 1.3 million located in urban areas, (iv) Pastorals from Nepal constituting about 250,000, (v) Marwaris numbering about 70,000, businessmen and traders located in towns, (vi) Hindustanis numbering about 650,000 constituted by urban working class, middle class, traders and industrialists. While the present Assamese mobilization is explicitly against categories two and four, there was antecedent mobilization against categories three and five.

Several factors operated together resulting in the migration of a large number of persons with a wide variety of backgrounds, into Assam (Das 1980: 1–20). As the colonial power wanted to consolidate administration, exploit natural resources, develop the plantations, improve transport and communication, they encouraged migration. This had to be done either because the local population was usually to take up certain occupations or because they were unwilling to take up certain occupations or because they were not available in adequate numbers with requisite skills. Moreover, the low density of population and the easy availability of vast tracts of fertile land attracted agricultural colonizers. Further, inadequate occupational diversification of local population also contributed. But these factors by themselves would not have given rise to the current situation in Assam. Lack of regulatory laws and/or the inadequate implementation of these laws coupled with the political motives to make Assam a state with substantial Muslim population seem to have contributed in large measure towards the current crisis. Finally, the political instability in neighbouring countries, particularly East Pakistan/Bangladesh as manifested in the division of the country in 1971, the domination of Punjabis over Bengalis, persecution of minority Hindu and tribal population etc., have led to the large scale entry of foreigners into the Indian States. And this problem is acutely felt by the Assamese as the migrants speak a different language and feel threatened. As for the Bengali infiltration from Bangladesh into West Bengal and Tripura, the two Bengali speaking Indian states, the local attitude seems to be somewhat different. In so far as the Assamese feel threatened about their culture and 'nationality' through large scale influx of migrants, it should be regulated, whether the migrants are foreign or Indian.

## Re-organization of Indian States and the Problem of Outsiders

Since the turn of this century the question of re-organizing Indian states has been exercising the minds of Indian leaders and there was widespread consensus that language affords a ready basis of doing it. But as I have noted earlier, this in effect meant re-organization based on the few dominant languages of India and finally India was re-organized in 1956. The broad principles enunciated by the Government of India for state re-organization were: (i) preservation and strengthening the unity and security of India;

(ii) linguistic and cultural homogeneity; (iii) financial, economic and administrative considerations etc. (see, Report of the State Re-Organization Commission, 1955). But distribution of speech communities or size of language groups does not follow administrative need on financial viability. Yet, finally administrative re-organization was done based on a single Principle, namely linguistic and cultural homogeneity. Thus we have states with substantial variations in size: some of which are administratively unmanageable and others financially unviable. This in turn created a feeling among all cultural groups that if they do not have a home state, that they are second class citizens and those who got such home states started feeling that they alone have the right to live and prosper in these states.

Over a period of time we have shifted from the linguistic cultural criterion. With the conceding of Punjabi Suba, religion came to be recognized as a principle for state re-organization. Gradually, a new criterion namely tribe came to be recognized as the basis of state formation, leading to the creation of some of the smallest states on the North-Eastern border, which are neither financially nor administratively viable. The principle of cultural and linguistic unity also became redundant in conceding the demands of separate statehood for some of these tribes as they have adopted English as the official language of their states. It is also important to note here that while demands have been put forward for the formation of new states in a large number of cases, only in those cases where the bargaining power of the agitators is substantial that such demands are actually conceded. The major sources of bargaining power in these cases seem to be their geo-political resources, being border states, and having easy communication with other nation-states bordering India.

A new implication of accepting criteria such as religion or tribe as the basis of state formation is that the outsiders get redefined and additional criteria are available to exclude them. Thus as language was the sole factor which was invoked hitherto to define outsiders legitimately, now religion and tribe could be added on to identify outsiders. When the tribal populations ask for a separate state even when they are a minority in a region (as in Jharkhand) or when the Sikhs talk of Hindu imperialism, the implications of conceding the demands for formation of states based on these criteria become self-evident.

At the time of State re-organization two broad views were articulated and to a certain extent these persist even today. These views were: (i) the unity of India must not be an imposed one but a fundamental unity recognizing her social pluralities and cultural diversity the strength of Indian union must be the strength it derives from its constituent units and (ii) in the past India was not an integrated political unit and the effort should be to create a united

India and the new concept of unity cannot be based on the reaffirmation or renunciation of old values such as religion, language etc., which are divisive rather than cohesive. Therefore, the unity of India should transcend community and language and recognize the nation as one integrated unit, (see, S.R.C. Report, 1955). As one looks at the situation in India today one finds neither of these principles is adhered to, the praxiological aberrations are far too many to conform to one of the principles enunciated.

The problem of outsiders in India, then, will have to be seen against this background. Indian social heterogeneity is stupendous viewed as a whole, but her homogeneity is strikingly seen in parts; 95% of her population live in the states in which they are born. Internal migration amounts to only about 6% and much of this migration is within same states usually occasioned by marriage ties. Even when migration occurs across states but within the same region perceived as culturally homogeneous such as the Hindi speaking states it does not generate much social tension and conflicts. Conversely even when migration occurs within the same state it may lead to conflicts. Therefore, the problem of outsiders is one that crystallizes in the context of migration across regions which are perceived to be different.

There are four kinds of situations that can be identified in contemporary India in this context. First, when the entire state is engulfed by varieties of outside migrant as is the case with Assam today. This leads to cumulative domination by the outsiders enveloping all aspects of life: The economic domination by Marwari and Punjabi capitalists, the cultural, educational and occupational domination by Bengali Hindus from West Bengal, the domination of rural economy through agricultural colonization by Bengali Muslim peasantry and Nepali Hindu peasantry and political domination by the majority groups among the migrants, particularly Bengalis. Such a situation leads to a 'loss of nerve' on the part of locals and the only course open to them is political action for self-preservation as is witnessed in the case of Assam.

The second type of situation is found within a sub-region in a state as exemplified in the case of Chotanagpur. The tribal population of Chotanagpur claim that they are the original inhabitants and there is a hierarchy of outsiders or Dikhus: Bengali, Marwari and North-Biharis. As is clear the first two categories do not belong to Bihar but even the third category, which belongs to the same state, is considered to be outsiders by the south Biharis. The solution that the people of Chotanagpur see to end the domination by outsiders is the formation of a separate tribal state, Jharkhand. However, the possibility of such a demand being conceded is limited for two reasons. First, the tribals are in a minority in the region and second, their geo-political positioning is not a threat to the nation-state. Being an encysted tribal group they are not in a position to put forward any secessionist demand, unlike the tribals of North-East frontier. An alternative is to pursue a policy of regionalism, ignoring the difference between outsiders and locals, tribals and non-tribals, Christian tribals and non-Christian tribals etc. But the North Biharis are not likely to accept the appellation outsiders along with Bengalis and Marwaris; the possibility of reconciling sectional interests among the local population too is somewhat limited. As the animist and Hindu tribals see it the policy of protective discrimination should benefit only them, the upper caste Hindu on the other hand views the policy as the blocking of opportunity, thereby thwarting the process of development. This means a policy equally satisfying to the heterogeneous population of Chotanagpur is not likely to emerge easily (see, Weiner, 1978).

The third situation where the problem of outsiders crystallizes is exemplified in the case of metropolitan cities such as Bombay, Bangalore etc. The formation of local political parties such as the Shiv Sena in Bombay and Kannada Chaluvaligars in Bangalore to assert particularly the rights to employment and admission to educational institutions for the 'sons of soil' is the typical response in such cases. The outsiders here are those who belong to another cultural region and speech community and irrespective of the longevity of their stay in the city they are defined as outsiders. By and large mobilizations in such contexts are directed against middle class white collar workers, professionals and small businessmen, and confined to particular cities within the region.

The fourth situation wherein the tension against outsiders is articulated is found within the same state, formed on the basis of linguistic and cultural homogeneity. The typical example of these are the Telangana regional movement in Andhra Pradesh, the Vidarbha movement in Maharashtra, the tension between Jammu, Kashmir and Ladakh in Jammu and Kashmir, the tension between the eastern, western and hill districts of Uttar Pradesh etc. The reasons for such tensions are: (i) disparity between economic development and levels of skills and education. Historical circumstances such as princely rule in Telangana and British rule in Coastal Andhra, usually contributing to disparities. (ii) Emergence of new economic opportunities in underdeveloped legions of the state being captured by the people of the more prosperous region through large scale migration. (iii) Expansion of education, in the underdeveloped regions of the state producing an army of the educated without a matching expansion in employment avenues. All of these lead to the surfacing of the hitherto submerged discontent and deprivation. And once mobilizations begin against usurpers even the minor differences are blown out of proportion so that more and more participants are attracted to and sustained in the movement (Weiner, 1978).

## Concluding Comments

Our analysis of the cases of foreigners, refugees and outsiders in India dearly indicates that conflicts between them and the local population—'sons of soil', emerge when the latter category is dominated by the former. And the intensity of these conflicts would depend upon the intertwining of the contexts and velocity of dominance. The contexts of dominance are economic, political and cultural and the categories involved are the following:

(a) The industrial entrepreneurs and agricultural colonizers,
(b) White collar employees and professionals,
(c) The industrial working class.

Most of the industrial enterprises in India's urban centres are owned by outsiders (including ex-refugees) drawn from specific 'ethnic' backgrounds: Marwaris, Parsees, Gujaratis, Punjabis, Sindhis, etc. Opposition against them is not organized or systematic except in rare cases when the local population perceives discrimination in the employment policies pursued by these entrepreneurs. The conflicts are usually between the local rising bourgeoisie and the entrenched outside entrepreneurs. Basically an economic conflict, once it triggers off primordial sentiments are invoked by the locals to expel the outsiders.

The conflicts between agricultural colonizers and locals are far too few in India although not non-existent. Thus the prosperous refugee Sikh farmers of Terai region of Uttar Pradesh or tough Bengali Muslim peasants of Assam have come in for attack latterly from the local population. The domination of agricultural colonizers in not simply economic but invariably political too given their large numbers.

The white collar employees and professionals are the most attacked and despised of the outsiders. Conflicts between them and local population are widespread and found in almost all big towns and cities in India. This is because they are effective competitors with the local rising middle class. Not only that they are blockers of economic opportunities but they also penetrate the local cultural milieu thereby trying to dominate over the locals intellectually. This cultural 'onslaught' by the outsiders is a highly inflammable situation which can provoke animosity against them which in turn would facilitate quick mobilization by locals. Then a situation of occupational cum cultural domination by outsiders have high conflict potentiality.

While the above two categories dominate over the locals the working class are a dominated category. They do not usually evoke feelings of envy and competition except when there exists close association between ethnicity and occupational specialization leading to the blockage of locals' entry into these fields. However, if their number increase substantially in a specific settlement, they can be a political threat in the electoral context, particularly when and if the locals perceive a divergence between their interests and that of these outsiders.

In most of the empirical situations that we know of in India today the dominance by outsiders is a dispersed one, that is, the dominance is confined usually either to the economic, or cultural context. In So far as the situation is of this nature, the locals seek to deal with it through administrative intervention: reservation of jobs, restriction of industrial and trade licences, prohibition of entry into educational institutions, shift in medium of instruction to local language etc. But when the dominance is cumulative, enveloping all dimensions they realize that administrative interventions are useless. For one thing, the outsiders' sheer number creates a demographic imbalance and hence their presence is a political threat. This situation facilitates economic and cultural domination over the locals by the outsiders. That is, the outsiders who are usually accommodated in the periphery of the system or whose dominance is tolerated in one of the contexts, move towards the very centre of the system relegating the locals into the periphery. This indeed is bound to generate acute and prolonged conflicts between the 'sons of soil' and the outsiders. Political mobilization is the only weapon which can successfully meet such an exigency.

# References


All Assam Student Union and Assam Gana Sangram Parishad. 1980. *Save Assam today to save India tomorrow*. Gauhati.

Bandopadhyay S. and Chattopadhyay K. 1965. 'Displaced persons from East Pakistan: Some findings of their social assimilation', Proceedings of the 53rd session of the Indian Science Congress (Abstract of papers) Part-III, Anthropological and Archaeology Section.

Bhuyan M. C. *Immigrant population of Assam* (An unpublished Ph.D. thesis, Gauhati University).

Chakravarti, N. C. 1948. *Report on the survey of refugee population in West Bengal*, mimeo., Calcutta.

Collins, Peter. 1971. *A mandate to protect and assist refugees.* Geneva: U.N. High Commissioner for Refugees.

Das, H. P. 1980. 'The problem of immigration in Assam: A geographical review and interpretation', Presidential address to National Association of Geographers of India, Jan. 18, 1980.

Douie, James. 1916. *The Punjab, North-West Frontier Province and Kashmir.* Cambridge University Press.

Gauhati Teachers Association. n.d. Leaflet No. 1, Coordination Committee, Gauhati.

Government of India. 1956. *State reorganization commission report.* New Delhi.

Government of India. 1957. *Rehabilitation in retrospect.* New Delhi: Ministry of Rehabilitation.

Government of West Bengal. 1951. *Report on the sample survey estimating the socio-economic characteristics of displaced persons migrating from East Pakistan to the state of West Bengal.* Calcutta: State Statistical Bureau.

Government of West Bengal. 1956. *Rehabilitation of refugees: A statistical survey.* Calcutta: State Statistical Bureau.

Keller, Stephen L. 1975. *Uprooting and social change: The role of refugees in development.* Delhi: Manohar Book Service.

Moon, Penderel. 1964. *Divide and quit.* London: Chatto & Windus.

Mukherjee, P. N. 1974. 'The great migration of 1971', *Economic and political weekly,* Vol. IX, Nos. 9,10,11, March 2nd, 9th & 16th.

Nayyar, Baldev Raj. 1966. *Minority politics in the Punjab.* Princeton: Princeton University Press.

Pakrasi, K. B. 1976. *The uprooted: A sociological study of the refugees in West Bengal.* Calcutta: Editions India.

Prasad, Rajendra. 1946. *India divided.* Bombay: Hind Kitabs.

Ramamurthi, P. 1980. *Real face of the Assam agitation.* New Delhi: Communist Party of India (Marxist).

Rao, Bhaskara U. 1967. *The story of rehabilitation.* Delhi: Deptt. of Rehabilitation Ministry of Labour, Employment and Rehabilitation, Government of India.

Saxena, R. N. 1961. *Refugees: A study in changing attitudes.* Bombay: Asia Publishing House.

Sen, Satyabrata. 1967. *The sample survey of displaced persons in urban areas of Bombay state.* Calcutta: The Cabinet Secretariat, Government of India.

Tandon, Prakash. 1963. *Punjabi century.* London: Chatto & Windus.

Weiner, Myron. 1978. *Sons of soil; migration and ethnic conflict in India.* Delhi: Oxford University Press.

# 11

# Negotiating Gender and Disability in Rural Haryana

*Nilika Mehrotra*

Disability remains an obstruction in attaining the full potential of an individual. Each community has its characteristic way of understanding disability and coping with its disabled population. Disability locates the individual in a compromised position not only for biological reasons, but also as a consequence of a complex combination of such non-biological factors as gender, caste, class, neighbourhood relations, and the nature of kinship and family structure. This paper explores the conceptual and empirical implications of the proposition that 'disability is culturally constructed and socially negotiated'. If disability creates obstacles for individuals in discharging their social responsibilities, there are inbuilt cultural mechanisms and social networks available to them as coping strategies within the family, kinship, caste and community.

Voluntary agencies and the state machinery, through various empowerment initiatives, are making consistent efforts to minimise, if not eliminate, the social hindrances and constraints that result from physical disability.[1] Since a large number of the disabled lives in rural areas, the absence of accurate information on the magnitude of the problem has hampered planning of realistic policies and services for them. In urban areas, the disabled are recognised as a social category for their special needs. There are attempts to integrate them into the social mainstream through institutions like special schools and training centres. The situation is different in rural areas. Here the disabled do not constitute a socially recognised group; they often continue to function as normal members of society. In order to understand disability in a rural area, it is necessary to recognise its social organisation of production, cultural values and the structure of gender relations.

Furthermore, disabilities are managed with available resources in the household and economy. The disability management group varies in terms of composition, authority structure, interpersonal relationships, and generation and management of resources within the society. The question of gender is important here: the feminists challenge the picture of the sharing, supportive family structures, and expose the gap between the ideological and the real-life household arrangements. The feminists also critique the notion of altruism as characteristic value of the domestic sphere by portraying the family as a site of oppression and community interests working against women (see Palriwala and Risseeuw 1996).

This paper explores the nature and form of disability afflicting the individual and social life of women in rural Haryana, in terms of both physical and mental parameters.[2] It describes the community, family and individual strategies in negotiating disability. It elucidates the social and physical handicaps faced by women of different age groups and different castes with respect to family, work and society in various stages of their life cycle.

In India, women with disabilities face double discrimination due to the prevalence of traditional gender roles and expectations, argue Maya Thomas and M. J. Thomas (2002). Disabled women activists, of late, have demonstrated that disabled women suffer oppression on account of both their gender and disability. They accuse the disability movement to be dominated by men's concerns, as it largely ignores issues of women's social and economic discrimination, sexuality, stereotypical images, and oppressive mores relating to childbearing and motherhood. They have also been critical of feminist movement for neglecting their problems by failing to recognise the disability perspective (Lloyd 2000).

Disability activists argue that marriage and motherhood prospects of disabled women are marred by physical disabilities, as society views such persons as incomplete. They are perceived to be in need of care themselves, and as being unable to fulfil a caring mothering role. Such women may be married off to 'wrong' persons or those who are already married, as they are construed as burden on the family. They are more likely to be divorced or abandoned than normal women. There are misconceptions about their disability being inherited by their children and about them being poor homemakers due to the belief that household chores and childcare need physical fitness and mobility (Thomas and Thomas 2000).[3] The validity of such propositions is examined in this paper.

## Social Stereotypes of Disabled

Disabled individuals in this region are often stereotyped as clever, hot tempered, sexually impotent, and unreliable. Such stereotypes are reflected in the local sayings and folk songs such as follows:

*Aa gai ghar me takhi na chodegi chulha chakhi.*

(When a woman with a squint is married into the family, the property of the house is at risk.)

A women with a squint is thus viewed with suspicion and distrust.

*Pair ke langde me aur aakh ke langde me ek rag faltu hota hai.* (A person who is impaired in one leg and one who is impaired in one eye has an extra nerve.)

The extra nerve signifies hot temper. Thus, one-legged and one-eyed persons are thought to be short-tempered.

*Mere gali me tota dole, mere sang jaegi ki tote sang jaegi yo se pucho yo bajro na khae gi. Lado mange bichuli jalebi mange titali.*

In this folk song, a woman is challenged to go with a disabled man, implying that she will never be sexually satisfied. A disabled individual is regarded as being sexually incapable or incompetent.

Thus, the disabled are not seen as complete or normal persons. They are also stereotyped as sexually incompetent. Their handicaps are often exaggerated and they are made to feel inferior. Ridicules are hurled at them, and often they are addressed by terms like *surdas* (visually disabled), *langdi* (limb deformed) or *bawali* (mentally challenged) instead of their names. The official terminology for the disabled includes *aashrit, viklang* and *apang*. However, several colloquial terms—*lula* and *langda*, for the limb-deformed; *kana* and *andha*, for the one-eyed and visually challenged; *goonga* and *behra*, for the deaf and dumb; and *bhola* and *bawali*, for the mentally challenged—are used to refer to and address the disabled persons. The severity of the disability plays a significant role in the manner it is reacted to: the more severe forms of disability are treated sombrely, but the less sever forms are treated jocularly.

The various factors responsible for disability in an individual form a mutual cause and effect relationship with 'fate'. The causes of the disability can be viewed either exclusively or in combination with each other, but the supervening belief in 'fate' holds good in all the cases of disability. The belief in the theory of *karma* has often led to the acceptance of the disability. Beliefs about the cosmic intervention of the malevolent and the benevolent vis-à-vis the possession by spirits play a significant role in the conceptualisation of disability. People seek treatments for a disability according to its symptom, causation and severity; they also visit the ritual and magical practitioners.

## Disabled Women: A Profile

How disability is culturally conceived and understood by the people, and how disabled persons negotiate, adjust and manage disability through their life cycle can best be seen on the basis of the life histories of women with disability.[4] While we had gone to the field with the apprehension of whether or not we will find any disabled people, we were surprised to see a large number of limb deformity cases (29). Polio, clubbed feet and other polio-like conditions due to medical mishaps or abnormality in the skeletal structure are common. Speech and hearing disability (3) is comparatively rare.

Disability does not discriminate between caste, class, gender, etc. However, the cultural values, social structure, and the availability of economic and social resources make an immense impact on the conception and management of disability. Thus, to study the variables of the allotment of resources, life histories on the basis of caste status—distinguishing between the scheduled castes and other castes—were taken. Of the 45 intensively studied cases, 13 are that of the scheduled castes while 32 belong to the other castes (see Table 11.1).

**Table 11.1:** Caste and Disability Type

| | *Type of Disability* | | | | | |
|---|---|---|---|---|---|---|
| *Caste* | *Limb deformity* | *Blindness* | *Mentally challenged* | *Speech and hearing disorder* | *Amputation* | *Total* |
| Brahmin | 2 | 1 | 1 | 0 | 0 | 4 |
| Jat | 5 | 1 | 2 | 2 | 1 | 11 |
| Ahir | 5 | 1 | 2 | 0 | 0 | 8 |
| Gujar | 1 | 0 | 0 | 0 | 0 | 1 |
| Yadav | 1 | 0 | 0 | 0 | 2 | 3 |
| Khati | 2 | 1 | 0 | 0 | 0 | 3 |
| Kumhar | 1 | 0 | 0 | 0 | 0 | 1 |
| Nai | 1 | 0 | 0 | 0 | 0 | 1 |
| Dhanak | 2 | 1 | 0 | 0 | 0 | 3 |
| Chamar | 1 | 1 | 0 | 0 | 0 | 2 |
| Harijan | 5 | 1 | 1 | 1 | 0 | 8 |
| Total | 26 | 7 | 6 | 3 | 3 | 45 |

The number of limb deformity cases is the largest among the Jats and the Ahirs, but they are the numerically dominant caste in the area. Limb deformity among the scheduled castes is also found to be very high. The distribution of blind women remains more or less the same across the castes, while the mentally challenged cases are rather high among the other castes. All the reported cases of amputation were from the other prosperous castes, the Yadav and the Jat, who are the cattle-owning community. Being economically stable, they can afford to buy fodder-cutting machines, used mainly by the women of the household who incidentally meet with accidents using them.

The highest number of limb deformity is found among women in the 15–45 age group; this number is the lowest in the age group of < 15 years for both the other castes and the scheduled castes (see Table 11.2). The reduction of limb deformity cases in the lowest age group may be explained by the effective implementation of the polio immunisation programme. The highest number of mentally challenged is in the < 15 years age group of the other castes.

**Table 11.2:** Disability Type According to Caste and Age Group

| | *Type of disability* | | | | | |
|---|---|---|---|---|---|---|
| *Caste and age group* | *Limb deformity* | *Blindness* | *Mentally challenged* | *Speech and hearing disorder* | *Amputation* | *Total* |
| *Other Castes* | | | | | | |
| < 15 | 2 | 0 | 4 | 1 | 0 | 7 |
| 15–45 | 11 | 2 | 1 | 0 | 3 | 17 |
| 45 > + | 5 | 2 | 0 | 1 | 0 | 8 |
| Total | 18 | 4 | 5 | 2 | 3 | 32 |
| *Scheduled Castes* | | | | | | |
| < 15 | 2 | 0 | 1 | 1 | 0 | 4 |
| 15–45 | 6 | 2 | 0 | 0 | 0 | 8 |
| 45 > | 0 | 1 | 0 | 0 | 0 | 1 |
| Total | 8 | 3 | 1 | 1 | 0 | 13 |
| *All Castes* | | | | | | |
| < 15 | 4 | 0 | 5 | 2 | 0 | 11 |
| 15–45 | 17 | 4 | 1 | 0 | 3 | 25 |
| 45 > | 5 | 3 | 0 | 1 | 0 | 9 |
| Total | 26 | 7 | 6 | 3 | 3 | 45 |

A large number of the disabled women studied (21) are unmarried (see Table 11.3). Obviously, disability delays marriage; all these women are, however, below 20 years of age and they still have prospects of marriage.

In what follows, we shall describe and analyse the life history of nine disabled women, representing the three age groups, and elucidate the different types of disabilities and their social management in various castes.

**Table 11.3:** Disability Type According to Caste and Marital Status

| | *Type of Disability* | | | | | |
|---|---|---|---|---|---|---|
| *Caste and marital status* | *Limb deformity* | *Blindness* | *Mentally challenged* | *Speech and hearing disorder* | *Amputation* | *Total* |
| *Other Castes* | | | | | | |
| Married | 11 | 4 | 1 | 1 | 3 | 20 |
| Unmarried | 7 | 0 | 4 | 1 | 0 | 12 |
| Total | 18 | 4 | 5 | 2 | 3 | 32 |
| *Scheduled Castes* | | | | | | |
| Married | 2 | 2 | 0 | 0 | 0 | 4 |
| Unmarried | 6 | 1 | 1 | 1 | 0 | 9 |
| Total | 8 | 3 | 1 | 1 | 0 | 13 |
| *All Castes* | | | | | | |
| Married | 13 | 6 | 1 | 1 | 3 | 24 |
| Unmarried | 13 | 1 | 5 | 2 | 0 | 21 |
| Total | 26 | 7 | 6 | 3 | 3 | 45 |

# Case Studies

## *Young Girls (<15 Years)*

*1. Name: Monu; age: 13 years; caste: Ahir; disability: mentally challenged.*

Monu did not talk until she was 3 years old and, when she did, her speech was distorted. She refused to walk, did not learn toilet manners and maintained ill health. Her uncle, a Registered Medical Practitioner, took her for the first three years to a number of small-time doctors. Being diagnosed with a liver problem, she was treated accordingly. Monu's liver problem was cured, she picked up on her appetite, but remained mentally slow. She had also been referred to a local *Vaid* (Ayurvedic physician) at the age of 2, and her family had been convinced that Monu would gain normalcy with time. When this did not happen even at the age of 3, the family took her to a well-known doctor in Jaipur. She continued his medicine for three months. Monu's parents claim that her condition has worsened and, for the time being, all medication has been stopped.

Monu is very particular about what she wears. She bathes twice a day and likes to keep herself clean. She is a very moody girl: if she wants to sleeps, then she sleeps all day; sometimes, she might not sleep at all. Monu was admitted in a public school at Nangal only when she was 9 years old, and she is now in class III. Her brothers and sisters accompany her to school. Her sister is her full-time playmate and the two girls keep each other company. Whether or not she wants to study is her prerogative. She needs to be given special attention, otherwise she gets lost in her own world in the middle of a task. Monu is often ridiculed and called as *bawali* (insane) by other children, but she does not react to such comments. But, when she gets angry, she hits out. She can look after herself, and she helps in household chores as and when she feels like it.

*2. Name: Renu; age: 15 years; caste: Dhanak; disability: left-foot deformity.*

Renu was two-and-a half-months old when she developed high fever. A Registered Medical Practitioner treated her locally for fever. As she grew older, she failed to stand up. Initially the family believed that the child's hip joint had been dislocated, but they later learnt that she had had an attack of polio. Medication was sought from a retired army doctor in a neighbouring village. Later, her maternal grandfather took her to Alwar, to her maternal granduncle's (MMB) house, for treatment at Bhagat Singh Hospital. Till date, Renu experiences weakness in her legs and needs a stick to support herself while walking.

Renu has two brothers and two sisters. Her father is poor and he suffers from Tuberculosis. Thus, he has readily transferred to Renu's (maternal) grandparents the responsibility to provide for the treatment and care of his daughter. She can perform most of her household chores, but has problems in fetching water. She tries to live her life like the normal children in the village, but faces a problem when it comes to playing games like running and skipping. Renu attended school for sometime, but has dropped out due to lack of interest in studies She still goes to the *Anganwadi* for the mid-day meal. Her family hopes to get her married in the next year or two.

Haryana has been notorious for high rates of female infanticide and, of late, for the misuse of sex-selection technologies leading to large number of foeticides. Clinics performing such tests and consequent abortions are mushrooming in all its towns. Since the 1981 Census, declining sex ratio has become a serious concern. Large-scale dowries, anti-women attitudes and strong male-preference are often cited as reasons for this. Strong patriarchal traditions, widespread prevalence of the dowry system, devaluation of women, and the life-long liability of the girl's family to endow her with gifts after her marriage mean that the girl child is a burden. Women largely remain unwanted as evidenced in the skewed sex ratio.

Scholars have highlighted the prevalence of anti-women attitudes in Haryanavi society, expressed through abuses, folk tales and stereotypes (see Chowdhry 1994). Girl children and women remain discriminated in terms of food distribution and access to health care. Obviously, a girl child, and that too with a disability, would be totally unwanted in such a society. The case studies reflect the initial neglect of a disabled girl child, and some parents even admitted their eager anticipation of the child's death. Marjina, a 7-year-old girl, who suffers of congenital limb deformities, was so named because her family members had lost all hopes of her living on: *mar* (death) and *jina* (life), meaning one who is alive after death. However, what is significant, when the child is able to cope with the disability, fighting all odds in spite of neglect, the family comes together to support her/him. The delayed response to the symptoms of abnormality in case of a child is mainly to the inability of the family to understand the disability early on.

This neglect in providing basic health care to women of all ages is due to both gender discrimination and financial difficulties. Among the scheduled castes, economic hardships were mainly found to be working against the survival of the girl child. Women across all castes are socialised to take their health less seriously. Ramesh has partial hearing and partial eyesight; she had an attack of small pox during her childhood and the disabilities followed. No medication was pursued at that time, as small pox is traditionally attributed to the visit of the *Mata* (the goddess), and it is believed that there is no remedy for the condition.

The role of family in disability management is significant. Mother and other female relatives look after the child and make the early diagnosis. Pooja, a mentally challenged girl enjoys a lot of indulgence from her mother who said, '*ye mar to rahi nahi thi*' (she wasn't dying, thus we decided to look after her). The mother refused to acknowledge any form of disability in the child. The possibility of a speech disability in Ramesh was first pointed out by her grandmother. Female relatives and the siblings play an important role in bringing up such a child and helping her cope with disability. Men usually take the responsibility of taking her around for cure.

In Renu's case, whose father was poor, the maternal grandparents took over medication and treatment of her left-foot deformity. In a patrilineal society, social links maintained with the woman's natal family are an important social resource. Moreover, with regard to cure and rehabilitation, social networks of relatives and neighbours are used. People who have moved out of the village often act as facilitators in establishing information networks, moving beyond the boundaries of household and kin relations. Lacking both economic and social resources, poor groups like the scheduled castes face difficulties in post-natal care and accessing general health care; both Pooja and Sunny could avail better post-natal care due to financial resources of the family and mobilisation of influential relatives. The scheduled caste parents hardly make any effort to take their children out for treatment, perhaps due to lack of social resources. Thus, though caste does not create problems directly, given their lower economic, educational and social status, disabled children of the scheduled castes tend to get discriminated.

Disability is conceived primarily in terms of effects of *karma* (fate) and often attributed to supernatural powers, spirits, etc. Remedial efforts are made on a trial and error basis, trying out every accessible and affordable cure. Here the economic status of an individual plays an important role than the caste status *per se*, but that does not deter people from pursuing possible alternative modes. The biomedical system of cure is highly sought after leaving the people vulnerable to quacks and other non-professionals. Going by the local conceptions of disability, all possible resources are availed to find the cure for disability. However, the effort is towards finding a cure, rather than rehabilitation. Disability might be totally ignored unless it comes in the way of smooth functioning of everyday life.

Young girls are socialised in traditional gender roles, as capacity to do hard manual work is a key factor deciding their marriage and future. These girl children are not in any sense different from others, as depending on the severity of their problem, they like to indulge in girls' play. Generally, they are not excluded from games. Their siblings are often protective about them. The restrictions on other 'normal' girl children are also applicable to them. There is very little playtime for these girls as most of them learn to look after the younger children of the household and help their mothers in household chores.

Although the disabled girls are also sent to school, not much value is attached to their education. A woman's destiny is still viewed in terms of marriage. This is in contrast to the disabled boys: people are aware of the concessions provided by the government for such boys, and they are educated with the hope that higher studies would help them get jobs. While the disabled girls are made to gain proficiency in household work, the disabled boys are encouraged to become economically stable.

## *Women (15–45 Years)*

*3. Name: Mukesh Pholsingh; age: 19 years; caste: Chamar; disability: blindness.*

Mukesh has been absolutely blind since she was 8 years old. One night around *Janmashtami* (Lord Krishna's birthday), she was sleeping in the *galli* (street) outside the house, but got up in the morning to find that she had lost her eyesight. In spite of constant probing, the family insisted that there was no other symptom that could be followed up to the condition. The family defines the situation as *'kisi ne ham per apni aafat dal di* (someone has put his problems onto us). It is maintained that there are men known as *sevra* (shaman) who usually perform black magic. In Mukesh's case, the family insisted that someone else's problems had fallen on then, but only by chance, because Mukesh was in the way of the *aafat* (evil spirit) and it affected her. The rumours went that the night on which Mukesh lost her eyesight someone had seen a*sevra* walking naked through the village.

Mukesh did not complain of any pain in the eye, and the family said that there were no home remedies to be pursued in this case. When the problem first arose, Mukesh was taken to the eye hospital at Rewari to no avail, and the pursuit was stopped. The mother complained that one trip to the hospital cost not less than Rs. 500. It took Mukesh quite a few years to adjust to the situation. She would go berserk asking what had happened to her. Physically, she adjusted to her problem more easily, she started performing her own tasks quite independently and her mother played an important role in this adjustment. Today, Mukesh can do all her work by herself: she can bathe, wash clothes, clean the house, cut vegetables, etc. and can even fetch water from the well (1 km from their house) with her *bhabhi*'s (brother's wife) help. She cannot perform any labour-intensive task outside the house. The family is landless and they work as agricultural labourers in the village. Because of Mukesh's condition they are now one member short for labour.

Before losing her eyesight, Mukesh had not been to school. After that, a teacher asked her to attend school. He taught her Braille. She went to school for five years with her brother or her neighbour's children, but then gave up because this teacher was rather irregular, and other teachers were not ready to keep her. Sending Mukesh to school seems to be a family strategy of managing her so that she could be kept busy while her parents left to pursue labour. Now Mukesh accompanies her mother whenever she goes out for work and sits the whole day in some corner of the field.

Mukesh's teacher had introduced the family to the idea of disability pension and helped them to get a medical certificate. Mukesh's parents get old-age pension as well. An account had been opened in the post office in Mukesh's name, and her brother claimed that her pension is deposited in this account. Now the family is looking out for a suitable groom for her.

*4. Name: Maya Devi; age: 32 years; caste: Ahir; disability: problem in right leg, laced muscles and deformed foot.*

When Maya Devi was 7 months old, she had a boil on her right inner upper thigh, and it was operated upon in a nearby by town. This operation, it is maintained, created nerve damage leading to deformity in the child's leg. The condition is described as '*nas khich gai thi*' (the nerve got stretched). She could not walk till she was 3 years old. She was taken by her *tau* (paternal uncle) to Bandikui for treatment where she stayed for the next three years. Maya Devi ultimately ended up with twenty stitches vertically down the thigh. When she was 11 years old, the doctor suggested a second operation, but her illiterate father, feared further complications. Thus, further medical pursuits were dropped.

Since Maya Devi was very young when she became disabled, she adjusted to it very well. She learnt all the household and agricultural chores. She was married off when she was 15 years old. Her in-laws' was a joint household: there were four *bahus* (daughters-in-law) and each of them had her share of household work. The household is now divided, but the brothers live close by. Maya Devi's husband has 1 *kila* of land, which he tills, but the income from this is not sufficient to meet the household expenses. He also works for a Registered Medical Practitioner to supplement the household income.

Maya Devi says that her stitches still hurt; she finds working strenuous and avoids lifting heavy weights. She does not use any household remedies; she knows that her condition is permanent and cannot be rectified. Her father-in-law, who learnt of the disability pension, had taken Maya Devi and helped her to get a disability certificate. She has been receiving pension for the past eleven years. Maya Devi says, 'her pension is consumed into the household budget because in today's costly world it is very difficult to make all ends meet'.

*5. Name: Chandbai; age: 35; caste: Jat; disability: right-hand amputation at the elbow.*

Chandbai was 16 years old when her hand got cut in an electric fodder-cutter. She lost consciousness at that moment She was first taken to a doctor in the village and then to Alwar. At Alwar she underwent three different operations and had to stay at the government hospital for three months. Her parents accompanied her during this time, while her brother shuttled between their natal village and the hospital carrying food, milk, etc. everyday. When her hand had got cut, Chandbai had gone almost hysterical, but she got a lot of support from her mother who stayed with her all the time.

Chandbai had been engaged, but the engagement was broken after the accident. Her parents managed to find another groom and, within a year, she was married off. She is very proud of her husband, and she claims that while her mother-in-law was never too supportive, her husband took on all her responsibilities. She insists that he had not claimed any extra money as dowry either. Chandbai also found support from her sister-in-law, who tried to help her as best as she could. Chandbai views her condition as '*bhagya ki bat* (a matter of fate). She says that she has never been ridiculed by any one, not even her mother-in-law; she, however, feels inferior to normal people.

Chandbai now lives in a nuclear family. Her husband has no land; his main occupation is sharecropping. Chandbai regrets that she cannot help her husband in any agricultural work; having only one hand, she is no good for *lavni* (reaping crop), etc. The only help that she can provide is to take food to him in the field.

Chandbai can do all the household chores including looking after the animals and cutting fodder for them. She can knead flour and cut vegetables with the help of her feet. She can make *rotis* (bread), and wash utensils and clothes, but these take her longer than they would take an individual with two hands. The house now has a tap connection, but earlier she would go to the well to fetch water. She would pull the rope with one hand then hold it with her feet and then pull the rope again. The women at the well would raise her pot to her head and her husband would remove it at home. When her husband was not around, she brought water in a bucket. She now has three daughters to look after the house for her.

Chandbai used to have pain in her hand till three or four years back. She learnt about the disability pension through the *Sarpanch* of the village. At a camp she was given a disability certificate and her pension form was filled in. Two-and-a-half years back, she was given an artificial hand and trained in how to wear and use it, but she has discarded it as it was heavy and painful and does not stay in place.

*6. Name: Munnidevi Lalsingh; age: 45 years; caste: Brahmin; disability: deformity in the right leg.*

Munnidevi belonged to a family of six brothers and sisters. She was 5 years old when she had high fever, after which her right foot got deformed. She was taken to Surajgad by her father for treatment, but to no avail. Her condition remained the same for the next three years, a time during which she was constantly administered therapy. This consisted of leg massages by her mother every afternoon for the next three years. She was once kept in a pit full of cow dung throughout the afternoon. She was not totally bed ridden; she could look after herself but her movements were restricted. After the therapy, she recovered to the extent that she could perform all household activities as well as agricultural activities. However, she still has problem moving around. In her younger days if she was taunted by her friends, she would fight verbally.

There was nothing wrong with Lalsingh, but his first marriage negotiations had been cancelled because he was into politics. This delayed his marriage prospects and he had trouble finding a bride. Then Lalsingh's marriage was fixed with Munnidevi. They got married when she was about 15 and he, around 21. Munnidevi's mother-in-law was very rude to her; she never gave her any concessions as far as work was concerned. Munnidevi had to, at times, carry up to 60 kg of wheat and fetch water in *matka* (pitcher) everyday. In the initial years of her marriage, she lost three kids; her mother-in-law would taunt her on this account saying that all her children would get buried under the earth. Munnidevi remained secluded. She now has four children; her first child was a daughter and then she had three sons. Munnidevi's daughter has now been married off, but before marriage, her daughter used to share a load of her work. Now Munnidevi has trained her youngest son Haripal to contribute significantly in the household chores. Munnidevi now lives in a nuclear household now. Her husband and his brothers have separated but they share a cordial relationship.

Munnidevi's leg has deteriorated over time and it still hurts. In winter, the pain is more and it continues for two or three days. It begins from the upper thigh and runs to the foot; she can feel palpitation at the centre of the feet. There are times when she applies *mehendi* (henna) on her feet (as a remedy) and, at other times, the pain reduces only after taking an injection. She also suffers severe pain in her legs and hips during her periods. Initially she had told her mother-in-law about it; since nothing was done about it, she spoke to her husband and he brought her medicines from a local Registered Medical Practitioner.

Munnidevi learnt about the disability pension plan through the *Sarpanch.* Munnidevi's husband had taken her to Rewari to get her medical certificate of disability and she was sanctioned the pension. Munnidevi is a confident woman and says that she is no less than any others: in spite of her disability, she performs all her chores successfully. She says that when her husband beats her in a drunken state, she hits him back, because she has strong natal support.

A disabled woman in the reproductive age group is most vulnerable, as she is pushed towards performing work like any normal individual in the society. This is explained in terms of the rigid division of labour and indispensability of woman's manual work within the domestic as well as agricultural sphere, especially after her marriage. No special concessions are made for disability, (that is, redesigning the house, exempting her from work, etc.); a girl child is initiated into all possible responsibilities. No special care is extended in terms their specific physical/mental disability. For instance

Urmila, a mentally challenged woman, never got any attention of a psychiatrist. She was even married and had children. Rural society does not perceive disabled as people with any special requirements. Mental illness especially is not recognised as illness or disability. Their actions are often perceived as either innocuous or nonconformist. Sometimes they are also seen as shirking work in the guise of disability. Their traditional gender roles as worker and reproducer are strictly enforced as in case of any normal woman.

Men play a vital role in arranging the girl's marriage. A woman is subjected to intensive scrutiny concerning her disability. The negative stereotypes, which construe her as incomplete, asexual, unreliable and hot tempered, also come in the way of finding groom for her. The major concern expressed in negotiating marriages is her fecundity, and whether or not she would prove to be a good worker. Thus, marriage for a severely disabled woman would prove to be difficult. However, the social security of every woman lies in her marriage; the dearth of women in the society due to male preference, acts to a disabled woman's advantage.

It is believed that if a woman is born with a congenital problem her disability will be passed on to her children. In most cases, however, the disability goes unnoticed at birth, due to lack of medical facilities and attention to preliminary indications. Thus, the stigma that would otherwise be attached to a woman due to congenital problems is removed due to late detection of disabilities in her children. It is also believed that man begets the child. It is said that the crop depends on the type of seed sown and not so much on the soil. This is a simile for the woman who is like a fertile ground where the man provides the seeds. Thus, the disability of the woman, it is believed, does not have a direct bearing on the child.

The most professed support that a woman with disability can get is the sharing of her responsibilities with her sisters. For this, the disabled girl is often married into the same household as her sister, usually with a consecutive brother and at times to the same man as her sister. This type of marriage practice often comes to the aid of a disabled woman. Other characteristics associated with the marriage of a disabled woman is that she is usually married to a disabled man, a widower, in a household whose economic condition is lower than her natal home, or to a man who cannot find a spouse for whatever reason. There were also reports of heavy dowries paid by parents of disabled girls. There were a few cases among the older women who insisted that disability had not got in the way of their marriage, but the point is debatable.

In South Asia, the care of the aged, the helpless and the young is considered the duty of the family (Dube 1998: 91). The women of the family, usually the mother and the sisters and other female relatives, distribute the household chores to best accommodate the disabled individual. Efforts are made to ensure that the disabled individual is accompanied at all times. Although she is made to do all possible jobs, there might be a relaxation in the amount of load she carries, or the time she takes to perform a particular task. Work might also be distributed in a manner that the disabled shoulder a greater load of the household chores while the others pursue agricultural labour. She often gets lot of support in her natal home. However, in her marital home, she is expected to do all the household chores. Dube points out that in rural and semi-urban areas, patrilineal kin and others tend to live contiguously, where a certain quality of relationship is expected and there is sharing of responsibilities (*ibid*).

The Brahmin women enjoy a slight advantage because they are not expected to contribute to agricultural labour, unless the household is in dire economic condition. The Jat and Yadav women face greater strain because tending to the animals is also taken to be a part of the household chores. New technology like fodder machines often work to the disadvantage of women, as we found several cases of amputation due to their use. Nirmala and Chandbai lost their hands in using electric fodder-cutter. Nirmala got much support, being in a joint family, especially from her sister (also married into the same family) who shared most of the household chores giving her time to recoup. But the accident has created a void between Nirmala and her husband. She has been experiencing so much marital strain that she has now stopped observing the ritualistic fasts for the welfare of her husband. Disability, especially after marriage, has led to conflict and estrangement, despite the women working hard. Domestic violence is a routine occurrence and disability gives another excuse for wife beating. Disability is not seen as a crisis on a long-term basis, rather the family treats it as one among other difficult situations. For a scheduled caste woman, disability has an adverse impact, because, being landless and procurers of small animals, they are mainly dependent on agricultural labour for their income. Disability robs the household of a working member. Most disabled women continue to perform the household chores, including fetching water from the well, cutting fodder, cooking, cleaning, etc. stretching their maximum bodily limits.

Resources within the household are usually tailored for the disabled in domestic, kinship and in the public domain. In the case of Urmila, who was married to her aunt's brother-in-law, an incompetent person who had problems finding a match. Her aunt fixed the alliance and Urmila had a chance to be his spouse. Being mentally challenged but physiologically capable, she had normal deliveries and all her children are normal. They provide various types of care to their mother. When the children were small,

Urmila's sister-in-law, who was her paternal aunt as well, facilitated her care. We may infer from this case that the kin have control over resources and the allocation of roles.

Women conditioned by the patriarchal ideology neglect their own health and do not complain. In fact, in most cases, they did not see disability as an issue to be discussed. For instance, Ramesh does not get periodical medical check up, because it is viewed as a waste of money. She would rather take her son, who is suffering from an allergic skin rash, to the doctor. Moreover, three of her daughters have to be married, for which she needs to save money. These women always seem to give preference to the family needs than their own. Patriarchy ensures compliance.

## *Women (>45 Years)*

> *7. Name: Bodhi Devi; age: 65; caste: Jat; disability: paralysis and deformity of both hands and legs.*

When Bodhi Devi was 10 years old, she suffered a paralytic stroke. She was sitting under a Neem tree and broke into cold sweat. By the time her mother, who was working in the field, reached her, Bodhi Devi had lost her ability to walk. Bodhi Devi's case was defined as a case of *hawa lagna.*[5] Bodhi Devi was taken home and wrapped in a blanket and *given kadha* (a concoction of herbs). Nothing further was done about her condition, as all was left to fate. Bodhi Devi was not totally immobile; she learnt to move around by dragging herself against the floor; she looked after herself and attended to most household chores.

When Bodhi Devi was of marriageable age, she was married off to her younger sister's husband. Both the sisters were married together and it was hoped that Bodhi Devi would look after the children while the younger sister would go for agricultural labour with her husband. After marriage, Bodhi Devi looked after the house cooked, cleaned, tended the animals, and plastered the floor with cow dung. This arrangement worked well for about seven years, while Bodhi Devi had a daughter and her younger sister had three daughters and two sons. After this, Bodhi Devi and her sister had a fight, and Bodhi Devi was thrown out of the house while her daughter stayed back with her younger sister.

After being thrown out, Bodhi Devi joined her other sister at Gurgaon. Two of her sisters Bhaonani and Gindu Devi had been married into the same village. Bhaonani took her in. Bodhi Devi now shuttles between her natal village (Jhabua) and her sister's place at Gurgaon. Gindu Devi's son Satbir accompanies his aunt during her travels. It is he who took her to Bawal and got her disability pension sanctioned.

> *8. Name: Shanti Devi Ganga Prasad; age: mid-60s; caste: Shami; disability: complete blindness.*

Shanti Devi got married at the age of 14–15 years. Two years later, she had an attack of chicken pox and lost the vision in one eye. No medication was pursued and Shanti Devi went on with her life without any problems. She did all the household work, and worked in the field, too. She had seven children, and married them all off, after which the couple was left to themselves. As the couple grew old and were no more fit to do agricultural labour, they opened a small teashop near the village bus stop and started spending their time there.

Gradually, with age, Shanti Devi lost the vision of her second eye too at the age of 60 due to complications of cataract and lack of family support. The doctors also feared that Shanti Devi might not endure an eye surgery because of her age.

Shanti Devi now needs support for all her activities. She has to be held and taken from the tea stall to her house, accompanied to the toilet, bathed, helped with her clothes and looked after at all times. One of her five daughters or her son is always present at their natal house to look after their mother.

Shanti Devi and her husband receive old-age pension. Her pension is main source of economic support in the household, as the tea stall makes very little profit. Shanti Devi has been taken to various eye camps with the hope that some doctor might be able to improve her eye condition but to no avail. Although Shanti Devi does not complain of any pain in her eyes, they constantly water. Sitting in the tea stall amidst fumes certainly does not help her.

As is evident from the life histories, the condition of a disabled woman changes with her age and status. In the childhood she enjoys parental care and support, but is socialised into her duties as a woman. After marriage, she is put to work and this is the most strenuous phase of her life. With age, she gains more social and moral authority in household affairs. With the expansion of the family, there are more supporting hands in terms of sons, daughters, daughters-in-law and grandchildren for her social and physical support. She is able to stand up for herself, and does not consider herself any less than the others. Much of this usually depends on the nature of household she belongs to. Prem Chowdhry (1994) opines that women not only reinforce the social boundaries but also subvert them. Older women especially express protest and control. Old age nevertheless brings with it other illnesses that compound the problem of physical discomforts. Nuclearisation of household is leading to reduced support in the old age.

## Conclusion

The foregoing analysis reveals that disability is not the primary disadvantage of women in rural Haryana; rather it becomes an additional burden on her marginalised gender position. Disabled women are not a homogenous category; different types of disability affect women differently. For instance, limb deformities are considered to be more disabling than being deaf and dumb. Mental illness is not viewed as an illness or disability till it completely disables the person. As a group, however, they are the subject of several stereotypes that further marginalise them.

Disabled women experience disability and gendered roles simultaneously. Although stereotyped to be incomplete, they are expected to fulfil all the gendered duties and are primarily taken to be working members of the society. As Kamla Ganesh (1998: 121) emphasises, household is the site of gender bias; family socialises its members to accept and transmit this bias, and the ideology of the descent system devalues females.

The case studies show that family is the most important support structure in rural society. People find greater security in living in joint households. Resources within the family are mobilised to extend help. Elderly women, like the grandmother, often facilitate the initial diagnosis of disability. Patriarchal structure of the household nevertheless ensures that the men of the household play a major role in decision-making—for example, where the child should be taken for treatment, how she is to be taken, who accompany her, etc. They, however, have very little role to play in the individual's adjustments in everyday life. The women usually administer even the prescribed therapy and they are the main caregivers.

Families can be seen as units that both protect and control women (Dube 1998: 121). Women usually get more support from their natal family, from their mother and sisters. Kinship groups, despite separation in terms of household structures and the neighbourhood, provide support from time to time. In the marital home though, she has a harder life still sharing of responsibilities among the daughters-in-law was observed. As regards role allocation, excepting those with mental disabilities, women are entrusted with specific gender roles and duties. The mentally challenged and the blind may have higher degree of dependency, whereas those with speech and hearing disabilities are not treated any differently, as they are able to perform all household and agricultural tasks. Families and neighbours with deaf children cultivate skills in sign language, thereby precluding the possibility of exclusion. Only those with severe locomotor disabilities are seen as *aashrit* (literally, dependent) or *viklang*, and thus in need of support. As evidenced from the cases, mental illness is less recognised unless it severely retards the functioning of the woman's life.

Older women receive help from the daughters (who visit their natal home regularly) and daughters-in-law. The role of mother's brother is also significant, and his family is seen to be extending help on different occasions. One tends to agree with Rajni Palriwala and Carla Risseeuw who argue that

> marriage, family and kinship are social domains characterised by duality. They carry the elements of security, support and care as they entail elements of control—even oppression—limiting people's options to realise their own welfare and interests or of those for whom they take particular responsibility (1996: 39).

We see here that, apart from extending support and help in their work, families do not necessarily create special opportunities for the disabled in order to cope better.

Management of disability in the context of a community is often related to a crisis situation. The more permanent form of rehabilitation is centred in the household where a woman with disability lives and with the help of several social mechanisms learns to cope with her state. No professional help is sought in most cases. Unlike in the urban and western context where social participation of disabled women is a major issue, rural society accommodates the disabled and extends support at several levels. Disabled are not excluded; however, they are made useful by recognising their potential. They, however, continue to bear the brunt of their disability and gender in trying to prove that they are as normal as her non-disabled women.

State policies, on the other hand treat the individual as a unit of analysis. The disability act ignores gendered realities of everyday lives of disabled, situated in families and communities. Women's education is a highly neglected area, as dropout rate of girl children after primary level is alarmingly high. Girl children among the scheduled castes generally do not receive any education. Devaluation of woman's education is an important reason for the disabled woman in a rural context being unable to become self-dependent. Nowadays younger girls are sent to school but very few complete it. Women's work outside the family is still not taken as a viable option. They rarely pursue higher education and professional jobs, though now there is growing awareness of the opportunities. Despite legal rights in property, patriliny ensures that they remain dependent on men of the family. Land rights are rarely given to women, virtually rendering them resource less.

The state provides nominal pension to the disabled;[6] this information is disseminated through announcements by the *Panchayat* and women's informal networks. Health camps are held in easily accessible places. However, there is no provision of pension for children and those below 18 years of age, as the state government expects families to fend for them.

Whether or not the disability pension and other facilities have contributed to empowerment remains a point of debate, especially in a society ruled by patriarchal norms. In most cases, the pension gets absorbed in the household expenses. Similar other concessions provided by the state—for example, fellowships, concessions, job reservation—are hardly relevant, largely due to heavy bias of the policy in favour of the urban educated middle-class society. Since the needs of the disabled women in rural areas find no place in the policy framework, they remain marginalised in their relationship to the state. The role of the state agencies like the department of social welfare and *Panchayat* is only limited to spreading information and disbursing pension. There are no special schools or community-based rehabilitation programmes in this area. The NGO initiatives are also almost negligible.

## Notes

Thanks are due to Planning, Research, Evaluation and Monitoring (PREM) Division, Ministry of Social Justice an Empowerment, Government of India for funding this project, and to Dr S. M. Patnaik, Department of Anthropology, University of Delhi and Indrani Sen, for research support.

1. Persons with Disabilities, Equal Opportunities, Protection of Rights and Full Participation Act 1995 is a comprehensive piece of legislation. Under this Act, each state provides for the educational, employment, travel and pension requirements of their disabled people.
2. This study was carried out in six villages of Rewari district through intensive anthropological fieldwork during May–August 2002 (see Mehrotra 2002). For an abridged version, see Mehrotra (2004b). For details on the cultural conceptions of disability and their cure in rural Haryana, see Mehrotra (2002a).
3. Many of the generalisations in the literature on disability in India require empirical validation. Sociological research in this area remains scanty and scattered.
4. Of the six villages visited during the course of study, fifty life histories were collected from various castes and age groups. However, only forty-five cases have been analysed here.

5. Most limb deformities in the area are understood in terms of '*hawa lagna*', though most people are now aware of polio. When *hawa* (wind) affects an individual, it causes bodily deformities. The words polio, paralysis or *lakwa* are used almost interchangeably.
6. The Government of Haryana provides a monthly pension of Rs 200 to each disabled person with more than 70 percent disability. Most people complained that this criteria, was not fair and the pension amount to be very meagre.

# References


Chowdhry, Prem, 1994. *The veiled women: Shifting gender equations in rural Haryana 1880–1990.* New Delhi: Oxford University Press.

Dube, Leela. 1998. 'Trends in kinship and gender relations in South Asia,' in Carla Risseeuw and Kamla Ganesh (eds.): *Negotiation and social space: A gendered analysis of changing kin and security networks in South Asia* (87–112). New Delhi: SAGE Publications.

Ganesh, Kamla. 1998. 'Gender and kinship studies: Indian material and context', in Carla Risseeuw and Kamla Ganesh (eds.): *Negotiation and social space: A gendered analysis of changing kin and security networks in South Asia* (113–33). New Delhi: SAGE Publications.

Lloyd, Margret. 2000. 'The politics of disability and feminism: Discord or synthesis', *Sociology*, 35 (3): 715–28.

Mehrotra, Nilika. 2002. *A study of the disabled women in rural Haryana.* Unpublished report submitted to Ministry of Social Justice and Empowerment (PREM Division), Government of India.

———. 2004a. 'Understanding cultural conceptions of disability in rural India: A case from Haryana', *The journal of Indian anthropological society*, 39 (1): 33–45.

———. 2004b. 'Women, disability and social support in rural Haryana', *Economic and political weekly*, 39 (52): 5640–44.

Palriwala, Rajni and Carla Risseeuw. 1996. 'Introduction', in Rajni Palriwala and Carla Risseeuw (eds.): *Shifting circles of support: Contextualising kinship and gender in South Asia and sub Saharan Africa* (15–47). New Delhi: SAGE Publications.

Risseeuw, Carla and Kamla Ganesh (eds.). 1998. *Negotiation and social space: A gendered analysis of changing kin and security networks in South Asia.* New Delhi: SAGE Publications.

Thomas, Maya and M. J. Thomas. 2002. 'Status of women with disabilities in South Asia', *Asia Pacific disability—rehabilitation journal*, Series 2, January 2002, downloaded from <www.aifo.it/languages/english/apdrj>.

# About the Editor and Contributors

## The Editor

**Abhijit Dasgupta** is Professor of Sociology at the, University of Delhi. His research interests include agrarian structure, sociology of development and the sociology of minorities and marginalised communities. He has co-edited the following books: *Bengal: Communities, Development and States* (1994); *State, Society and Displaced People in South Asia* (2004); and *Minorities and the State: The Changing Landscape of Bengal* (2011). He has authored *Growth with Equity: The New Technology and Agrarian Change in Bengal* (1998).

## The Contributors

**B. K. Roy Burman** is a renowned anthropologist who worked on the tribals in the north-east India. He has published several books including the *Encyclopaedia on Scheduled Tribes, Scheduled Castes and Disadvantaged Peoples.*

**Maren Bellwinkel** was associated with the Department of Sociology, University of Delhi. She has carried out fieldwork on construction workers in the city of Delhi and has published several papers.

**Victor S. D'Souza**, the former President of Indian Sociological Society, was Professor at the Punjab University, Chandigarh. He has published several books and papers.

**Biswajit Ghosh** worked on 'Trade unionism in leather and book-binding industries in Kolkata' and has published several papers on the industrial workers.

**Ritambhara Hebbar** has worked on 'Ho community and their environment' and has published several papers. She is currently teaching at the Tata Institute of Social Sciences, Mumbai.

**Nilika Mehrotra** is currently teaching at the Centre for Social Systems, Jawaharlal Nehru University, Delhi. She has published several papers on gender inequalities and disabilities, and is the Managing Editor of the *Journal of Indian Anthropological Association.*

**T. K. Oommen** is an eminent sociologist and a former President of the International Sociological Association. He is author of several books and articles.

**Kanti Pakrasi** was a sociologist at the Indian Statistical Institute, Kolkata. He has published books and papers on the refugees in West Bengal.

**C. Parvathamma**, the first dalit woman sociologist of India, taught at the University of Mysore and published books and papers on dalits in India.

**N. R. Sheth** is an eminent industrial sociologist and author of several books and papers.

**John C. B. Webster** is a historian associated with the Presbyterian Seminary of India. He has authored several books including *Dalit Christians* and *History and Contemporary.*

# Index